PE̶
WELCOME!

1994

The Animal Lovers' Holiday Guide

33rd Edition 1994
ISBN 1 85055 177 4 © FHG Publications Ltd.

Cover design: Sheila Begbie
Cover photograph: Images Colour Library

Cartography by GEO Projects, Reading

Maps are based on Ordnance Survey Maps with the permission of the
Controller of Her Majesty's Stationery Office, Crown copyright reserved.

Set by Keyset Composition, Colchester.
Printed and bound in Great Britain by Guernsey Press, Guernsey

Published by FHG Publications Ltd, a member of the U.N. Group.
Abbey Mill Business Centre, Seedhill, Paisley PA1 1TJ
(Tel: 041-887 0428. Fax: 041-889 7204).

Distribution: **Book Trade:** WLM, 117 The Hollow, Littleover, Derby DE3 7BS
(Tel: 0332 272020. Fax: 0332 774287).
News Trade: UMD, Castle House, 37/45 Paul Street, London EC2A 4PB
(Tel: 071-490 2020. Fax: 071-490 1239).

PETS WELCOME!
1994

DID YOU KNOW that in June 1993 *Pets Welcome!* appeared as Number One in the book trade's Best-Seller List for travel and holiday publications? Regular readers won't be surprised. For years they have known, just as we have known, that the successive editions of this guide to holidays for pets and their owners have been a 'boon and a blessing' to thousands of animal lovers.

For 1994 we have two 'extras' – new features for even better value and added interest. Firstly, we have been pleased to collaborate with Beta Petfoods to produce a Supplement of 'Golden Bowl Award' pubs, inns and small hotels which offer special facilities for pets and owners. This is an amusing – and useful – read. There are further details on our Contents Page. Secondly, if you turn over a few pages you will find clearly marked pages of Vouchers/Coupons for FREE and REDUCED RATE ENTRY to a selection of popular holiday attractions for readers of *Pets Welcome!* FHG Publications has arranged this Readers' Offer with proprietors and managers and although in a few cases pets are not permitted, we hope that you'll cut out and use the coupons as appropriate.

Most importantly, of course, the pages of Pets Welcome offer holiday accommodation of all sorts throughout Britain to which holidaymakers who are accompanied by their pets will be made welcome. The extent to which pets are 'welcomed' can vary. We have tried to give some indication by symbols which show whether or not an additional charge is involved and where there are special facilities. If, however, you have any particular worries – or requirements – you should discuss these when you are making enquiries or bookings.

Most of our entries are of long standing and are tried and tested favourites with animal lovers. However as publishers we do not inspect the accommodation advertised in *Pets Welcome!* and an entry does not imply our recommendation. If you have any problems or complaints about accommodation, please raise them on the spot with the owner or his representative in the first place. We will follow up complaints if necessary but we regret that we cannot act as intermediaries nor can we accept responsibility for details of accommodation and/or services described here. Happily, serious complaints are few.

Finally, if you have to cancel or postpone a holiday booking, please give as much notice as possible. This courtesy will be appreciated and it could save later difficulties.

Please let us know if you have any unusual or humorous experiences with your pet on holiday. This always makes interesting reading! And we hope that you'll mention *Pets Welcome!* when you make your holiday enquiries and bookings.

Peter Clark
Publishing Director

CONTENTS

SYMBOLS

⚊ Indicates no charge for pets.
£ Indicates a charge for pets: nightly or weekly.
pw! Indicates some special provision for pets: exercise, feeding etc.

3

4

FHG

READERS' OFFER 1994

VALID during 1994 Season

Beale Wildlife Gardens

Church Farm, Lower Basildon, Reading, Berkshire RG8 9NH Tel: (0734) 845172

Admit **ONE CHILD FREE** with an accompanying adult

NOT TO BE USED IN CONJUNCTION WITH ANY OTHER OFFER

FHG

READERS' OFFER 1994

VALID during 1994 Season

Flambards Village Theme Park

Helston, Cornwall TR13 0GA Telephone: (0326) 574549

£1.00 OFF full admission price

NOT TO BE USED IN CONJUNCTION WITH ANY OTHER OFFER

FHG

READERS' OFFER 1994

VALID during 1994 Season

North Cornwall Museum and Gallery

The Cleare, Camelford, Cornwall Telephone: (0840) 212954

One **FREE** adult entry with every paid adult entry

NOT TO BE USED IN CONJUNCTION WITH ANY OTHER OFFER

FHG

READERS' OFFER 1994

VALID Easter to end November 1994 except 30/31 July

South Tynedale Railway

Alston, Cumbria CA9 3JB Telephone (0434) 381696

Reduction of 40p on adult ticket and 20p on child ticket

NOT TO BE USED IN CONJUNCTION WITH ANY OTHER OFFER

FHG

READERS' OFFER 1994

VALID during 1994

Tullie House City Museum and Art Gallery

Castle Street, Carlisle, Cumbria CA3 8TP Telephone: (0228) 34781

One person admitted **FREE** for every adult admission purchased

NOT TO BE USED IN CONJUNCTION WITH ANY OTHER OFFER

Exotic birds, pets' corner, adventure playgrounds, river cruises etc, all set in acres of gardens, lakes and water meadows.

DIRECTIONS: on A329 one mile from Pangbourne.

OPEN: daily (closed January and February).

FHG PUBLICATIONS, ABBEY MILL BUSINESS CENTRE, PAISLEY PA1 1TJ

All-weather entertainment for all the family. Victorian Village, Britain in the Blitz, rides and much more.

DIRECTIONS: A394 to Helston.

OPEN: Easter to end October.

FHG PUBLICATIONS, ABBEY MILL BUSINESS CENTRE, PAISLEY PA1 1TJ

Life in Cornwall during the past century. Workmen's tools, domestic items, collection of Cornish and Devonshire pottery.

DIRECTIONS: off A39 18 miles south of Bude.

OPEN: Easter to end September daily except Sundays.

FHG PUBLICATIONS, ABBEY MILL BUSINESS CENTRE, PAISLEY PA1 1TJ

England's highest narrow-gauge railway. Steam and diesel engines carry passengers through the scenic North Pennines.

DIRECTIONS: station is just off A686 Hexham road north of Alston town centre.

OPEN: service operates April to November (daily July and August).

FHG PUBLICATIONS, ABBEY MILL BUSINESS CENTRE, PAISLEY PA1 1TJ

The story of Carlisle's place in turbulent Border history focusing on the Romans, historic railways, and the notorious Reivers.

DIRECTIONS: follow signs for Castle and Cathedral in Carlisle.

OPEN: daily except Christmas Day.

FHG PUBLICATIONS, ABBEY MILL BUSINESS CENTRE, PAISLEY PA1 1TJ

A selection of costumes and accessories (changed each year) on show in one of the oldest and most interesting houses in the heart of Totnes.

DIRECTIONS: part of the Butterwalk which is near main town car park.

OPEN: Spring Bank Holiday to October 1st (closed Saturdays).

FHG PUBLICATIONS, ABBEY MILL BUSINESS CENTRE, PAISLEY PA1 1TJ

The home of rare breed conservation, with over 50 breeding flocks and herds. Adventure playground, pets' corners, gift shops etc.

DIRECTIONS: M5 Junction 9, B4077 Stow-on-the-Wold road. 7 miles from Stow-on-the-Wold and Bourton-on-the-Water.

OPEN: daily March to October.

FHG PUBLICATIONS, ABBEY MILL BUSINESS CENTRE, PAISLEY PA1 1TJ

Magnificent Norman Keep with banqueting hall and minstrels' gallery. Beautiful grounds with woodland and lakeside walks; light refreshments.

DIRECTIONS: on B1058, one mile from A604 between Cambridge and Colchester. Within easy reach of M25, M11 and A12.

OPEN: Easter to end October.

FHG PUBLICATIONS, ABBEY MILL BUSINESS CENTRE, PAISLEY PA1 1TJ

Magnificent home of the Berkeley family for over 850 years. Full of treasures including paintings, tapestries, porcelain.

DIRECTIONS: off A38 midway between Bristol and Gloucester.

OPEN: April to October.

FHG PUBLICATIONS, ABBEY MILL BUSINESS CENTRE, PAISLEY PA1 1TJ

Cider Museum and Distillery telling the fascinating story of traditional cider making through the ages. Displays include reconstructed farm cider house and cider brandy distillery.

DIRECTIONS: off A438 towards Brecon.

OPEN: April to October daily 10am-5.30pm; November to March Mon-Sat 1-5pm.

FHG PUBLICATIONS, ABBEY MILL BUSINESS CENTRE, PAISLEY PA1 1TJ

Founded by the second Baron Rothschild; unusual museum containing a fine collection of mammals, birds, reptiles and insects in a unique Victorian setting.

DIRECTIONS: Tring is on A41 between Berkhamsted and Aylesbury.

OPEN: all year.

FHG PUBLICATIONS, ABBEY MILL BUSINESS CENTRE, PAISLEY PA1 1TJ

From the Romans to World War II, Dover's historic past comes alive using the latest audio-visual techniques.

DIRECTIONS: from London A2(M2) or A20(M20); within walking distance of Dover Priory BR station.

OPEN: daily except Christmas Day.

FHG PUBLICATIONS, ABBEY MILL BUSINESS CENTRE, PAISLEY PA1 1TJ

Restored by a charitable trust, historic steam engines run through scenic countryside between Tenterden and Northiam.

DIRECTIONS: on A28 between Ashford and Hastings.

OPEN: Weekends in March, April, May, October, November; daily June–September.

FHG PUBLICATIONS, ABBEY MILL BUSINESS CENTRE, PAISLEY PA1 1TJ

Western theme park with rides and attractions for all the family.

DIRECTIONS: on coast 8 miles south of M6 Junction 35.

OPEN: daily.

FHG PUBLICATIONS, ABBEY MILL BUSINESS CENTRE, PAISLEY PA1 1TJ

Five main gallery areas tell the story of the county's rich industrial heritage. Hands-on *Science Alive!*, nature trail and picnic areas.

DIRECTIONS: 12 miles north-west of Leicester.

OPEN: daily except Christmas and Boxing Days.

FHG PUBLICATIONS, ABBEY MILL BUSINESS CENTRE, PAISLEY PA1 1TJ

Rescues and rears abandoned seal pups before returning them to the wild.
Specialised collection includes penguins, reptiles etc.

DIRECTIONS: coastal resort 19 miles north-east of Boston.

OPEN: daily except Christmas Day, Boxing Day and New Year's Day.

FHG PUBLICATIONS, ABBEY MILL BUSINESS CENTRE, PAISLEY PA1 1TJ

Family-run zoo offering an opportunity to experience the sights, sounds and smells
of wild animals including many endangered species.

DIRECTIONS: on the coast 16 miles north of Liverpool.

OPEN: daily except Christmas Day.

FHG PUBLICATIONS, ABBEY MILL BUSINESS CENTRE, PAISLEY PA1 1TJ

A fun way to understand the links between farming, food and the land.
Lots of friendly animals, activity centre.

DIRECTIONS: off the A614 at Farnsfield, 12 miles north of Nottingham.

OPEN: daily all year round.

FHG PUBLICATIONS, ABBEY MILL BUSINESS CENTRE, PAISLEY PA1 1TJ

Beautiful walled garden with nearly 900 types of herbs,
woodland walk, nursery, shop. Guide dogs only.

DIRECTIONS: 6 miles north of Hexham, next to Chesters Roman Fort.

OPEN: daily March to October/November.

FHG PUBLICATIONS, ABBEY MILL BUSINESS CENTRE, PAISLEY PA1 1TJ

The golden age of the Great Western Railway – steam trains, original equipment; picnic
area and refreshment room. Rides on trains all Sundays June to August,
Bank Holidays – enquire for other times.

DIRECTIONS: 10 miles south of Oxford, signposted from M4 (Junction 13) and A34.

OPEN: weekends all year; daily April to September.

FHG PUBLICATIONS, ABBEY MILL BUSINESS CENTRE, PAISLEY PA1 1TJ

A museum of the Oxfordshire countryside, with Manor House, working farm, riverside walks etc, plus daily demonstration of cooking on the kitchen range.

DIRECTIONS: follow signs from A40, close to Witney town centre.

OPEN: 2nd April to end October. Closed Mondays except Bank Holidays,

FHG PUBLICATIONS, ABBEY MILL BUSINESS CENTRE, PAISLEY PA1 1TJ

See how cider has been made for centuries in the traditional way.
Cider shop – try before you buy.

DIRECTIONS: approximately 2 miles from Ilminster, 3 miles from Cricket St Thomas.

OPEN: all year except Sunday afternoons.

FHG PUBLICATIONS, ABBEY MILL BUSINESS CENTRE, PAISLEY PA1 1TJ

Trace the history of the world from 4500 million years ago to the present day.
Journey through time and see how plants and animals lived 200 million years ago.
Other attractions include World of Dinosaurs and Miniature Railway.

DIRECTIONS: signposted "Garden Paradise" off A26 and A259.

OPEN: all year.

FHG PUBLICATIONS, ABBEY MILL BUSINESS CENTRE, PAISLEY PA1 1TJ

Europe's only indoor theme park with roller coaster, kiddies' railway,
live entertainment and lots more – a great day IN.

DIRECTIONS: A1(M), south of Newcastle-upon-Tyne.

OPEN: daily all year round.

FHG PUBLICATIONS, ABBEY MILL BUSINESS CENTRE, PAISLEY PA1 1TJ

Working narrow gauge steam railway, railway museum
and over 70 replica brasses to rub.

DIRECTIONS: on the A447 six miles north of Hinckley.

OPEN: second Saturday each month.

FHG PUBLICATIONS, ABBEY MILL BUSINESS CENTRE, PAISLEY PA1 1TJ

World's largest collection of Worcester Porcelain,
including magnificent Chicago Exhibition Vase.

DIRECTIONS: M5 Junction 7 to city centre, then left at 3rd set of traffic lights.

OPEN: daily except Sundays.

FHG PUBLICATIONS, ABBEY MILL BUSINESS CENTRE, PAISLEY PA1 1TJ

Dracula returns to Whitby in this ultimate horror story – special sound and
lighting effects to set the hairs on your neck tingling.

DIRECTIONS: near harbour in Whitby centre.

OPEN: April to October.

FHG PUBLICATIONS, ABBEY MILL BUSINESS CENTRE, PAISLEY PA1 1TJ

"Elsie Wagstaff's War" – just one of the exciting educational journeys through time
with lots of other extra surprises

DIRECTIONS: off Clifford Street in central York.

OPEN: daily from mid-January to end November.

FHG PUBLICATIONS, ABBEY MILL BUSINESS CENTRE, PAISLEY PA1 1TJ

Birds of prey from all round the world in re-created natural habitats.
Free-flying demonstrations daily.

DIRECTIONS: A65 by-pass from Settle to Kendal; 2nd left after Giggleswick station.

OPEN: daily except Christmas Day.

FHG PUBLICATIONS, ABBEY MILL BUSINESS CENTRE, PAISLEY PA1 1TJ

Intricate models and audio-visual exhibits explain how canals were built and used.
Enjoy a horse-drawn boat trip or take a narrowboat across the aqueduct.

DIRECTIONS: A5 to Llangollen.

OPEN: open daily Easter to end October (limited opening March and October).

FHG PUBLICATIONS, ABBEY MILL BUSINESS CENTRE, PAISLEY PA1 1TJ

35 acres of landscaped grounds and gardens with animals, birds, reptiles and fish.
Children's play area, cafeteria etc.

DIRECTIONS: off B4318 between Tenby and Carew.

OPEN: open daily Easter to end September.

FHG PUBLICATIONS, ABBEY MILL BUSINESS CENTRE, PAISLEY PA1 1TJ

Journey back in time with the audio-visual presentation "Black Gold" and experience the
unique character and culture of the Rhondda. Children's play area.

DIRECTIONS: two miles west of Pontypridd.

OPEN: all year.

FHG PUBLICATIONS, ABBEY MILL BUSINESS CENTRE, PAISLEY PA1 1TJ

Set in the heart of Snowdonia, award-winning underground audio-visual tours.
Magnificent stalactite and stalagmite formations.

DIRECTIONS: one mile from Beddgelert on A498 towards Capel Curig.

OPEN: all year.

FHG PUBLICATIONS, ABBEY MILL BUSINESS CENTRE, PAISLEY PA1 1TJ

Regular flying displays throughout the day when birds are flown free. Numerous species
including Sea Eagle with 8' wingspan. Falconry tuition course available.

DIRECTIONS: follow signs off A96 Aberdeen to Inverness trunk road near Huntly.

OPEN: daily March to October.

FHG PUBLICATIONS, ABBEY MILL BUSINESS CENTRE, PAISLEY PA1 1TJ

Find out about life 3000 years ago at this award-winning Community Project
and Heritage Museum. Lots to see and do.

DIRECTIONS: within a mile of the city centre.

OPEN: Monday to Friday except public holidays.

FHG PUBLICATIONS, ABBEY MILL BUSINESS CENTRE, PAISLEY PA1 1TJ

READERS' OFFER 1994
VALID April to October 1994

Scottish Maritime Museum

Harbourside, Irvine, Ayrshire KA12 8QE Telephone: (0294) 278283

Admit **ONE CHILD FREE** with adult paying full entry price

NOT TO BE USED IN CONJUNCTION WITH ANY OTHER OFFER

FHG

READERS' OFFER 1994
VALID during 1994

Edinburgh Crystal Visitor Centre

Eastfield, Penicuik, Midlothian EH26 8HB Telephone: (0968) 675128

TWO adult entry tickets to factory tour for the price of one

NOT TO BE USED IN CONJUNCTION WITH ANY OTHER OFFER

FHG

READERS' OFFER 1994
VALID during 1994

Myreton Motor Museum

Aberlady, East Lothian EH32 0PZ Telephone: (0875) 870288

One child under 16 **FREE** with full paying adult

NOT TO BE USED IN CONJUNCTION WITH ANY OTHER OFFER

FHG

READERS' OFFER 1994
VALID during 1994 season

Crail Museum & Heritage Centre

62-64 Marketgate, Crail, Fife KY10 3TL Telephone: (0333) 450869

FREE entry

NOT TO BE USED IN CONJUNCTION WITH ANY OTHER OFFER

FHG

READERS' OFFER 1994
VALID during 1994

New Lanark Visitor Centre

Lanark, Lanarkshire ML11 9DB Telephone: (0555) 661345

One **FREE** child entry with each full paying adult

NOT TO BE USED IN CONJUNCTION WITH ANY OTHER OFFER

Floating collection of historic vessels; special exhibition, shop, tearoom. Guided tours of engine shop and historic fleet; special events and craftsmen's demonstrations.

DIRECTIONS: 400 yards from Irvine rail station. By road follow signs to Irvine Harbourside.

OPEN: all year.

FHG PUBLICATIONS, ABBEY MILL BUSINESS CENTRE, PAISLEY PA1 1TJ

Guided tour showing glassblowing, cutting and engraving; world's largest collection of Edinburgh Crystal; historic crystal exhibition. Factory shop, coffee shop.

DIRECTIONS: 10 miles south of Edinburgh on A701 Peebles road.

OPEN: daily; tours Monday to Friday, plus weekends May to September.

FHG PUBLICATIONS, ABBEY MILL BUSINESS CENTRE, PAISLEY PA1 1TJ

Motorcars from 1896, motorcycles from 1902, WWII British Military Vehicles; period advertising and motoring ephemera.

DIRECTIONS: near Aberlady between A198 and B1377.

OPEN: daily.

FHG PUBLICATIONS, ABBEY MILL BUSINESS CENTRE, PAISLEY PA1 1TJ

Small museum in 18th century house illustrating the history of this Royal Burgh and fishing village, with its picturesque harbour.

DIRECTIONS: A918 from St. Andrews, A917 from Leven.

OPEN: Easter week; 1st June – mid September; weekends in April, May and rest of September.

FHG PUBLICATIONS, ABBEY MILL BUSINESS CENTRE, PAISLEY PA1 1TJ

Award-winning 200-year-old conservation village with Disney-style "dark" ride, exhibition, gift and coffee shop. Play area and riverside walks.

DIRECTIONS: off A73 south-east of Glasgow.

OPEN: daily all year round (except 25/26 December and 1/2 January).

FHG PUBLICATIONS, ABBEY MILL BUSINESS CENTRE, PAISLEY PA1 1TJ

BEACH BUNGALOW
OUR WORLD BY THE SEA

Executive Beach Bungalow, in its own grounds, quiet secluded cove, with your own beach, moments from your Patio door. Every comfort in an area of outstanding natural beauty. On flat coastal strip with sub-tropical plants confirming Gulf Stream mild climate. Tour beautiful Snowdonia, 'The Castles' and the famous Llyn Peninsula and beaches. Tastefully furnished by Parker Knoll. Modern split level lounge-dining room, overlooking lawn, beach and sea. 3 bedrooms, vanitory units. TV's and duvets; 1 & 2 Double & Single; 3 Single or double; 4 children's upstairs 4 singles; 2 Bathrooms en-suite. Teletext colour TV' video, compact disc tape and music centre, dishwasher, microwave, fridge, freezer, washing machine, tumble dryer, electric blankets, telephone and central heating, patio furniture, parking 5 cars. P.O. and shop handy. Safe bathing and water sports, sea/river fishing. Nearby Restaurants, Bar Snacks, take-aways and most leisure activities, including golf, rambling, pony trekking, three modern Leisure Centres. Featured by BBC and Wales Tourist Board (top grade 5 award). Come and inspect any time, between Caernarfon and Nefyn on A499 (Llyn Peninsula). Try a £49 Minibreak.

JAN	FEB	MARCH	APRIL	MAY	JUNE	JULY	AUG	SEPT	OCT	NOV	DEC
1 -£109	5 -£99	5 -£139	2BH -£369	7 -£219	4 -£329	2 -£429	6 -£549	3 -£415	1 -£269	5 -£159	3 -£99
8 -£89	12 -£99	12 -£149	9 -£229	14-£229	11 -£339	9 -£499	13-£549	10 -£389	8 -£229	12 -£149	10 -£99
15 -£79	19 -£109	19 -£156	16 -£199	21 -£259	18 -£379	16 -£529	20 -£529	17 -£359	15 -£229	19-£129	17 -£299
22 -£79	26 -£109	26 -£199	23 -£189	28BH-£429	25 -£389	23 -£549	27BH-£499	24 -£319	22 -£299	26 -£119	24 -£399
29 -£89			30MD-£199			30 -£549			29 -£249		31 -£259

Deposit ¹/₄ of total. Minimum £50 p.w. and Insurance £3 nightly. Sleeps 10, over 5 persons £5 per night each.
Free electric allowance £7. Central Heating 70° £35 weekly. (Dogs £5 nightly, 2 only. Never left alone.) Weekend, Midweek or Week Breaks Phone 0286 660400

VILLA CHALET

Your own beach, moments from your lounge patio sliding door, overlooking lawn, beach and sea. Every comfort, Lounge dinette, exclusive 3 piece suite. Teletext colour TV, Electric fire, bed settee, 3 separate bedrooms. 1 Double, vanitory basin, en-suite to bathroom, electric blankets and heater. 2 Double, or 2 singles, two drop-down beds for children. 3 Single with drop-down bed. Blankets and pillows provided. Bring linen, towels or own duvet? Kitchen area. Microwave, electric hob & oven, fridge-freezer, slow cooker, kettle, toaster and Hoover. Bathroom, Sit-down shower-bath, wash basin, toilet. Well heated, patio furniture, much up market Dragon Award. **Featured by the BBC and Wales Tourist Board.** View any time. Try a £25 Minibreak.

WALES *It's magic*

MARCH	APRIL	MAY	JUNE	JULY	AUGUST	SEPT	OCT
12 -£78	2BH -£178	7 -£158	4 -£238	2 -£278	6 -£328	3 -£268	1 -£148
19 -£98	9 -£128	14 -£178	11 -£248	9 -£288	13 -£328	10 -£228	8 -£148
26GF-£128	16 -£96	21 -£188	18 -£258	16 -£308	20 -£328	17 -£198	15 -£108
	23 -£108	28BH-£318	25 -£268	23 -£328	27BH-£318	24 -£178	22 -£168
	30MD-£128			30 -£328			

New 2 Bedroomed, Similar, Deduct £25 from above rates. Deposit ¹/₄ of total. Minimum £50 p.w. and Insurance £2 nightly. Sea view £3 nightly. Full Heating 70° £5 nightly. Limited to 8, over 5 persons £3 per night each. (Dogs £3 nightly, never left alone, 2 only). Weekend, Midweek or Week Breaks Phone 0286 660400

BEACH HOLIDAY HOME

BEACH MODERN LUXURY HOLIDAY HOME (Tourist Board approved caravan)
Your own beach, moments from your door. Top Grade 5 award. 6-berth B type, 2 bedrooms: 8 berth A type, 2 bedrooms limited to 6: 10 berth A type, 3 bedrooms limited to 8. Lounge, Kitchen, Dinette, Bedrooms, 1st, one Double; 2nd, some have a Single with a drop-down Bed, or 2 Singles to make a Double; 3rd, Single or Twins, some make a Double. Request on phone and on white booking form. In some a Double Bed Settee makes up in the Lounge/Dinette. Blankets and pillows provided. Bring linen and towels or own duvet? Bathroom, shower, wash basin, toilet. Well heated, remote control Colour TV, Fridge, Large Cooker, Electric Blanket, Kettle and Hoover. Featured by the BBC, Wales Tourist Board, and British Holiday Home Parks. **Superior Dragon Award Holiday Homes with heated Bedroom, £2 nightly.** View any time. Try a £12 minibreak.

MARCH Date	6 berth	8 berth	10 berth	APRIL Date	6 berth	8 berth	10 berth	MAY Date	6 berth	8 berth	10 berth	JUNE Date	6 berth	8 berth	10 berth	JULY Date	6 berth	8 berth	10 berth	AUGUST Date	6 berth	8 berth	10 berth	SEPTEMBER Date	6 berth	8 berth	10 berth	OCTOBER Date	6 berth	8 berth	10 berth
12	£35	£38	£40	2BH	£49	£69	£79	7	£43	£55	£57	4	£69	£89	£95	2	£109	£129	£139	6	£155	£189	£199	3	£79	£99	£109	1	£39	£45	£53
19	£37	£39	£42	9	£39	£49	£52	14	£45	£57	£59	11	£79	£99	£105	9	£115	£139	£145	13	£155	£189	£199	10	£65	£79	£85	8	£35	£45	£49
26GF	£39	£55	£59	16	£39	£45	£47	21	£49	£67	£69	18	£89	£115	£119	16	£135	£169	£179	20	£155	£189	£199	17	£49	£65	£75	15	£35	£47	£49
				23	£39	£45	£47	28BH	£99	£129	£155	25	£99	£119	£129	23	£155	£189	£199	27BH	£129	£159	£169	24	£45	£55	£63	22	£45	£59	£65
				30MD	£41	£49	£53					30	£155	£189	£199	30	£155	£189	£199												

12 foot wide super luxury holiday homes, 20% more spacious. Add £35 to above prices. Deposit £25 p.w. and Insurance £1 nightly. Sea view £2 nightly.
Twin bedded room £2 nightly. Microwave £1 nightly. Superior Dragon Award, with heated bedroom £2 nightly, latest model, recent model, up market model, double glazed model heated to 70°, special position, upgraded etc £5 nightly each. Request quotation. Over 6 persons £3 per night each. (Dogs £2 nightly). Weekends, Midweek or Week Breaks Phone 0286 660400.

BEACH HOLIDAY, WEST POINT, THE BEACH, PONTLLYFNI, CAERNARFON, NORTH WALES LL54 5ET

PERSONAL ATTENTION, BROCHURE
& RESERVATIONS TEL 0286 660400

AVON

COUNTRY HOLIDAYS. Thousands of quality cottages across Britain in the most
picturesque areas. Long holidays or short breaks. Pets welcome in most properties.
COUNTRY HOLIDAYS, SPRING MILL, EARBY, COLNE, LANCASHIRE BB8 6RN
(0282 445216).

Bath

The best-preserved Georgian city in Britain, Bath has been famous since Roman times for its
mineral springs. It is a noted centre for music and the arts, with a wide range of leisure facilities.

TOWN AND COUNTRY COTTAGES. Wide choice of quality cottages in Bath,
Cotswolds, Somerset and Herefordshire. Over 50 welcome pets. Personal attention
and free brochure. APPLY – 22 CHARMOUTH ROAD, NEWBRIDGE, BATH BA1
3LJ (0225 481764). [🐕]

Bristol

Busy university city on River Avon (spanned by Brunel's famous suspension bridge). SS Great Britain, Brunel's iron ship, is moored in the old docks. Many historic buildings including cathedral and Theatre Royal. Gloucester 35 miles, Bath 13.

LINDEN HOTEL, HIGH STREET, KINGSWOOD, BRISTOL BS15 4AR (0272 674331; Fax: 0272 615871). Ideal for visiting National Trust properties; Wookey Hole and Cheddar Gorge within easy travelling distance. 30 bedrooms, most en suite. Car park. Dogs most welcome – owners tolerated! *[🐕]*

ALANDALE HOTEL, 4 TYNDALL'S PARK ROAD, BRISTOL BS8 1PG (0272 735407). An elegant warm and friendly hotel, centrally situated with car park. Colour TV, telephone and tea/coffee making facilities in all bedrooms. All pets welcome. ETB 2 Crowns. *[🐕]*

Ubley

Village 2 miles east of Blagdon Lake.

MRS C. B. PERRY, CLEVE HILL FARM, UBLEY, NEAR BRISTOL BS18 6PG (0761 462410). Two self catering units on working dairy farm. Nearby trout fishing, birdwatching, walking. Maisonette with double bedroom, single bed on the landing, kitchen/diner, bathroom; second unit has double room, twin bedded room, lounge, kitchen/diner, bathroom. Fully equipped except linen. SAE for terms. *[🐕]*

Weston-super-Mare

Popular resort on the Bristol Channel with a wide range of entertainments and leisure facilities. An ideal base for touring the West Country.

MR AND MRS C. G. THOMAS, ARDNAVE CARAVAN PARK, KEWSTOKE, WESTON-SUPER-MARE BS22 9XJ (0934 622319). Caravans 4-6 berth, deluxe with colour TV, electric lighting, showers and toilets in caravans, 2-3 bedrooms. 4-Star two-bedroom caravans; all facilities, colour TV. Parking. Dogs allowed. Graded 4 ticks. *[🐕pw!]*

BRAESIDE GUEST HOUSE, 2 VICTORIA PARK, WESTON-SUPER-MARE BS23 2HZ (0934 626642). Delightful, family-run hotel, close to shops and sea front. All rooms en suite; colour TV; tea/coffee making. November to April THIRD NIGHT FREE. See display advertisement. *[🐕]*

CHESHIRE

CHESHIRE   *Chester*

Chester

County town of Cheshire and former Roman city on the River Dee. Well-preserved City walls, beautiful 14th century Cathedral and fine timbered houses all make it one of the most magnificent medieval cities. Shrewsbury 42 miles, Liverpool 25.

WESTMINSTER HOTEL, CITY ROAD, CHESTER CH1 3AF (0244 317341). A well established hotel offering good service in a friendly atmosphere. Ten minutes' walk from the city centre, it's an ideal base for exploring the historic city. 3 Crowns. [🐾]

FROGG MANOR HOTEL AND RESTAURANT, FULLERS MOOR, NANTWICH ROAD, BROXTON, CHESTER CH3 9JH (0829 782629). Not far from the madding crowd, a Georgian house set in 10 acres of landscaped gardens. Restaurant has an Anglo/French menu and an atmosphere of pure romance. 4 Crowns Commended, AA and RAC***. [🐾]

CLEVELAND

Saltburn-by-the-Sea

Family resort with 5-mile stretch of sand, rock pools, cliffs. Lovely gardens. Good sporting facilities. Whitby 19 miles, Middlesbrough 13, Redcar 5.

MR & MRS BULL, WESTERLANDS GUEST HOUSE, 27 EAST PARADE, SKELTON, SALTBURN-BY-SEA (0287 650690). Situated alongside Cleveland Way, Westerlands is a quiet, modern detached house with beautiful views. Ideal base for touring Moors and East Coast resorts. Evening meals by arrangement; special meals available. All bedrooms with private bathrooms and/or showers. Open March until end September. [🐾]

CORNWALL

CORNWALL   *Praa Sands*

Jasmine and Two Ways
PRAA SANDS, NEAR PENZANCE
Delightful modern bungalows set in very large, well-kept gardens. One not overlooked, set on its own with parking for 3 cars. Sleeps 9 in 4 bedrooms. One overlooking sea. Sleeps 6 in 3 bedrooms. Both superb accommodation. Ideal for pets, all breeds welcome.

Apply—MRS JANE LAITY,
CHYRASE FARM, GOLDSITHNEY, PENZANCE TR20 9JD
Tel: 0736 763301

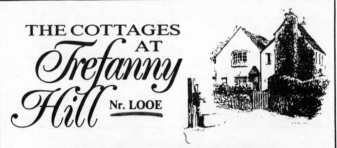

THE COTTAGES AT Trefanny Hill
Nr. LOOE

GORGEOUS OLD WORLD COUNTRY COTTAGES

Sleep 2, 4 and 6, with beams, lovely furnishings and fabulous views. Open all year. Everything from nightstore heating and log fires in winter to heated summer pool. Dishwasher, washing machine/tumble dryer, colour TV and video. Meals service, full and generous linen and much, much more.

An abundance of country walks from your garden gate and coastal walks only 4 miles away.

Free colour brochure:

**O. Slaughter
St. Mary Manor
Trefanny Hill
Duloe, Liskeard
Cornwall PL14 4QF**

Telephone: 0503 220622

CORNWALL *Bissoe, Bridgerule, Bude, Crackington Haven*

IVY COTTAGE, BISSOE, CORNWALL
200-year-old south-facing COUNTRY COTTAGE 5 miles south-west of Truro. Kitchen/dining room, lounge, two bedrooms (sleeps up to 5/6). Garage, garden, separate play area. All facilities incl. TV and microwave. £110–£285. Convenient for all Mid and West Cornwall. **Telephone 0872 70768 for brochure.**

A family run 16 acre woodland site of outstanding natural beauty set well away from main roads, with freedom for the children and peace and quiet for adults. All this and yet just 10 minutes drive from the beach.
On-site facilities include
Licensed bar & clubroom with children's adventure area. Shop, take-away, laundry, off-licence & All-modern amenities.
Open all year.
*Static & touring caravans for hire, Caravan storage available. Dogs/pets welcome, **Daily dog kennelling facility.***

For a brochure, write or call:
Hedley Wood Caravan & Camping Park
Bridgerule, Holsworthy, Devon EX22 7ED
Tel & Fax 0288 81 404

  Listed Site   RAC Appointed Site

Gunnedah
Crackington Haven, Near Bude.
Telephone: 0840 230265

Superior self–contained Bungalows and Cottages with balcony and/or patio with individual entrance for each unit. Electricity by meter. 2–4 bedrooms. Comfortable lounge with dining area. Colour TV. All with fully equipped kitchens and bathrooms. All bed linen provided. Garage/parking on the premises. Launderette. All units but one overlook the sea with sandy beach only 200 yards away. Wonderful views and scenery. Suitable for occupation all year round Special out-of-season terms.
Send for brochure and terms to Resident Proprietors:
John and Ann Connell

Stamford Hill Hotel
"A Country House Hotel"

Set in five acres of gardens and woodland overlooking open countryside yet only a mile from the sandy beaches of Bude. Our spacious Georgian Manor House with
15 en-suite bedrooms with TV and tea/coffee making facilities, outdoor heated pool, tennis court, badminton court, games room and sauna is the ideal place for a relaxing holiday or short break. Daily Bed and Breakfast from £21.00, Three–day Break Dinner, Bed and Breakfast from £85.00. Pets welcome.

Contact: Ian and Joy McFeat, Stamford Hill Hotel, Stratton, Bude EX23 9AY Tel: (0288) 352709.

 **CARAVAN & CAMPING PARK**
CRACKINGTON HAVEN, NEAR BUDE, CORNWALL
✓✓✓ Peaceful caravan/camping park in Area of Outstanding Natural Beauty. Glorious Coastal walks, watersports, riding, ideal touring centre. Luxury Holiday Caravans, touring and camping pitches. Take-away farmhouse meals, free library. Families and pets welcome.
Tel: 0840 230365; Fax: 0840 230514   OPEN ALL YEAR

30

CORNWALL

Crackington Haven, Crafthole, Falmouth, Gorran Haven, Hayle

CORNWALL   *Helston, Holywell Bay, Liskeard*

Mr & Mrs Donald, "Halwyn", Manaccan, Helston TR12 6ER
Tel: 0326 280359/565694
Situated in an area of outstanding natural beauty, near the Coastal Footpath, "Halwyn" is an ancient Cornish farmstead. The original old farmhouse and former farm buildings have been converted to a choice of holiday homes. There are two acres of delightful gardens with an indoor heated swimming pool, sauna and solarium. A perfect "away from it all" holiday retreat. Open all year with special low rates, log fires and storage heaters out of season.
Terms from £95 per week inclusive.

HOLYWELL BAY
Two self-catering Bungalows two minutes from National Trust beach. Two bedrooms, sleep 6. Colour TV, modern conveniences throughout. Private gardens, pets welcome. Terms £100 to £280 per week.
Apply: **M. Devonshire, White Surf, Pentire, Newquay TR7 1PP.**
Tel: (0637) 871862

Woodlay Farm Holidays
Herodsfoot, Liskeard PL14 4RB
Tel: 0503 220221 Fax: 0503 220802

200 ACRES OF PETS PARADISE
Luxury accommodation set in landscaped gardens amidst 200 acres of beautiful Cornish countryside. Converted 16th century barn and cottage to accommodate between 2-6 people.

Tastefully modernised to a very high standard to include fitted carpets, colour TV, central heating, electric blankets, etc.

Short drive to Looe, Polperro, Mevagissey, and many lovely secluded beaches. Golf, riding, sea fishing all available close by. Woodlay also offers free coarse fishing to residents only.

AA, West Country Tourist Board listed.
Colour brochure available — stamp appreciated.

Liskeard, Cornwall. Tel: Liskeard (0579) 20332
Bed and Breakfast   Evening Meal optional
H/C in all rooms. Ground-floor twin-bedded room with washbasin and toilet. Good touring area. Television. All comforts. Central heating. Good Food. Main Road. Open all year. Fire Certificate. Moderate terms.
Mrs Northcott, Pendower, East Taphouse, Liskeard PL14 4NH

Readers are requested to mention this guidebook when seeking accommodation (and please enclose a stamped addressed envelope).

Cutkive Wood Chalets

Six only detached, self catering cedarwood chalets in 41 acres of private woodland. Personally supervised; the owners take great pride in the cleanliness and condition of these two and three bedroomed chalets which are fully equipped, including bed linen, colour TV, full size cooker, fridge and microwave oven. Picturesque resorts of Looe and Polperro a short drive away; Plymouth 30 minutes; St. Mellion Championship Golf Course five miles. On-site shop, milk and papers daily. Pets corner with goats, pigs, ducks, hens, geese. Children welcome to help feed the animals and milk the goats. Three-hole golf course, games room, adventure playground. Dogs welcome.

**Mrs. E. Coles, Cutkive Wood Chalets,
St. Ive, Liskeard PL14 3ND
Tel: 0579 62216**

PARC BRAWSE HOUSE
Penmenner Road, The Lizard, Cornwall TR12 7NR (0326 290466).

Small Georgian-style hotel in superb coastal position offers every comfort. Home cooking, including vegetarian. Sea views. Cosy bar. En-suite available. Tea making facilities and radio/alarms. Dogs welcome.　　　　RAC Acclaimed　　　　ETB 🏵🏵 Approved

CORNWALL'S LIZARD PENINSULA

Small hotel set in 1½ acres lawned gardens with superb view across Kynance Cove. Peaceful, comfortable and relaxing. All rooms with shower, or shower and toilet. Interesting choice of menus. Cosy bar.
Mount's Bay House Hotel, Penmenner Road, The Lizard TR12 7NP
(0326) 290305/290393

ETB 🏵🏵 Commended　　　　　　　　　　　　　　　　　　ACCESS/VISA

TALLAND, BARTON CARAVAN PARK
Talland Bay, Looe, Cornwall PL13 2JA

This is a small family-run farm site situated in peaceful countryside between Looe/Polperro, yet only a few minutes' walk from the beaches at Talland Bay. We offer a variety of caravans with colour TV and full services, from luxury three and two-bedroomed 33' to economy priced 25'. Part weeks and weekend bookings acceptable in low season. The site has a shop, licensed member club, toilet/shower block, laundry room, play area and swimming pool.
Pets are welcome—plenty of room for walks as our land extends to half-mile of coast and runs right down to the beach, joining up with the coastal walks to Looe & Polperro.

For colour brochure—SAE appreciated, or ring (0503) 72429.

DOWNDERRY BEACH HOLIDAY PARK
— NEAR LOOE, CORNWALL —

Modern holiday bungalows & Cottages in a sheltered sunny south facing valley. Very close to Downderry Beach. Accommodation, sleeps 2-8 persons with 1, 2 or 3 bedrooms. Shops, village Inn etc only 3 mins walk.

JOHN FOWLER HOLIDAYS

GENEROUS EARLY BOOKING DISCOUNTS

FOR COLOUR BROCHURE **0271 866666**

John Fowler Holidays, Department 36, Marlborough Road, Ilfracombe, Devon EX34 8PF

35

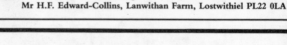

Bissoe

Village four miles south-west of Truro.

IVY COTTAGE, BISSOE, CORNWALL. 200-year-old country cottage 5 miles from Truro. Kitchen/dining room, lounge, 2 bedrooms. All facilities incl. TV and microwave. Terms £110–£285. For brochure phone 0872 70768. *[🛏]*

Bodmin

Quaint county town of Cornwall, standing steeply on the edge of Bodmin moor. Pretty market town and touring centre. Plymouth 31 miles, Newquay 20, Wadebridge 7.

COOMBE MILL, ST. BREWARD, BODMIN PL30 4LZ (0208 850344). Superb cottages and beautiful log cabins set in an idyllic 30 acre farm park. Prices from £100 (Off season short break for 2 people) to £720 (Cottage for 8 in August). Free colour brochure.

NEAR JAMAICA INN, BODMIN MOOR, A30. Character 4-bedroomed holiday farmhouse, sleeps 4–8. Lovely old farmyard, period barns, walled gardens, fabulous views. Own lake, no neighbours. 4 miles village, outstanding countryside, by lake, close local beauty spots. Tastefully furnished, log fires and nightstore heating, colour TV. GRAHAM WRIGHT, FURSWAIN FARM, COMMON MOOR, LISKEARD, CORNWALL PL14 6SB (0579 344080).

Boscastle

Picturesque village in tiny harbour. Rocky beach, some sand, fine scenery. Tintagel 4 miles.

BOTTREAUX HOUSE HOTEL, BOSCASTLE PL35 0BG (0840 250231). This seven-bedroom, privately run Hotel offers guests every amenity, from lovely en suite bedrooms to our candlelit restaurant. You will find a caring and relaxed atmosphere when you stay with us. Children and pets welcome. Parking. Free use of mountain bikes. *[🛏]*

THE WELLINGTON HOTEL, THE HARBOUR, BOSCASTLE PL35 0AQ (0840 250202). Historic 16th-century Coaching Inn in glorious National Trust area offers 21 bedrooms (16 en suite) with colour TV, tea/coffee facilities. Anglo-French restaurant; Free House with real ale. Log fires. Pets always welcome. 10 acres woodland walks. Free brochure. *[🛏]*

MRS M. CONGDON, TREMORLE, BOSCASTLE PL35 0BU (0840 250233). Peaceful, spacious self-catering bungalow in own grounds with views. Comfortable, heated and well equipped for 2–8. Lovely cliff, valley walks. Spring and autumn £80–£180 per week /pw! £10 per pet weekly.] ETB 3 Keys.

MRS PEGGY SAUNDERS, OLD POST HOUSE, BOSCASTLE PL35 0AX (0840 250342). Cottage for two. Cosy. Quaint. Large wooded garden. Pets paradise. National Trust/Conservation area. 5 minutes Elizabethan Harbour. From £98. *[pw!]*

Boscastle/Crackington Haven area. Modern bungalow sleeping 2-6. Near sandy beaches, cliff and valley walks. Heating Spring and Autumn. £80–£160 per week. MRS PROUT (0840 250289). *[£8 per week.]*

Bude

Popular seaside resort overlooking a wide bay of golden sand flanked by spectacular cliffs. Ideal for surfing; seawater swimming pool for safe bathing.

JOHN AND JULIA HILDER, MORNISH HOTEL, 20 SUMMERLEAZE CRESCENT, BUDE EX23 8HL (0288 352972). Homely and friendly with comfortable, well-equipped rooms. All en-suite with tea/coffee making facilities and television. Central heating. Residents' bar. *[£2 per day.]*

HEDLEY WOOD CARAVAN AND CAMPING PARK, BRIDGERULE, NEAR BUDE EX22 7ED (Tel and Fax: 0288–81 404). Superb 16-acre site amidst lovely countryside, 10 minutes from sandy beaches. All modern facilities. Licensed bar, club room, separate children's play area. [🐕pw!]

BUDE HOLIDAY PARK, MAER LANE, BUDE EX23 9EE (0288 355955). Caravans and holiday apartments sleeping 2-9, with colour TV, free gas and electricity. Nightly entertainment, amusements, pool room, mini-market, launderette. Large touring area. Pets welcome.

STAMFORD HILL HOTEL, STRATTON, NEAR BUDE EX23 9AY (0288 352709). Elegant Georgian manor, 5 mins from beaches. 15 en suite rooms, all with colour TV, tea/coffee makers. Heated pool, tennis court, badminton etc. Ideal for golf, fishing, walking.

JOHN AND ANN CONNELL, "GUNNEDAH", CRACKINGTON HAVEN, NEAR BUDE EX23 0JZ (0840 230265). Self-contained Bungalows and Cottages. All with fully equipped kitchens, bathrooms. Launderette. Pets by prior arrangement. [£5 per week.]

EDGCUMBE HOTEL, SUMMERLEAZE CRESCENT, BUDE EX23 8HJ (0288 353846). Overlooking sea and downs. All rooms colour TV, most en suite, tea/coffee facilities, radio/intercom. 2 minutes town centre, golf course. Dinner, Bed and Breakfast from £154.00 to £187.75 including VAT per week. Private parking. [pw!]

Beautiful Cottages in lovely rural setting 5 miles from Crackington Haven. Log fires, every comfort, furnished and equipped to a very high standard. Dogs welcome by arrangement. Open all year. 3 Keys Commended. APPLY: BERRY, TRENANNICK, WARBSTOW, LAUNCESTON PL15 8RP (056-681 443). [🐕]

Cawsand

Quaint fishing village with bathing beach; sand at low tide. Ideal for watersports. Plymouth (car ferry) 11 miles, (foot ferry) 3.

FRIARY MANOR HOTEL & RESTAURANT, MAKER HEIGHTS, TORPOINT, NEAR CAWSAND PL10 1JB (Tel and Fax: 0752 822112). Historic Manor House set in beautiful area bordering Mount Edgcumbe Country Park, opposite Plymouth on River Tamar. Spacious en suite rooms and family suites. B&B from £18; DB&B from £31.50. 3 Crowns Approved. [🐕]

MR AND MRS A. FIDLER, RAME BARTON GUEST HOUSE, RAME, CAWSAND PL10 1LG (0752 822789). Old Country House standing in own grounds on beautiful Rame Peninsula. Lovely coastline/beaches. Pets, children very welcome. Bed and Breakfast and Evening Meals. Licensed. [pw! £0.30p nightly.] SAE please.

Crackington Haven

Small coastal village in North Cornwall set amidst fine cliff scenery. Small, sandy beach. Launceston 18 miles, Bude 10, Camelford 10.

MR & MRS O. H. F. TIPPETT, TRELAY, ST GENNYS, BUDE EX23 0NJ (0840 230378). Lovely stone cottages on tranquil farm in area of outstanding natural beauty. Log fires, linen, fenced gardens/patios. Sandy beach and National Trust cliffs 2 miles. Three Keys Approved. [£7 per week]

BREMOR HOLIDAY BUNGALOWS AND COTTAGES, CRACKINGTON HAVEN, NEAR BUDE EX23 0JN (0840 230340). Delightfully furnished and equipped bungalows for 6. Linen provided. Enclosed garden. Pets free. Also cottage for two, recently renovated. Open beams, idyllic setting. 3 Keys. [🐕pw!]

HENTERVENE PINE LODGE CARAVAN AND CAMPING PARK, CRACKINGTON HAVEN, NEAR BUDE EX23 0LF (0840 230365, Fax: 0840 230514). 1½ miles unspoilt sandy beach. Area of outstanding natural beauty. Luxury caravans to let. First-class facilities for families and pets. Open all year. AA 3 Pennants. [pw! £10 per week.]

Peaceful wooded valley. Tourist Board 2, 3, 4 Keys Approved/Commended. Traditional Cornish Cottages and Bungalow. Sleep 4–8. Children and dogs welcome. [£7 per week.] APPLY – MRS H. TIPPETT, MINESHOP, CRACKINGTON HAVEN, NEAR BUDE EX23 0NR (0840 230 338).

Crafthole

Village near sea at Portwrinkle. Fine views over Whitsand Bay and River Lynner. Golf course nearby. Torpoint 6 miles.

MRS V. ANDREW, TREWRICKLE FARM, CRAFTHOLE, TORPOINT, WHITSAND BAY PL11 3BX (St Germans [0503] 30333). Homely farmhouse accommodation on Whitsand Bay. Land runs down to beach and adjoins golf course. Washbasins all rooms. Home-produced meat and home cooking. Large garden. Dogs welcome. Bed, Breakfast and Evening Dinner. (Optional).

Falmouth

Well-known port and resort on Fal estuary ideal for boating, sailing and fishing; safe bathing from sandy beaches. Of interest is Pendennis Castle (16th century). Exeter 97 miles, Newquay 26, Penzance 26, Truro 11, Redruth 10.

Ideally situated, spacious self-catering bungalow with secluded garden. Full heating. Ample parking. Children and dogs welcome. Sleeps 1-6. Low Season: £90 to £140; High Season: £165 to £240. Apply MRS J. A. SIMMONS, 215A PERRY STREET, BILLERICAY, ESSEX CM12 0NZ (0277 654425). [£5 weekly.]

MRS J. GOODWIN, 'GOOD-WINDS' GUEST HOUSE, 13 STRATTON TERRACE, FALMOUTH TR11 2SY (0326 313200). 'Good-Winds' is a large Georgian House with panoramic views over Flushing and Falmouth Harbour. En-suite rooms available with colour TV. Licensed. Self catering apartments also available. [pw!]

Gorran Haven

Coastal village, 3 miles from Mevagissey.

Self catering flats sleeping 2–7. Beautiful rural area, 600 yards from sandy beach and harbour. Colour TV, cooker, microwave, fridge freezer. Secluded garden, parking. Open all year. KEN AND SALLY PIKE, TREGILLAN, TREWOLLOCK LANE, GORRAN HAVEN PL26 6NT (0726 842452 24 hours). [🐕]

Hayle

Resort, shopping centre, seaport with excellent sands and dunes. Helston 10 miles, Redruth 10, Penzance 8, Camborne 5.

Modern self-contained family holiday Bungalows, sleeping 6. Only 200 yards shops and beach. Pets welcome. Private parking. APPLY - MAUREEN RICHARDS, SPRINGFIELD, LELANT DOWNS, NEAR HAYLE, CORNWALL TR27 6LL (0736 753625).

MR A. JAMES, ST. IVES BAY HOLIDAY PARK, 73 LOGGANS ROAD, UPTON TOWANS, HAYLE TR27 5BH (0736 752274). Park in sand dunes adjoining huge sandy beach. Choice of bars, free entertainment. Chalets, Caravan and Camping. Large indoor pool [£14 per week.]

Helston

Ancient Stannary Town and excellent touring centre. Noted for the quaint annual 'Furry' Dance. Nearby is Loe Pool, separated from the sea by a bar. Truro 17 miles, St. Ives 15, Falmouth 13, Lizard 11, Redruth 11.

CLASSIC COTTAGES (25), HELSTON, CORNWALL TR13 8NA (24 HOUR DIAL-A-BROCHURE 0326 565555). Choose your cottage from 300 of the finest coastal and country cottages throughout the West Country. *[£8 weekly.]*

MR & MRS DONALD, HALWYN, MANACCAN, HELSTON TR12 6ER (0326 280359/565694). Ancient Cornish farmstead converted to a choice of holiday homes. 2 acres of gardens with indoor swimming pool, sauna and solarium. Perfect for an "away from it all" holiday. Open all year. Terms from £95 per week. *[🔭]*

Holywell Bay

Faces west with extensive sands, cliffs, rocks, 5½ miles Newquay.

Two self-catering Bungalows 2 minutes from beach. Colour TV, private gardens. Pets welcome. £100–£280 per week. APPLY – M. DEVONSHIRE, WHITE SURF, PENTIRE, NEWQUAY TR7 1PP (0637 871862). *[🔭]*

Lanivet

Small, pretty village three miles south-west of Bodmin.

MENA BARN, MENA FARM, LANIVET, BODMIN. Detached barn conversion sleeps 9 adults, 2 children. Ideal for touring. Fully fitted kitchen with washing machine, dishwasher, fridge, cooker, microwave etc. Central heating, electricity and linen included in cost. Pets welcome. Stables and grazing available for your own horse. ALAN & LYNDA EVANS, WOODSIDE, HOOPERS BRIDGE, LANIVET, BODMIN (0628 484700).

Launceston

Historic inland town dominated by ruined Norman Castle. Views over Upper Tamar Valley. Good centre for sea and moors. Plymouth 25 miles, Bude 19, Okehampton 19, Holsworthy 14, Tavistock 14.

MR & MRS E. J. BROAD, TAMAR VIEW, DUTSON, LAUNCESTON PL15 9SP (0566 772607; Fax: 0566 773547). Comfortable, warm and spacious cottage, sleeps 2/8 plus cot. Pleasant walks around farm, salmon fishing on River Tamar, coarse fishing lake. Central for touring. Golf, riding, steam railway, otter sanctuary, etc within five miles. £120–£300 per week.

Liskeard

Pleasant market town and good centre for exploring East Cornwall. Bodmin moor and the quaint fishing villages of Looe and Polperro are near at hand. Plymouth 19 miles, St Austell 19, Launceston 16, Fowey (via ferry) 15, Bodmin 13, Looe 9.

Luxury accommodation in converted 16th century barn, tastefully modernised to a high standard, accommodating 2-6 people. Set in 200 acres near secluded beaches, towns, sporting amenities. AA/WCTB Listed. APPLY - ANN HAWKE, WOODLAY FARM HOLIDAYS, HERODSFOOT, LISKEARD PL14 4RB (0503 220221; Fax: 0503 220802). *[£15 per week.]*

MR AND MRS M. BARKER, RIVERMEAD FARM, TWOWATERSFOOT, LISKEARD PL14 6HT (0208 821464). Self-catering Apartments and Farm Cottages convenient for both coasts and moors. Fishing on River Fowey. Pets welcome! *[🔭]*

MRS V. M. NORTHCOTT, 'PENDOWER', EAST TAPHOUSE, LISKEARD PL14 4NH (0579 20332). All comforts. Open all year. Main road. Good food. Fire Certificate. *[🐕]*

MRS E. COLES, CUTKIVE WOOD CHALETS, ST. IVE, LISKEARD PL14 3ND (0579 62216). Self-catering chalets in 41 acres of woodland. 2/3 bedrooms; full equipped inc. linen, colour TV, fridge, cooker and microwave. On site shop. Pets corner for children. Dogs welcome. *[🐕]*

B. WRIGHT, TREWORGEY COTTAGES, DULOE, LISKEARD, CORNWALL PL14 4PP (0503 262730). Old World Country Cottages. Private garden. Heated summer swimming pool. Full linen. Home cooking. Colour TV, videos, dishwashers, microwaves and log fires. Golf, riding and fishing nearby. Looe 3 miles. Colour brochure available. *[pw! £11 per week]*

Gorgeous old world country cottages for 2, 4, 6 near Looe and Polperro. Open all year. Everything from nightstore heating and log fires in the winter to heated summer pool. Meals service, colour TV, linen, own private garden, plenty of country walks. O. SLAUGHTER, ST MARY MANOR, TREFANNY HILL, DULOE, LISKEARD PL14 4QF (0503 220622). *[One pet free, others £10 weekly.]*

Lizard

The most southerly point in England. Fine coast scenery and secluded coves. Sandy beach at Housel Bay. Truro 28 miles, Falmouth 22, Helston 11.

MR & MRS M. S. STEPHENS, ATLANTIC HOUSE, PENTREATH LANE, THE LIZARD TR12 7NY (0326 290753). Self catering. Coastal house (4 bedrooms). Apartment (2 bedrooms). Lovely sea views. Few minutes' walk coastal foothpath. Open all year. Low season short breaks. Dogs welcome. *[£10 per week]*

MOUNT'S BAY HOUSE HOTEL, PENMENNER ROAD, THE LIZARD TR12 7NP (0326 290305/290393). Set in 1½ acres lawned grounds with superb views across Kynance Cove. Peaceful, comfortable and relaxing. Interesting choice of menu. Cosy bar. Access/Visa. 2 Crowns Commended. *[£1 per night]*

PARC BRAWSE HOUSE, PENMENNER ROAD, THE LIZARD TR12 7NR (0326 290466). Small Georgian–style hotel in superb coastal position offers every comfort. Home cooking, including vegetarian. Sea views. Cosy bar. En-suite available. Tea making facilities and radio/alarms. Dogs welcome. RÁC Acclaimed. ETB 2 Crowns Approved. *[£1 per night]*

Looe

Twin towns linked by a bridge over the River Looe. Capital of the shark fishing industry; nearby Monkey Sanctuary is well worth a visit.

TRADITIONAL CORNISH HOLIDAY COTTAGES for 2,4,6,8. 250 yards Polperro harbour, 5 miles Looe. Either magnificently situated directly overlooking harbour, fabulous outlook, 14 miles sea views; or nicely positioned in the quaint old village centre, by river, gardens, parking, 2 minutes shops, beach, cliff walks. GRAHAM WRIGHT, THE MILL, POLPERRO, CORNWALL PL13 2RP (0579 344080).

Gorgeous old world country cottages for 2, 4, 6. Near Looe and Polperro. Open all year. Everything from nightstore heating and log fires in the winter to heated summer pool. Meals Service, Colour TV, Linen. Own Private Garden. Plenty of country walks. O. SLAUGHTER, ST MARY MANOR, TREFANNY HILL, DULOE, LISKEARD PL14 4QF (0503 220622). *[One pet free, others £10 weekly.]*

Self-catering Bungalows in sheltered, sunny valley. Free colour television. Close to the beach. Children welcome. Ample car parking. APPLY – JOHN FOWLER HOLIDAYS, DEPARTMENT 36, MARLBOROUGH ROAD, ILFRACOMBE EX34 8PF (0271 866666).

MRS JOY RYDING, APPLE TREES, PORTUAN ROAD, HANNAFORE, LOOE PL13 2DN (0503 262626). Well-furnished, self-contained bungalow flat. Sleeps 2/4. 150 yards sea. Dogs welcome, no charge. Open all year. SAE please. *[🐕]*

JOHN & NANCY JOLLIFF, TREMAINE GREEN, PELYNT, NEAR LOOE PL13 2LS (0503 220333). Dogs love our cosy and comfortable character cottages, Cornish countryside and coastal walks. Accompanying humans also welcome if well behaved. Splendid free colour brochure. *[£16.00 per week.]*

TALLAND BARTON CARAVAN PARK, TALLAND BAY, LOOE PL13 2JA (Polperro [0503] 72429). Caravans with electricity and running water, some with showers, flush toilets on family-run farm site close to beaches. Some available from Friday to Friday. Site has shop, licensed club, toilet and shower block, swimming-pool, laundry room. Ideal touring centre. Pets welcome. SAE for colour brochure.

Lostwithiel

Charming town on River Fowey 5 miles south-east of Bodmin. A medieval bridge spans the river and there is a 14th century church.

Fal Estuary/River Fowey - choice of 10 Apartments and Cottages, all personally owned and run with good friendly Cornish hospitality. See Display Advertisement in this guide. For brochure contact: MR H. F. EDWARD-COLLINS, LANWITHAN FARM, LOSTWITHIEL PL22 0LA (0208 872444). *[£10 per week.]*

Mawgan Porth

Modern village on small, sandy bay. Good surfing. Inland stretches the beautiful Vale of Lanherne. Rock formation of Bedruthan Steps is nearby. Newquay 6 miles W.

MR C. E. & MRS H. ROBINSON, SEAVISTA HOTEL, MAWGAN PORTH, NEAR NEWQUAY TR8 4AL (0637 860276). Small nine-roomed family-run Hotel with some en suite accommodation. All fresh produce used whenever possible. Terms £14 to £18 per day plus Evening Meal whenever required. Phone Carl or Hazel. *[🐕]*

THE MALMAR HOTEL, TRENANCE, MAWGAN PORTH, NEWQUAY TR8 4DA (0637 860324). Small licensed hotel. Reputable sea-fishing coast. Two good golf courses nearby. Good English cooking. Rooms with tea-making facilities, some en-suite. *[🐕 pw!]*

WHITE LODGE HOTEL, MAWGAN PORTH BAY, NEAR NEWQUAY TR8 4BN (0637 860512). Give yourselves and your dogs a quality holiday break at this family-run hotel overlooking beautiful Mawgan Porth Bay. Bedrooms en-suite, all rooms with washbasins, shaver points, heaters etc. Lounge bar, games room, sun patio, dining room. Car park. Phone for free brochure. 2 Crowns. AA. RAC. *[🐕 pw!]*

Mevagissey

Pretty little resort and fishing village. Interesting harbour, narrow streets. Sandy coves nearby. Bodmin 17 miles, Truro 17, St Austell 6.

Small family Park. Chalets, Caravans at Carnmoggas Holiday Park, Cornish Riviera. Indoor heated pool. Indoor Bowls 6/7 Rinks, Snooker, Pool, Clubhouse, Colour Televisions. Pets welcome. WCTB; ETB; 3 ticks. APPLY: P14 RYSDALE ROAD, BRISTOL, AVON BS9 3QU (0272 623792) or (0275 372590). *[£12 per week]*

Mousehole

Picturesque fishing village with sandy and shingle beach. Penzance 3 miles.

POLVELLAN HOLIDAY FLATS. Three S/C flats (sleep 2–4) at entrance to unspoilt fishing village. Fully equipped. Linen supplied FREE. Colour TV. Open all year from £70 per week. Pets welcome free of charge. APPLY – MAJOR J. T. KELLY, POLVELLAN, CLIFF ROAD, MOUSEHOLE, CORNWALL TR19 6PT (0736 731563). *[🐾]*

Mullion

Lizard peninsula village with fine Church (15th cent.). 1 mile S.W. is Mullion Cove (N.T.) sheltered by high cliffs. Other little coves in vicinity and impressive rock and cliff scenery. Helston 8 miles.

TRENANCE FARM COTTAGES, MULLION TR12 7HB (0326 240639). Very well-equipped and comfortable cottages, also B&B in the farmhouse, situated half way between Mullion village and Mullion Cove – field to exercise dogs. Public footpath to cliff top and lovely walks and views (¼ mile). Summer swimming pool. *[🐾 pw!]*

Newquay

Popular family holiday resort surrounded by miles of golden beaches. Semi-tropical gardens, zoo and museum. Ideal for exploring all of Cornwall.

ROSEMERE HOTEL, WATERGATE BAY, NEAR NEWQUAY TR8 4AB (0637 860238). Relaxed, informal, family-run Hotel; large grassed area, beach and Coastal Footpath all within 100 yards. 44 rooms, 36 en suite. Licensed bar, entertainment. Open all year. *[🐾]*

CORISANDE MANOR HOTEL, PENTIRE, NEWQUAY TR7 1PL (0637 872042). A Hotel of unique turreted Austrian design, quietly situated and commanding an unrivalled position in three-acre secluded landscaped gardens. Private fore-shore. 17 en suite bedrooms with TV, tea-making facilities. Same chef proprietors since 1968. DB&B weekly £165–£200 pp inc. VAT. For brochure and menus telephone David and Anne Painter. AA**RAC, ETB Three Crowns Commended, Les Routiers. *[🐾]*

MR D. P. W. HUMPHREY, MEADOW, HOLYWELL BAY, NEWQUAY (0872 572752). Modern Bungalows and Caravans. Available all year. Close beach. Television. Pets welcome.

CY AND BARBARA MOORE, THE RANCH HOUSE, TRENCREEK, NEWQUAY TR8 4NR (0637 875419). Detached bungalow with lovely gardens and superb views. Choice of bedrooms (two en-suite); shower rooms; lounge. Parking. Children and pets welcome. Bed and Breakfast from £13 daily. *[£10 per week.]*

WHITE LODGE HOTEL, MAWGAN PORTH BAY, NEAR NEWQUAY TR8 4BN (0637 860512). Give yourselves and your dogs a quality holiday break at this family-run hotel overlooking beautiful Mawgan Porth Bay. Bedrooms en-suite, all rooms with washbasins, shaver points, heaters etc. Lounge bar, games room, sun patio, dining room. Car park. Phone for free brochure. 2 Crowns. AA. RAC. *[🐾 pw!]*

Padstow

Bright little resort with pretty harbour on Camel estuary. Extensive sands. Nearby is Prideaux Place (Eliz.). Launceston 35 miles, Truro 24, Bodmin 15, Newquay 15, Wadebridge 8.

RAINTREE HOUSE HOLIDAYS, WHISTLERS, TREYARNON BAY, PADSTOW PL28 8JR (Tel and Fax: 0841 520228). We have a varied selection of accommodation. Small or large, houses and apartments, some by the sea. All in easy reach of our lovely beaches. Please write or phone for brochure. *[🐾]*

Pleasant Victorian House. Well converted to 3 fully equipped apartments. Sleep 4/6. Large garden. Car park. Dogs love us! MRS WATTS, "WHISTLERS", TREYARNON BAY, PADSTOW PL28 8JR (Tel and Fax: 0841 520228). *[🐾]*

Penzance

Well-known resort and port for Scilly Isles. Sand and shingle beaches. Bodmin 48 miles, Truro 27, Falmouth 26, Redruth 18, Helston 13, Land's End 10, St. Ives 8.

ALEXANDRA HOTEL, ALEXANDRA TERRACE, SEAFRONT, PENZANCE TR18 4NX (0736 62644/66333). Seafront hotel, 32 bedrooms (30 en-suite), all with colour TV, telephone, central heating and tea/coffee making facilities. Excellent cuisine. Lounge and licensed bar. Sun terrace. Parking. Bed and Breakfast from £140.

SALLY AND PETER HOGG, TRENANT PRIVATE HOTEL, ALEXANDRA ROAD, PENZANCE TR18 4LX (0736 62005). Comfortable, friendly Hotel near seafront. Colour TV, teamaker, B&B from £14 nightly, £90 weekly. En-suite, fourposter bedrooms and ground floor twin available. Dinner optional. Licensed. Early Breakfasts. All welcome from stick insects to elephants! AA, WCTB 2 Crowns, Cornwall Tourist Board. *[🐾]*

PENWITH COTTAGES, CHYANDOUR OFFICE, PENZANCE TR18 3LW (0736 65306). Holiday Cottages, Farmhouses set in beautiful Cornish countryside. Well equipped. SAE for brochure *[pw! £10 per week.]*

Perranporth

Popular family resort with wide sands and cliffs. Surf-bathing. Of interest is St. Piran's Church (6th cent). Redruth 10 miles, Truro 10, Newquay 9.

ATLANTIC VIEW LICENSED HOTEL, PERRANPORTH (0872 573171). Beside the beach. Sky colour TV. Free drinks. En suite facilities. Riding, golf, fishing. Free child places. DB&B from £135 per week. Christmas Breaks. Pets welcome. ETB Two Crowns.

Polperro

Picturesque and quaint little fishing village, harbour. Of interest is the 'House on the Props'. Fine coast scenery. Fowey 9 miles, Looe 5.

POLPERRO 250 YARDS HARBOUR. Holiday cottages for 2,4,6,8. Either magnificently situated directly overlooking harbour, fabulous outlook, 14 miles sea views; or nicely positioned in quaint old village centre, by river, gardens. Parking. Colour TV. 2 minutes shops, beach, cliff walks. GRAHAM WRIGHT, THE MILL, POLPERRO, CORNWALL PL13 2RP (0579 344080).

CLAREMONT HOTEL, THE COOMBES, POLPERRO PL13 2RG (0503 72241). All rooms en suite with colour TV and tea-making facilities. Bar. Restaurant. Ideally located for walking and touring Cornwall. Short Breaks. Open all year. ETB 3 Crowns, AA/RAC 1 Star. Logis. *[£1 per night.]*

Gorgeous old world country cottages for 2, 4, 6 near Looe and Polperro. Open all year. Everything from nightstore heating and log fires in the winter to heated summer pool. Meals service, colour TV, linen, own private garden, plenty of country walks. O. SLAUGHTER, ST MARY MANOR, TREFANNY HILL, DULOE, LISKEARD PL14 4QF (0503 220622). *[One pet free, others £10 weekly.]*

Polzeath

Small, friendly resort on cliffs near Padstow. Fine sands, good bathing, surfing. Sheltered by Pentire Head (N.T.) to the north. Wadebridge 8 miles.

D. & L. SHARPE, PINEWOOD FLATS, POLZEATH PL27 6TQ (020-886 2269). Flats, Chalets and Cottage. Table tennis, swingball, launderette, baby-sitting. Superb touring centre.

Port Gaverne

Hamlet on east side of Port Isaac, near Camel Estuary.

Luxury Cottages for six in bygone fishing hamlet. Set around a peaceful courtyard garden with further gardens and private parking. Full central heating, fridge/freezer, washer/dryer, dishwasher, microwave, colour TV, video. Weekly: £140 (February), £450 (August). Also daily rates off-season. Open all year. APPLY: CAROLE & MALCOLM LEE, GULLROCK, PORT GAVERNE, PORT ISAAC PL29 3SQ (0208 880106). [🐶]

Port Isaac

Attractive fishing village with harbour. Much of the attractive coastline is protected by the National Trust. Camelford 9 miles, Wadebridge 9.

LONG CROSS HOTEL & VICTORIAN GARDENS, TRELIGHTS, PORT ISAAC PL29 3TF (0208 880243). Set in magnificent public gardens with tavern in the grounds. Pets' corner. Perfect base for touring. Excellent food served all day. Bargain Spring/Autumn Breaks.

Cottages sleep 6/8. Central location. Approximately 5 miles beautiful beaches, moors, golf course and bike trails. Brochure. MRS S. STEPHENS, CASTLE GOFF, LANTEGLOS, CAMELFORD PL32 9RQ (0840 213535).

Portscatho

Tiny cliff-top resort on Roseland Peninsula overlooking beach of rocks and sand. Harbour; splendid views. Falmouth 5 miles.

ROSEVINE HOTEL, PORTHCURNICK BEACH, PORTSCATHO, TRURO TR2 5EW (0872 580206/580230). A friendly, family-managed country house hotel in a peaceful setting with delightful sea views. Top class cuisine, fresh local fish a speciality. AA/RAC***, Ashley Courtenay Highly Recommended. [pw! £2.75 per night.]

TREWINCE MANOR, PORTSCATHO TR2 5ET (0872 580289). Self-catering units on estate overlooking St. Mawes and the sea with small touring site. Private woods and quay for boating enthusiasts. Family-run site. 1 to 3 Keys WCTB/CTB. [pw! £16 per week.]

Poundstock

Attractive village with interesting frescoes on church wall. Nearby Penfound Manor is mentioned in Domesday Book. Bude 4 miles.

Two cottages in an area of outstanding natural beauty. Sleep 6 and 8. 100 yards from unspoilt beach. Open all year. Pets and children welcome. [£7 per week.] APPLY – MR AND MRS H. CUMMINS, MINESHOP, CRACKINGTON HAVEN, BUDE EX23 0NR (0840 230338).

Praa Sands

Magnificent stretch of sands and dunes. Nearby is picturesque Prussia Cove. Penzance 7½ miles, Helston 6.

Superb well-appointed Bungalow. Sleeps two families. Private lake fishing, large garden, beaches 2 miles. Central heating and electricity included. APPLY - LAITY, BOSTRASE, MILLPOOL, GOLDSITHNEY, PENZANCE TR20 9JG (0736 763486). *[🐾]*

Superb Bungalows sleeping 6 and 8, plus cot. One overlooking sea at Praa Sands. One 2 miles Praa Sands, secluded situation. Well furnished and large gardens all round. All breeds welcome. APPLY - MRS J. LAITY, CHYRASE FARM, GOLDSITH-NEY, PENZANCE TR20 9JD (0736 763301). *[£10 per week.]*

St. Agnes

Patchwork of fields dotted with remains of local mining industry. Watch for grey seals swimming off St. Agnes Head.

MARC WATTS, TREVAUNANCE POINT HOTEL, ST AGNES TR5 0RZ (087 255 3235). Old world clifftop Hotel, ships timbered rooms, sea views, candlelight cuisine. Sea-food specialities. Open all year. Winter breaks. *[🐾pw!]*

THE SUNHOLME HOTEL, ST. AGNES TR5 0NW (0872 552318). This country Hotel enjoys one of the finest views in the South West. Ideal for touring, cliff walks, beaches. Fine cuisine, service. All bedrooms en suite. 3 day breaks available. Brochure available.

THE DRIFTWOOD SPARS HOTEL, TREVAUNANCE COVE, ST. AGNES TR5 0RT (0872 552428). Take a deep breath of Cornish fresh air at this comfortable Hotel ideally situated for a perfect seaside holiday. Wonderful food, traditional Cornish home cooking. Children and pets welcome.

ROSEMUNDY HOUSE HOTEL, ST AGNES TR5 0UF (0872 552101). An elegant Queen Anne residence set in 4 acres of informal garden and woodland. Swimming pool, games room, croquet, putting. Half board from £140. Send or telephone for colour brochure. *[🐾pw!]*

St. Austell

Old Cornish town and china clay centre with small port at Charlestown (1½ miles). Excellent touring centre. Newquay 16 miles, Truro 14, Bodmin 12, Fowey 9, Mevagissey 6.

ROSETOWN LUXURY BOARDING KENNELS AND CATTERY, THE BUNGALOW, PITSMINGLE, ROCHE, ST AUSTELL PL26 8LZ (0726 890531). Holiday with your pet in mid-Cornwall. Comfortable B&B accommodation in luxury bungalow. Double room en suite, twin room with shared bathroom. Details on request.

P. W. MILLN, BOSINVER FARM, ST. AUSTELL PL26 7DT (0726 72128). Quality self-catering Cottages and Bungalows on small estate. Sleep 2,4,6,7,11 – one suitable for a wheelchair. Children and dogs welcome. Personally supervised by owners. Colour brochure. *[pw! £7 per week.]*

ST. MARGARET'S HOLIDAY PARK, POLGOOTH, ST. AUSTELL PL26 7AX (0726 74283). Family-run 27 Bungalows and Chalets in sunny wooded valley. Village inn, shop, golf 500 yards. Children and pets welcome. From £80 per week. *[pw! £7 per week.]*

St. Ives

Picturesque resort, popular with artists, with cobbled streets and intriguing little shops. Wide stretches of sand.

THE LINKS HOLIDAY FLATS, CHURCH LANE, LELANT, ST. IVES TR26 3HY (0736 753326). Self-catering Holiday Flats on 2-acre site 5 minutes from beach. All flats are self-contained with colour TV. Write or phone for brochure. *[pw!]*

Country Cottages at Hellesveor, one mile St. Ives Harbour. Sleeps 4–6. Luxuriously equipped; sheets, central heating; garden, parking; farm views, cliff walks. Children welcome. Available all year. Terms £85 to £150 (Winter) and £130–£260 (Summer); includes sheets and heating. Tourist Board Category 3. APPLY: MRS P. H. SEABROOK, 30 NEWCOMBE STREET, MARKET HARBOROUGH, LEICESTER-SHIRE LE16 9PB (0858 463723).

PRIMROSE COTTAGE, PORTHMINSTER, ST. IVES TR26 2ED. Superb granite family house on path to beach (two minutes). Three bedrooms (two on ground floor); two bathrooms, 24 ft. lounge, etc. Magnificent views. Large sheltered gardens. Private parking reserved, if required. SAE, or phone (0736 62185 or 796783).

ST IVES, PENZANCE, HAYLE, ST AGNES, CALLINGTON. Choice of five delightful self-catering holiday villages in woodland and seaside settings. All with indoor pool, children's play area etc. Brochure from CORNISH MANOR HOLIDAYS (DEPT PW), QUAYSIDE HOUSE, NEWHAM ROAD, TRURO TR1 2DP (0872 225525).

CARLYON GUEST HOUSE, 18 THE TERRACE, ST IVES TR26 2BP (0736 795317). Warm, friendly atmosphere with good English cooking. All bedrooms with TV and tea/coffee facilities; some with showers. Bed and Breakfast, with Evening Meal optional.

St Mawgan

Delightful village in a wooded river valley. Ancient church has fine carvings.

DALSWINTON COUNTRY HOUSE HOTEL, ST. MAWGAN, NEAR NEWQUAY TR8 4EZ (0637 860385). Old Cornish house standing in nine and a half acres of secluded grounds. All rooms en-suite, colour TV, tea/coffee facilities. Heated swimming pool. Open all year including Christmas and New Year. ETB 3 Crowns, AA 2 Stars. *[🐶]*

Tintagel

Attractively situated amidst fine cliff scenery. Small rocky beach with some sand. Famous for associations with King Arthur, whose ruined Castle on Tintagel Head is of interest. Also worthy of note is Barras Head and Glebe Cliff (N.T.), Church and Old Post Office. Bodmin 20 miles, Bude 19, Wadebridge 16, Camelford 6.

MRS M. LEEDS, WILLAPARK MANOR HOTEL, BOSSINEY, TINTAGEL PL34 0BA (0840 770782). Beautiful character house amidst 14 acres and only minutes from the beach. All en suite rooms. Children and pets welcome. Open all year. SAE for brochure. ETB 3 Crowns Commended. *[🐶]*

VIC & MARGARET GROSS, PENDRIN HOUSE, ATLANTIC ROAD, TINTAGEL PL34 0DE (0840 770560). Pendrin sits snugly in King Arthur's country, a short walk from a breathtaking coastline with much myth, magic and beauty to explore. Well-behaved owners are welcome. Telephone Vic or Margaret for rates. *[🐶]*

TRENOWAN HOTEL, TREKNOW, TINTAGEL PL34 0EJ (0840 770255). Small family-run hotel. Stunning scenery. Good home cooking. All rooms en suite, colour TV and teamaking. Phone for brochure. *[🐶]*

BOSSINEY FARM CARAVAN AND CAMPING PARK, TINTAGEL PL34 0AY (0840 770481). Family-run park. Two ranges of caravans – semi-serviced with toilet, fridge etc. Fully-serviced with H&C, shower and room heater. All with TV. On the coast at Tintagel. Colour brochure available.

Treknow

Village near north coast of Trebarwith Strand. Camelford 4 miles.

MRS S. M. ORME, "HILLSCROFT", TREKNOW, TINTAGEL (0840 770551). Comfortable accommodation near surfing beach in beautiful National Trust country-side. Walks, riding, sea-fishing all nearby. Car parking. Good home cooking. All rooms tea/coffee facilities. Pets welcome. Bed and Breakfast.

Truro

Pleasant cathedral city. An excellent touring centre with both north and south coasts within easy reach. Many tourist attractions including fine shops. There are numerous creeks to explore and boat trips may be made across the estuary to Falmouth. Penzance 27 miles, Bodmin 25, Helston 17, St. Austell 14, Falmouth 11, Redruth 8.

MICHAEL AND KITTY ECCLES, HUNDRED HOUSE HOTEL, RUAN HIGHLANES, TRURO TR2 5JR (0872 501336). Country House, 3 acre garden. Friendly atmos-phere. Imaginative English cooking. All rooms en suite. Colour television. ETB category 3 Crowns. Brochure and tariff. *[£2.50 per night.]*

MARCORRIE HOTEL, 20 FALMOUTH ROAD, TRURO TR1 2HX (0872 77374; Fax: 0872 41666). A former Victorian family house close to city centre, in a quiet area, centrally situated to visit nearby country houses, gardens or coastal footpaths. Edwardian Restaurant serves traditional food. Comfortable en-suite rooms, ample parking. Double/twin en-suite room from £40 B&B. *[£2.50 per night]*

Wadebridge

Town on River Camel six miles N.W. of Bodmin. Oldest working roadbridge in Britain, dates from 1485. Piers said to be built on woolpacks.

E. P. JONES, HENDRA COUNTRY GUEST HOUSE, ST KEW HIGHWAY, NEAR WADEBRIDGE, BODMIN PL30 3EQ (0208 84343). I am Henry, a Collie, and just love meeting new friends. I have a lovely field to explore. Please bring your humans to holiday here with you. "Bone and Basket" (B&B) from £18.00 per night. Please ring my master Eddie Jones. 3 Crowns Commended, RAC Acclaimed. *[£1 per night]*

CUMBRIA

CUMBRIA *Allonby*

EAST HOUSE GUEST HOUSE
Allonby, Maryport CA15 6PQ. Tel: 0900 881264 or 881276

Overlooking Solway Firth; sea approximately two minutes. Safe bathing, central for Lakes, Carlisle. Tennis, golf at Silloth and Maryport (five miles). Riding school. Open all year. Three family, two double, two twin rooms (all washbasins). Children, dogs welcome. Parking. BB&EM £90 per week; Full Board £120 per week. En suite rooms – B&B £14 nightly; BB&EM £17 nightly, £100 weekly.

QUEENS HOTEL
Market Place, Ambleside, Cumbria LA22 9BU

CENTRAL AMBLESIDE: Ideal location for all the Lakes. All bedrooms ensuite with colour TV, radio/intercom, telephone, tea/coffee making facilities. Full central heating. Bar meals and snacks. Real ales served. Two bars; table d'hôte menu. Non-smoking areas. Pets allowed in all areas except dining room.
Tel: 05394 32206

ETB 👑👑👑

SKELWITH BRIDGE HOTEL
NEAR AMBLESIDE, CUMBRIA LA22 9NJ AA★★RAC
Tel: 05394 32115 Fax: 05394 34254

Those in pursuit of not only the quiet life but the good life will be charmed by this lovely traditional seventeenth century Lakeland Inn. Well appointed en suite bedrooms offer every comfort including colour TV, radio, tea and coffee facilities, direct-dial telephone and hairdryer, and residents have two private lounges at their disposal, as well as the oak panelled Library Bar, sun terrace and gardens. Children are most welcome here, and parents will be delighted with the very reasonable rates charged for family rooms.

KINGSWOOD OLD LAKE ROAD
AMBLESIDE. TEL. 053-94 34081

Near town centre yet off main road. Ample car parking. Comfortable, well-equipped bedrooms with washbasins, tea/coffee making facilities. Colour TV. Central heating. Non-smoking. Pets welcome. Bargain Breaks off season. Phone for rates and details.

THE BRITANNIA INN
ELTERWATER
TEL: 05394 37210
FAX: 05394 37311

👑👑👑
Commended

This genuine old-world, 400-year-old inn overlooking the village green in the delightful unspoilt village of Elterwater is renowned for its fine food and excellent wine cellar, and is also open to non-residents for dinner in the evening. There are seven double bedrooms, five of which have en suite shower and toilet; two twin-bedded rooms, one of which has shower and toilet. All have tea and coffee making facilities, hair dryers, colour television, telephone and central heating. With open fires burning cheerfully in the bars, this lively inn is popular for its bar meals, menu and choice of traditional ales. A warm welcome is assured by the resident proprietor, David Fry and his staff. Facilities nearby include fishing, sailing, fell walking, pony trekking and hound trails. The inn is closed at Christmas.

The Britannia Inn, Elterwater, Ambleside, Cumbria LA22 9HP

ϒ ϒ ϒ/ϒ ϒ ϒ ϒ (Up to Highly Commended)

All home comforts provide a relaxing country holiday in peaceful setting. Luxury self-catering lodges and cottages, two or three bedroomed to sleep 2–7. Central heating, microwave, telephone, linen and towels, bath/shower–second WC in three-bedroomed properties. Laundry. Warm for your arrival. 30 minute drive; Lake Ullswater, Keswick, Gretna Green. Golf 5 miles. Open all year. Resident owners.

Terms from £135–£425 per week.

Green View Lodges, Welton, Nr Dalston, Carlisle CA5 7ES
Tel: 06974 76230 Fax: 06974 76523

COMMENDED   4 Keys Commended

Tel: 0228 577308

NEW PALLYARDS, HETHERSGILL, CARLISLE CA6 6HZ

One modern bungalow, 3/4 bedrooms, sleeps 8; 2 lovely cottages on farm. Bed and Breakfast, Half Board. En suite double/family, twin/single rooms. Disabled welcome. We are proud to have won the National Award for the Best Breakfast in Britain and have been filmed for BBC TV.

Bed and Breakfast £16-£18, Dinner from £9.50
Self Catering £80-£325

LAKESHORE LODGES Scandinavian pine Bungalows beautifully situated amongst 50 acres of English woodland designated an 'Area of Special Scientific Interest'. Perfect base for touring Lake District, Scottish Borders and Yorkshire Dales National Park. Dream location for Fly Fishing Holiday with Brown and Rainbow Trout, Boats and tackle available. For brochure and fishing details: *Mrs Sheelagh Potter, Lakeshore Lodges, The Lough Trout Fishery, Thurstonfield, Carlisle CA5 6HB*

Telephone: 0228 576552

ETB   Commended **CRAIGBURN FARM**   AA Listed
Catlowdy, Penton, Carlisle CA6 5QP

Enjoy the delights of the beautiful Cumbrian countryside and life on our 250-acre working farm. Ideal for relaxing on a ''get away from it all'' holiday. Selection of ''rare breeds'' and small park for children. Delicious farmhouse cooking - Mrs Lawson holds award for cooking - and with 25 years' experience in the business, there is a comfortable, friendly atmosphere. Convenient for travel to/from Scotland/Northern Ireland. Central heating. All bedrooms en suite, tea making. FOUR-POSTER BED, perfect for honeymoons. Residential Licence. Games room. Short Break discounts, 20% discounts weekly bookings. Pets most welcome.

Mrs Jane Lawson Tel: (0228) 577214

Allerdale Court Hotel

Market Square, Cockermouth, Cumbria CA13 0AN
Tel: 0900 823654

Situated in the centre of the ancient market town of Cockermouth–birthplace of Wordsworth. Ideally placed for touring the Lakes and the Border country, the Allerdale Court offers all the comforts and amenities you expect of a first class holiday. Most rooms are en suite and have colour television, radio and tea/coffee making facilities AND your pets are made to feel at home. In addition there are three bars with marvellous local atmosphere, and the 'Pickwick Restaurant' which has justly earned a first class reputation. There is also a newly opened Italian Bistro Restaurant, to add an international flavour.

So, for a memorable holiday or a competitively priced short break phone or send for our colour brochure. **"Enjoy a family atmosphere with a professional approach"**

OVERWATER, NR IREBY, KESWICK CUMBRIA CA5 1HH TEL: (07687) 76566

♕♕♕ Commended

Elegant 18th Century Country House Hotel. Family run and cared for, offering the best in traditional comforts and service. Excellent food. Peacefully secluded location yet within only a short drive of the popular centres of Lakeland. *Dogs very welcome in your room. 18 acres of woodlands and gardens for your dog to enjoy unleashed.*
Mini breaks from £44.25 per person per night, Dinner, Room and Breakfast.
Weekly terms £295 per person. Please telephone for a brochure.

Rickerby Grange
PORTINSCALE, KESWICK, CUMBRIA CA12 5RH
Tel: KESWICK (07687) 72344

♕♕♕
COMMENDED
Quiet location in the pretty village of Portinscale, ¾ mile west of Keswick. Ideal base for explorers of the Lakes by foot or car. Family-run, 14 bedroom hotel (most rooms en suite), all with tea/coffee making facilities, direct-dial telephone, colour TV and central heating. Three ground floor bedrooms and four-poster available. The lounge and cosy bar offer a relaxing atmosphere before a delicious home-cooked meal in the elegant dining room. Private car park. Dinner, Bed and Breakfast from £32 per person. Brochure sent with pleasure:

contact
Gordon and Marian Turnbull
on 07687 72344

DERWENTWATER
PORTINSCALE, KESWICK, CUMBRIA CA12 5RE
AA *** RAC

ON THE LAKE SHORE - IN THE HEART OF THE LAKE DISTRICT

Set in 16 acres of conservation grounds on the shores of Lake Derwentwater, yet only 1 mile from the centre of Keswick. Two country style houses offer:-

Traditional Hotel Accommodation
or
Self-catering Apartments with Style
Many facilities available - Children and Pets Welcome.

FULL COLOUR BROCHURE TEL: (07687) 72538
A WARM WELCOME AWAITS
ASHLEY COURTENAY RECOMMENDED

KESWICK
'AYSGARTH', CROSTHWAITE ROAD, KESWICK.

Aysgarth is a lovely secluded semi-detached house on the outskirts of Keswick–the jewel of the Lake District. Furnished to a high standard, Aysgarth features a 27' long sitting room with colour TV, kitchen, bathroom and 3 bedrooms sleeping up to 6. There is a lovely garden and ample private car parking.

The centre of the town, with its shops and attractions, is a 10 minute walk through the park, and Lake Derwentwater with all sorts of boating, just 15 minutes' walk. Pets and children welcome and well catered for.

Apply: Mrs J. Hall, Fisherground Farm, Eskdale CA19 1TF Tel: 09467 23319

"YOUR PET(S)–YOUR HOLIDAY"
Combine COMFORT, PEACE & QUIET, RELAX, FISH, STROLL OR WALK:
SECLUDED COTTAGES AND LEISURE FISHING.

Tranquil quality cottages overlooking two lakes amid Lakeland's beautiful Eden Valley countryside, only 30 minutes' drive from Ullswater, North Pennines, Hadrian's Wall and Scottish Borders.

* Well fenced areas for pets' freedom & exercise
* Guaranteed clean * Well equipped and maintained * Linen provided
* Beds freshly made for your arrival * Centrally located
* Exceptional wildlife and walking area
* Laundry area * **Pets welcome** * Trout & Coarse Fish too–11lb weight caught
* Honest brochure-clear prices * Open all year–breaks/weeks

Relax & escape to "YOUR" home in the country, why settle for less...
Tel: 0768 896275 7 days 8am–10pm. (Fax available).
Answering machine only 10pm–8am.
24hr Auto. Brochure line 0768 898711(manned most Saturdays).

SAE CROSSFIELD COTTAGE, KIRKOSWALD, PENRITH, CUMBRIA CA10 1EU

   RING NOW! It's never too early or too late! | No silly rules

67

Swinside Inn

**NEWLANDS
KESWICK
CUMBRIA**
Telephone (07687) 78253

This warm, cosy and friendly inn has breathtaking views across the Newlands Valley, and is ideally placed for fell walking, climbing, sailing and windsurfing, with Keswick close at hand.

* Extensive bar menu at reasonable prices *
* Good selection of wines *
* Two bars - one with open fire and beamed ceiling *

Eight brightly decorated bedrooms (some en suite) - all with satellite TV and tea/coffee making facilities.

Bed and Full English Breakfast from £15.00 per person.
Reductions for children   Access and Visa accepted

RAC Acclaimed

SAWREY HOUSE COUNTRY HOTEL

**Near Sawrey,
Hawkshead LA22 0LF
Tel: (05394) 36387
Fax: (05394) 36530**

Sawrey House Hotel offers a special combination of comfort and elegance set amidst the stunning beauty and tranquillity of the Lakeland fells. The perfect place to escape for a few days, with personal service, comfortable rooms and delicious food, yet close to excellent fishing, water sports, golf and, of course walking. An ideal centre for touring the area. The Hotel has a lounge and lounge bar, is centrally heated and has log fires too. We are open March to December including New Year. Children & pets welcome. Colour brochure available.

CUMBRIA **LISCO** **PENRITH**
TROUTBECK, PENRITH CA11 OSY TEL: THRELKELD 07687 79645

LISCO has beautiful views of Saddleback and the Fells. Three miles from Keswick Golf Club, six from Derwentwater and five from Ullswater. A good base for touring lovely Lakeland. Comfortable accommodation offered in one double and two family rooms, all with tea/coffee making facilities and washbasins. Bathroom with shower. Lounge and separate Dining Room. Bed and Breakfast, optional Evening meal. Good home cooking. Colour TV. Children welcome. Outside accommodation available for dogs. Large dogs also welcome.

SAE or phone Mrs Mary Teasdale for further information/terms.
PETS WELCOME

Allonby

Small coastal resort with sand and shingle beach. 5 miles north-east of Maryport across Allonby Bay.

EAST HOUSE GUEST HOUSE, ALLONBY, MARYPORT CA15 6PQ (0900 881264 or 881276). Overlooking Solway Firth, two minutes sea. Central Lakes, Carlisle. Riding, tennis, golf near. Bed and Breakfast from £11.00 nightly. Bed, Breakfast, Evening Meal £14.00 nightly. [🐕]

Ambleside

Popular centre for exploring Lake District at northern end of Lake Windermere. Picturesque Stock Ghyll waterfall nearby, lovely walks. Associated with Wordsworth. Penrith 30 miles, Keswick 17, Kendal 13, Windermere 5.

ROSEMARY AND DAVID RUSS, CROYDEN HOUSE, CHURCH STREET, AMBLE-SIDE LA22 0BU (05394 32209). Croyden House offers B&B with en suite facilities from £16, including generous breakfast, in warm, friendly atmosphere. Central location, private parking. Dogs with responsible, loving owners welcome. Contact Rosemary or David for brochure/tariff. *[Donation to Animal Concern]*

SKELWITH BRIDGE HOTEL, NEAR AMBLESIDE LA22 9NJ (05394 32115; Fax: 05394 34254). Traditional 17th Century Lakeland Inn has well-appointed en suite bedrooms which offer every comfort including colour TV, radio, tea/coffee facilities. Children welcome. Sun terrace and gardens.

'KINGSWOOD', OLD LAKE ROAD, AMBLESIDE LA22 0AE (053 94 34081). Near town centre yet off main road. Ample parking. Rooms have washbasins, tea/coffee making facilities. Colour TV; central heating. Pets welcome. Phone for rates and details. *[🐕]*

THE OLD VICARAGE, VICARAGE ROAD, AMBLESIDE LA22 9DH (05394 33364). "Rest awhile in style". Tranquil wooded grounds in heart of village. Car park. All rooms ensuite. Kettle, clock/radio, TV, hair dryer. Quality B&B from £18pp/pn (low season). Reductions for longer stays. Friendly service where your pets are welcome. Phone Ian or Helen Burt.

MRS EDITH PEERS, FISHERBECK FARMHOUSE, OLD LAKE ROAD, AMBLESIDE LA22 0DH (05394 32523). Comfortable 16th century Farmhouse (not working farm). Singles, doubles/twins, family rooms. Washbasins, tea/coffee making facilities, parking. Relais Routiers recommended, Tourist Board 2 Crowns.

BRITANNIA INN, ELTERWATER, AMBLESIDE LA22 9HP (05394 37210). 400-year-old inn renowned for fine food and excellent cellar. All bedrooms with colour TV, tea/coffee facilities etc; most en suite. Fishing, sailing, pony trekking nearby. *[🐕]*

QUEENS HOTEL, MARKET PLACE, AMBLESIDE LA22 9BU (05394 32206). Central location for all the Lakes. All bedrooms en suite; colour TV, radio/intercom, telephone, tea/coffee making. Central heating. Bar meals, real ales. Table d'hôte menu. ETB 3 Crowns. *[£2.50 nightly]*

KIRKSTONE FOOT HOTEL, KIRKSTONE PASS ROAD, AMBLESIDE, CUMBRIA LA22 9EH (05394 32232). Country house hotel with luxury self-catering Cottages and Apartments sleeping 2/7. Set in peaceful and secluded grounds. Adjoining lovely Lakeland fells, great for walking. Special winter breaks. *[pw! £2.50 per night.]*

Appleby

Pleasant touring centre on River Eden, between lofty Pennines and Lake District. Of historic note are the Castle (12th and 17th cent.) and Moot Hall (16th cent.). Good trout fishing, swimming pool, tennis, bowls. Kendal 24 miles, Penrith 13, Brough 8.

"JUBILEE COTTAGE". Sleeps 5/6. 18th century cottage situated between North Lakes and Pennines. Car essential; off road parking for two cars in front of cottage. Well behaved pets welcome. Terms £90-£150. MISS L.I. BASTEN, DAYMER COTTAGE, LEE, NEAR ILFRACOMBE, DEVON (0271 863769). *[🐕]*

Borrowdale

Scenic valley of River Derwent, splendid walking and climbing country.

MARY MOUNT HOTEL, BORROWDALE, NEAR KESWICK CA12 5UU (07687 77223). Set in 4½ acres of gardens and woodlands on the shores of Derwentwater. 2½ miles from Keswick in picturesque Borrowdale. Superb walking and touring. All rooms en suite with colour TV and tea/coffee making facilities. Licensed. Brochure on request. [🐕]

Buttermere

Between lake of same name and Crummock Water. Magnificent scenery. Of special note is Sour Milk Ghyll waterfall and steep and impressive Honister Pass 2½ miles S.E. Golf course. Keswick 15 miles, Cockermouth 10.

BRIDGE HOTEL, BUTTERMERE CA13 9UZ (07687 70252 - three lines). 22 bedrooms all with private bathroom. Full central heating. Direct dial telephones. Excellent food and large selection of wines. Real ale. Walking, fishing and birdwatching. Dogs welcome. Self catering apartments available. [£3 per night.]

Carlisle

Important Border city and former Roman station on River Eden. The Cathedral (12-14th cent.) has famous East window. 12th cent. Castle is of historic interest, also Tullie House Museum and Art Gallery. Good sports facilities inc. football and racecourse. Kendal 45 miles, Dumfries 33, Penrith 18.

GREEN VIEW LODGES, WELTON, NEAR DALSTON, CARLISLE CA5 7ES. Luxury self-catering lodges and cottages, sleeping 2–7 – two/three bedroomed. Peaceful setting. Central heating, microwave, telephone, linen and towels, bath/shower. Lake Ullswater, Keswick, Gretna Green nearby; golf 5 miles. Terms £135–£425 per week. 4/5 Keys (up to Highly Commended). Telephone: MRS IVINSON (06974-76230).

MRS SHEELAGH POTTER, LAKESHORE LODGES, THE LOUGH TROUT FISHERY, THURSTONFIELD CA5 6HB (0228 576552). Scandinavian pine Bungalows with verandahs overlooking 30 acre lake surrounded by unspoilt English woodland. 3 Keys. Dream location for fishing holiday. Boats and tackle available.

NEWPALLYARDS, HETHERSGILL, CARLISLE CA6 6HZ (0228 577308). ETB 4 KEYS COMMENDED. Relax and see beautiful North Cumbria and the Borders. Self-catering accommodation in one Bungalow, 3/4 bedrooms; two lovely Cottages on farm. Also Bed and Breakfast or Half Board – en suite rooms. [£3/£5 per week.]

DALSTON HALL CARAVAN PARK, DALSTON HALL, DALSTON, NEAR CARLISLE CA5 7JX (0228 710165). 4 Ticks. Exit 42 off M6, follow signs for Dalston. Small family-run park set in peaceful surroundings. Electric hook-ups, shop, playground, launderette, fly-fishing, nine-hole golf course. [pw!]

Catlowdy

Ideal for touring Roman Wall, Lake District and Southern Scotland.

MRS JANE LAWSON, CRAIGBURN FARM, CATLOWDY, PENTON, CARLISLE CA6 5QP (0228 577214). Beautiful countryside, superb food, friendly atmosphere. All bedrooms en suite with tea-making facilities. Residential licence. Games room. Pets most welcome. 3 Crowns Commended.

Cockermouth

Market town and popular touring centre for Lake District and quiet Cumbrian coast. On Rivers Derwent and Cocker. Fine fell scenery to the east. Birthplace of Wordsworth. The ruined Norman Castle is of interest. Penrith 30 miles, Carlisle 26, Whitehaven 14, Keswick 12, Workington 8, Maryport 7.

ALLERDALE COURT HOTEL, MARKET SQUARE, COCKERMOUTH CA13 0AN (0900 823654). 'Enjoy a family atmosphere with a professional approach.' Ideal for touring the Lakes and Border country. Most rooms are en suite. Tea and coffee making facilities in your room. Send or telephone for your colour brochure. *[🐾]*

HUNDITH HILL HOTEL, LORTON, COCKERMOUTH CA13 9TT (Cockermouth [0900] 822092). Comfortable, quiet family Hotel. Ideal centre for Lakes. Dogs welcome. Bed and Breakfast from £20. *[£2.00 per night.]*

Elterwater

Beautifully situated at entrance to Great Langdale. Ambleside 4 miles.

MRS M. JONES, ROSEGATE, ELTERWATER, NEAR AMBLESIDE LA22 9HW (05394 37605). Comfortably furnished three-bedroom house. Pretty garden, pets welcome. Charming Lakeland village, ideal for exploring the beautiful Lake District. Ambleside, Windermere and Hawkshead all nearby. Please send SAE for further details. *[🐾]*

Eskdale

Lakeless valley, noted for waterfalls and ascended by a light-gauge railway. Tremendous views. Roman fort. Keswick 35 miles, Broughton-in-Furness 10 miles.

PAT AND EDDIE DARLINGTON, BROOK HOUSE HOTEL, BOOT, ESKDALE CA19 1TG (09467 23288). Bed, Breakfast and Evening Dinner in beautiful Eskdale Valley. Open all year. Licensed bar. Pets welcome. Good home cooking. Parking available.

MRS J. P. HALL, FISHERGROUND FARM, ESKDALE CA19 1TF (09467 23319). Self-catering to suit everyone. Scandinavian Pine Lodges and Cottages – on a delightful traditional farm. Adventure playground. Pets' and children's paradise. Brochures available. ETB 4 Keys. *[🐾]*

Grasmere

Village famous for Wordsworth associations; the poet lived in Dove Cottage (preserved as it was), and is buried in churchyard. Museum has manuscripts and relics.

GRASMERE HOTEL, GRASMERE, NEAR AMBLESIDE LA22 9TA (05394 35277). 12-bedroomed licensed Hotel set in the centre of the Lakes. Ideal for walking or sightseeing. All rooms have en suite facilities, TV etc. Gourmet food and interesting wines. *[🐾]*

Hawkshead

Quaint village in Lake District between Coniston Water and Windermere. The 16th century Church and Grammar School, which Wordsworth attended, and the Old Court House (N.T.) are of interest. Ambleside 5 miles.

BETTY FOLD GUEST HOUSE, HAWKSHEAD HILL, AMBLESIDE LA22 0PS (05394 36611). Guest house with self-catering Flat and Cottage. Set in peaceful and spacious grounds. Ideal for the walker and dog. Open all year. 2 Crowns Highly Commended, 3 Keys Approved. *[£2 per night.]*

IVY HOUSE, HAWKSHEAD, NEAR AMBLESIDE LA22 0MS (Hawkshead [05394] 36204). Dogs welcome. Attractive Georgian residence. Restaurant licence. Well-appointed private suites available. Excellent cuisine, central heating, colour television. Hot drinks facilities in bedrooms. Brochure on request.

Ireby

Quiet Cumbrian village between the fells and the sea. Good centre for the northern Lake District. Cockermouth 11 miles, Bassenthwaite 6.

WOODLANDS COUNTRY HOUSE, IREBY CA5 1EX (06973 71791). In private wooded grounds four miles from Bassenthwaite, ideal for Lakes and Borders. All bedrooms en-suite with tea making facilities. Children welcome. Residential licence. B&B from £20. 2 Crowns Commended. [⚲ pw!]

Keswick

Famous Lake District resort at north end of Derwentwater. Of interest are Crosthwaite Church (11th cent. and later) and museum. Carlisle 30 miles, Penrith 18, Ambleside 17, Cockermouth 12.

MARION AND IAN ROBINSON, THELMLEA COUNTRY GUEST HOUSE, BRAITH-WAITE, KESWICK CA12 5TD (07687 78305). Set in 1¾ acre grounds, ideal base touring/walking. En-suite available. Tea/coffee; colour TV; central heating all rooms. Bed and Breakfast from £13.50. Optional evening meal. Parking. Open all year. ETB 3 Crowns [pw!]

Threlkeld village (Keswick 4 miles). Tourist Board 4 Keys Commended. Delightful Bungalows. Sleep 4/6. All amenities, fridge, electric cooker, night storage heaters, colour TV, telephone. Laundry room. Own grounds with ample parking. £95 minimum to £360 maximum. Bargain breaks low season. Children and pets welcome. APPLY – MRS F. WALKER, THE PARK, RICKERBY, CARLISLE CA3 9AA (0228 24848). [⚲ pw!]

JOHN & JEAN MITCHELL, 35 MAIN STREET, KESWICK (Tel and Fax: 0768 772790). Luxurious Lakeland flats and cottages located in one of Keswick's most desirable areas. All gas central heating. Some with two bathrooms (one en suite).

ROYAL OAK HOTEL, ROSTHWAITE, KESWICK CA12 5XB (07687 77214). Traditional Lakeland hotel with friendly atmosphere. Home cooking, cosy bar and comfortable lounge. Ideally situated 6 miles south of Keswick. Brochure available. ETB 3 Crowns Commended. [⚲ pw!]

J. A. GRANGE, LAKELAND COTTAGE HOLIDAYS, KESWICK CA12 3ES (07687 71071). Warm, comfortable Cottages, Houses and Bungalows in Keswick and beautiful Borrowdale. Most cottages welcome your dog. ETB inspected and approved.

ALLAN AND VIVIENNE CAIRNS, SWAN HOTEL, THORNTHWAITE, KESWICK CA12 5SQ (07687 78 256). Bed, Breakfast and Evening Meal in quiet country hotel in beautiful surroundings. Keswick 4 miles. Fully licensed. Pets welcome. RAC Merit Award. [pw! £1.25 per night.]

OVERWATER HALL, OVERWATER, NEAR IREBY, KESWICK CA5 1HH (07687 76566). Elegant Country House Hotel in spacious grounds. Excellent food. Dogs very welcome in your room. Mini breaks from £44.25 per person per night. Dinner, Room and Breakfast. 3 Crowns Commended. [⚲ pw!]

HARNEY PEAK, PORTINSCALE, NEAR KESWICK. Eight beautifully converted apartments in an old Lakeland-stone building – the very best in self-catering accommodation. Situated in the village of Portinscale only a mile from Keswick. Brochure available. APPLY – MRS J. SMITH, 55 BLYTHWOOD ROAD, PINNER, MIDDLESEX HA5 3QW (081-429 0402, 24 hours). *[pw! £10 per week.]*

Wide choice of self-catering Cottages, Chalets, Apartments and Holiday Home Caravans in and around the Northern Lake District. APPLY – GREY ABBEY PROPERTIES, DEPARTMENT PW, COACH ROAD, WHITEHAVEN CA28 9DF (0946 693346/693364) 24 hours.

SWINSIDE INN, NEWLANDS, KESWICK CA12 5UE (07687 78253). Ideal for fell walking, climbing, sailing etc. Extensive bar menu; eight comfortable bedrooms (some en-suite), all with satellite TV and tea making. Reductions for children. *[🐕]*

MRS J. HALL, FISHERGROUND FARM, ESKDALE CA19 1TF (09467 23319). Situated on the outskirts of Keswick 10 minutes from town centre. Furnished to high standard with 3 bedrooms sleeping up to 6. Garden and private parking.

MR ASTON, THE DERWENTWATER HOTEL, PORTINSCALE, KESWICK CA12 5RE (07687 72538; Fax: 07687 71002). The Hotel has 83 bedrooms, all en-suite, some with view of Lake Derwentwater. All with TV, radio, telephone etc... Single rooms and Four Poster suite available. Restaurant, 2 lounges and conservatory. Also putting and fishing. *[£4 per night.]*

A traditional 17th-century farmhouse, one acre grounds with lovely garden. Ideal for numerous walks. Good home cooking. Pets and children welcome and catered for. Open all year. 3 Crowns Approved. MURIEL BOND, THORNTHWAITE HALL, THORNTHWAITE, NEAR KESWICK CA12 5SA (Tel. and Fax: 07687 78424). *[🐕]*

GORDON AND MARIAN TURNBULL, RICKERBY GRANGE, PORTINSCALE, KESWICK CA12 5RH (07687 72344). Delightfully situated in quiet village. Licensed. Imaginative home cooked food, attractively served. Open almost all year. *[£1 per night.]*

Kirkby Lonsdale

Small town on River Lune, 14 miles north-east of Lancaster. Of interest – the motte-and-bailey castle, mid-19th century Market House and the 16th century Abbots Hall.

Delightful market town. Spacious centrally heated flats sleep 4/6, overlooking river. Parking, garden. Lakes, Dales nearby. £130–£205. Brochure. B&B in 17th century farmhouse on working farm 4 miles from Kirkby Lonsdale. From £13.00. PAT NICHOLSON, GREENLANE END, LUPTON, CARNFORTH LA6 2PP (05395 67236).

Kirkoswald

Village in the Cumbrian hills, lying north-west of the Lake District. Ideal for touring. Penrith 7 miles.

SECLUDED COTTAGES AND LEISURE FISHING, KIRKOSWALD, CA10 1EU 0768 896275 7 days 8 am–10 pm (Fax available). Answering machine only 10 pm–8 am. 24 hr auto-brochure line 0768 898711 (manned most Saturdays). Tranquilly secluded quality cottages, guaranteed clean, well equipped and well maintained. Centrally located for Lakes, Pennines, Hadrian's Wall, Borderland. Enjoy the Good Life in comfort.

Near Sawrey

This beautiful village on the west side of Windermere has many old cottages set among trees and beautiful gardens with flowers. The world-famous writer Beatrix Potter lived at Hill Top Farm, behind the Tower Bank Arms. When she died in 1943 she left the house and much of the surrounding land to the National Trust. A ferry travels across the Lake to Hawkshead. Hawkshead 2 miles, Far Sawrey ½.

SAWREY HOUSE COUNTRY HOTEL, NEAR SAWREY, HAWKSHEAD LA22 0LF (05394 36387; Fax: 05394 36530). Elegant family-run hotel in three acres of peaceful gardens with magnificent views across Esthwaite Water. Excellent food, warm friendly atmosphere. Lounge, separate bar. Children and pets welcome. 3 Crowns, RAC Acclaimed. *[£2.50 per night.]*

Penrith

Historic market town and centre for touring Lake District. Of particular interest is the ruined Castle (14th cent.), Gloucester Arms (dated 1477) and Tudor House, believed to have been the school attended by Wordsworth. Excellent sporting facilities. Kendal 27 miles, Windermere 17, Carlisle 18, Keswick 18.

MRS MARY TEASDALE, LISCO, TROUTBECK, PENRITH CA11 0SY (07687 79645). Open all year for Bed and Breakfast, optional Evening Meal. Good Home Cooking. All rooms tea/coffee facilities. Lounge, Dining room, TV. Children welcome. Ideally placed for Lake District. Moderate terms *[pw!]*

WESTWOOD, CLIBURN, NEAR PENRITH. Comfortable modern bungalow (sleeps 8 in 3 bedrooms), with self-contained granny flat (sleeps 2/4) set in large private garden. Panoramic Lakeland views; midway Penrith/Appleby. Both units with fitted kitchens. Central heating. Fuel/electricity included. Linen hire. Parking. 2 dogs per unit. ETB 3 Keys Commended. Contact: MRS J. DAY, 7 NADDLEGATE, BURN-BANKS, PENRITH CA10 2RL (0931 713376). *[🛏]*

SECLUDED COTTAGES AND LEISURE FISHING, KIRKOSWALD, PENRITH CA10 1EU 0768 896275 7 days 8 am–10 pm (Fax available). Answering machine only 10 pm–8 am. 24 hr auto-brochure line 0768 898711 (manned most Saturdays). Tranquilly secluded quality cottages, guaranteed clean, well equipped and well maintained. Centrally located for Lakes, Pennines, Hadrian's Wall, Borderland. Enjoy the Good Life in comfort.

Roadhead

Hamlet 9 miles north of Brampton.

In an undiscovered corner of Cumbria two lovely cottages with 280 tranquil acres of flora and fauna to explore (maps provided). Central for Hadrian's Wall and Gretna Green. 4 Keys Highly Commended. Apply: MRS J. JAMES, MIDTODHILLS FARM, ROADHEAD, CARLISLE CA6 6PF (06977 48213). *[£10.00 per week]*

Silloth

Solway Firth resort with harbour and fine sandy beach. Mountain views. Golf, fishing. Penrith 33 miles, Carlisle 23, Cockermouth 17.

MR AND MRS G. E. BOWMAN, TANGLEWOOD CARAVAN PARK, CAUSEWAY HEAD, SILLOTH (06973 31253). Friendly country site, excellent toilet and laundry facilities. Tourers welcome or hire a luxury caravan. Telephone or send stamp for colour brochure. *[🛏]*

Thornthwaite

Peaceful village, 3 miles north-west of Keswick.

THWAITE HOWE HOTEL, THORNTHWAITE, NEAR KESWICK CA12 5SA (07687 78281). Country hotel in own grounds. All bedrooms en-suite, with colour TV etc. Excellent base for touring. Regret no children under 12. Brochure available. *[pw! £1 per night.]*

Windermere

Famous resort on lake of same name, the largest in England. Magnificent scenery. Car ferry from Bowness, 1 mile distant. Kendal 9 miles.

LOW SPRINGFIELD HOTEL, THORNBARROW ROAD, WINDERMERE LA23 2DF (05394 46383). Fashion (Boxer) and Treacle (Heinz 57) would like to welcome you to their peaceful Hotel in its own secluded gardens. Lovely views of the Lakes and Fells. All rooms en suite with colour TV etc. Some four-posters. Brochure available. ETB 3 Crowns. [pw! 🅃]

FIRGARTH PRIVATE HOTEL, AMBLESIDE ROAD, WINDERMERE LA23 1EU (05394 46974). Elegant Victorian house close to Lake viewpoint on outskirts of Windermere village. Good breakfast. Private parking. All bedrooms with colour TV, tea/coffee facilities. B&B from £17.00 per person with full en suite facilities. [£1 per night.]

HILLTHWAITE HOUSE HOTEL, THORNBARROW ROAD, WINDERMERE LA23 2DF (05394 43636; Fax: 05394 88660). Set in three acres of secluded gardens, with superb views of lakes and fells. En suite bedrooms with colour TV, telephone etc. Leisure facilities. Pets welcome.

JENNIFER WRIGLEY, UPPER OAKMERE, 3 UPPER OAK STREET, WINDERMERE LA23 2LB (05394 45649/0831 845547). Built in traditional Lakeland stone and situated close to park. Warm, clean and very friendly. Single people welcome. Pets preferred to people. B&B £13.75, Dinner optional. [🅃]

BOWNESS LEISURE LTD., BURNSIDE HOTEL, KENDALE ROAD, BOWNESS-ON-WINDERMERE, CUMBRIA (05394 42211). Self catering cottages sleeping six persons and luxurious hotel set in 3 acres of gardens. All residents have full use of all-weather leisure club. Freephone 0800 220688 for bookings.

APPLEGARTH HOTEL, COLLEGE ROAD, WINDERMERE LA23 1BU (05394 43206). Elegant Victorian mansion house; all rooms with private facilities. Ideally situated for shops, restaurants and touring. Close to bus and rail stations.

Many attractive self-catering holiday homes in a variety of good locations, all well equipped and managed by our caring staff. Pets welcome. For brochure, contact: LAKELOVERS, THE TOFFEE LOFT, ASH STREET, WINDERMERE LA23 3RA (05394 88855 Fax: 05394 88857). [£10.50 per week.]

DERBYSHIRE

DERBYSHIRE   *Ashbourne*

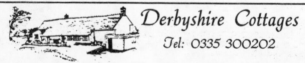

Derbyshire Cottages
Tel: 0335 300202

Derbyshire Cottages are set in the grounds of our 17th century inn, overlooking the Staffordshire Moorlands. Very close to Peak District, Dovedale, Alton Towers and the quaint town of Ashbourne. Each cottage is built of stone and has its own patio with tables and chairs overlooking open countryside. Fully fitted kitchen, including fridge and split-level cooker. Colour TV, radio and direct-dial telephone with baby listening. Children and pets welcome.
Call Mary for further details.

BERESFORD ARMS HOTEL
Station Road, Ashbourne, Derbyshire DE6 1AA
Tel: 0335 300035 Fax: 0335 300065

Situated in the centre of Ashbourne, Gateway to the Peak District, The Beresford offers a warm welcome in a pleasant environment of 'Olde Worlde' charm and character, with pets and children being especially catered for. It makes a perfect starting point to explore the area or visit Alton Towers which is only 10 miles away.   **AA*****

DOG AND PARTRIDGE
Swinscoe, Ashbourne DE6 2HS Tel: 0335-343183

Mary and Martin Stelfox welcome you to a family-run 17th century Inn and motel set in five acres, 5 miles from Alton Towers and close to Dovedale and Ashbourne. We specialise in family breaks, and special diets and vegetarians are catered for. All rooms have private bathrooms, colour TV, direct-dial telephone, tea making facilities and baby listening service. Ideal for touring Stoke Potteries, Derbyshire Dales and Staffordshire moorlands. Restaurant open all day, non-residents welcome.

THORNHEYES PRIVATE HOTEL
Small owner-managed hotel of Victorian elegance

A warm & welcoming Victorian house, set in its own grounds. No evening meals, but hosts supply guide on where to eat, five minutes' walk from Hotel. Ample parking. 11 rooms to 3 Crown standard. Also two self catering cottage apartments.

137 London Road, Buxton SK17 9NW Tel: 0298 23539

PRIORY LEA HOLIDAY FLATS

Beautiful situation adjoining woodland walks and own meadows. Cleanliness assured; comfortably furnished and well equipped. Colour TV. Bed linen available. Sleeps 2/8. Ample private parking. Close to Poole's Cavern Country Park. Brochure available from resident owner. Open all year. 1994 terms from £75 to £190.

Mrs. Gill Taylor, 50 White Knowle Road, Buxton SK17 9NH. Tel: (0298) 23737 or 71661

THE CHARLES COTTON HOTEL
Hartington, Near Buxton SK17 0AL

The Charles Cotton is a small, comfortable hotel with a starred rating for the AA and RAC. The hotel lies in the heart of the Derbyshire Dales, pleasantly situated in the village square of Hartington, with nearby shops catering for all needs. It is renowned throughout the area for its hospitality and good home cooking. Pets and children are welcome; special diets catered for. The Charles Cotton makes the perfect centre to relax and explore the area, whether walking, cycling, brass-rubbing, pony trekking or even hang gliding.

TEL: 0298 84 229

Ashbourne

Market town on River Henmore, close to its junction with River Dove. Several interesting old buildings. Birmingham 42 miles, Sheffield 34, Nottingham 29, Stafford 26, Buxton 21, Burton-on-Trent 19, Derby 13.

BERESFORD ARMS HOTEL, STATION ROAD, ASHBOURNE DE6 1AA (0335 300035; Fax: 0335 300065). Situated in the centre of Ashbourne and offering a warm welcome, especially to pets and children. It makes a perfect starting point to explore the area or visit Alton Towers. *[*🐕*]*

MRS M. M. STELFOX, DOG AND PARTRIDGE, SWINSCOE, ASHBOURNE DE6 2HS (0335 43183). 17th century inn offering ideal holiday accommodation. Many leisure activities available. All bedrooms with washbasins, colour TV, telephone and private facilities. ETB 4 Crowns. *[pw!]*

DERBYSHIRE COTTAGES. Set in grounds of 17th century inn, close to Peak District, Alton Towers. Fully fitted kitchen, colour TV, radio, telephone. Pets and children welcome. Tel: 0335 300202 for details.

DERBYSHIRE

MRS M. A. RICHARDSON, THROWLEY HALL FARM, ILAM, ASHBOURNE DE6 2BB (0538 308202/308243). Self-catering accommodation in Farmhouse for up to 12 and cottage for seven people. Also Bed and Breakfast in Farmhouse. Central heating, washbasins, tea/coffee facilities in rooms. Children and pets welcome. Near Alton Towers and Stately Homes. Tourist Board 2 Crowns/4 Keys.

Buxton

Well-known spa and centre for the Peak District. Beautiful scenery. Good sporting amenities and entertainments. Leeds 50 miles, Stafford 37, Derby 34, Sheffield 28, Stoke-on-Trent 24, Matlock 20, Macclesfield 12.

THORN HEYES PRIVATE HOTEL, 137 LONDON ROAD, BUXTON SK17 9NW (BUXTON [0298] 23539). Small owner-managed Hotel in beautiful gardens. Full central heating. Tea-making facilities in every room; all rooms en suite and with colour television. Also two self-catering units to sleep 4/6, equipped to high standard. [🐕]

THE CHARLES COTTON HOTEL, HARTINGTON, NEAR BUXTON SK17 0AL (0298 84229). Small hotel, AA & RAC star rated. Good home cooking and hospitality. In heart of Derbyshire Dales. Special diets catered for. Ideal for relaxing, walking, cycling, hang gliding.

MRS LYNNE P. FEARNS, HEATH FARM, SMALLDALE, BUXTON SK17 8EB (0298 24431). Farm in Peak District, 4½ miles from Buxton. Quiet location. Many activities locally. Cot and babysitting available. Car essential. Bed and Breakfast from £13.50, reductions children and weekly stays.

MRS GILL TAYLOR, 50 WHITE KNOWLE ROAD, BUXTON SK17 9NH (0298 23737/71661). Priory Lea Holiday Flats close to Poole's Cavern Country Park. Fully equipped. Sleep 2/8. Cleanliness assured. Terms £75–£190. Open all year. [pw! £1 per night.]

MRS E. J. KNELLER, CANDLEMAS COTTAGE, DAMSIDE LANE, PEAK FOREST, NEAR BUXTON SK17 8EH (0298 24853). Centrally but peacefully situated in Peak National Park. Bed and Breakfast. Excellent Evening Meals locally. Sumptuous breakfasts. Tea-making and TV in bedrooms. Log fires. Lovely walks. [pw! from £4 per week.]

Matlock

Inland resort and spa in the Derwent Valley. Chesterfield 9 miles.

LANE END HOUSE, GREEN LANE, TANSLEY DE4 5FJ (0629 583981). A non-smoking Georgian farmhouse close to Chatsworth and Haddon. Lovingly refurbished by caring owners who serve delicious food at yesterday's prices. Walk in nearby fields or explore the wonderful countryside that surrounds us. AA and "Staying off the Beaten Track".

TUCKERS GUEST HOUSE, 48 DALE ROAD, MATLOCK DE4 3NB (0629 583018). Victorian house in central but secluded position. Spacious, well equipped rooms. Full English or vegetarian breakfast. Wonderful scenery and walks. So much to see and do. Pets welcome to stay in rooms. Bed and Breakfast £15. Open all year. [🐕 pw!]

DEVON

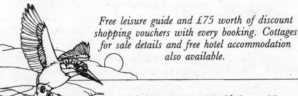

PETS STAY FREE

Sandy Cove Hotel

THE SEA FOOD HOTEL
**Combe Martin Bay,
Berrynarbor,
Devon EX34 9SR**
**Tel: (0271) 882243
or 882888**

YOUR PETS ARE WELCOME TO STAY ABSOLUTELY *FREE* IF YOU RETURN THIS ADVERT WITH YOUR BOOKING

How would you like to arrive for a week's holiday at an hotel overlooking a beautiful bay, the sea and Exmoor? The first thing you would notice would be the acres of gardens and woods running down to the cliff edge, and the heated swimming pool set in its midst. A warm bath then dinner in the restaurant, with excellent à la carte and table d'hote menus. The hot carvery and Swedish Smorgasbord on a Saturday will wet your lips. Enjoy live entertainment in season and dance on a Saturday night until midnight, use the heated pool (heated to 80°F), fitness room with gymnasium equipment, sauna, whirlpool and sun bed. CHILDREN ARE VERY WELCOME AND AT CERTAIN TIMES OF THE YEAR THEY HAVE ABSOLUTELY *FREE* ACCOMMODATION PROVIDING THEY SHARE THEIR PARENTS' ROOM–YOU JUST PAY FOR THEIR MEALS. Baby sitting can be arranged. Invalids catered for. We are happy if you bring pets with you. Open all the year–Christmas and Mini-weekend breaks a speciality. Some four poster bedrooms for romantic honeymoons. NEW pool enclosure means it can be indoors or outdoors–sliding sides and roof to enjoy the sun.

*34 bedrooms all ensuite, with colour TV, telephone and tea-making. Fully licensed
Combe Martin 1 mile. Ilfracombe 4 miles.*

Please write or ring for free colour brochure to:
*Dawn and Richard Gilson; DEPT (3), SANDY COVE HOTEL,
COMBE MARTIN BAY, BERRYNARBOR, N. DEVON EX34 9SR
Tel: Combe Martin (0271) 882243 or 882888*

DEVON   *Chagford, Combe Martin, Crediton*

FREE and REDUCED RATE Holiday Visits!
Don't miss our Readers' Offer Vouchers on pages 5 to 20.

DEVON *Dartmoor, Dawlish, East Allington, Eastleigh Barton, Exeter, Exmoor, Hartland*

ROGUES ROOST · DARTMOOR NATIONAL PARK
Two self-catering moorland properties, sleeping four and eight
Off beaten track   **Children and dogs welcome**
Telephone: 03643 223 for information, Susan Booty,
Rogues Roost, Poundsgate, Ashburton, Devon TQ13 7PS

BROOKDALE HOUSE
Self catering Flats sleeping 2/8 (some ground floor) in prime position with BR station, shops, buses and sea all within 100 yards.
NO HILLS TO CLIMB
Between October and May Flats from £70 per week. Discounts for couples in June.
SAE Mr & Mrs L. F. Papworth, 5 Brookdale Terrace, Dawlish EX7 9PF. Tel: 0626 865111

KINGSBRIDGE AREA
Farm Cottages sleeping 4/8. Pets welcome.
Within easy reach of coast and moors.
Mr. Matthews, Lower Combe Farm, East Allington, Totnes, Devon TQ9 7PY
Tel: 054-852 348

* The Barton Cottage *
EASTLEIGH BARTON, Nr BIDEFORD, N. DEVON   **Tel: 0271 860536**
Fully modernised Cottage with three bedrooms, bathroom and toilet, lounge, television, fitted carpets, modern kitchen, refrigerator, electric cooker. Log fires, part double glazing. Garage. Small enclosed garden. Only two miles from Bideford and Instow. FULLY EQUIPPED FOR 6-8 PERSONS EXCEPT FOR SHEETS AND PILLOW-CASES. COT ALSO AVAILABLE. **Mrs F. E. MAY**
Centrally situated for touring Dartmoor and Exmoor and near several beaches

TEIGN VALLEY FOREST
HALDON LODGE FARM, KENNFORD,
NR EXETER, DEVON EX6 7YG Tel: (0392) 832312

Delightful modern 34ft Caravan only five miles from Exeter and short distance Dawlish, Teignmouth and Torbay, from £65 per week. Lounge (TV), 2 bedrooms, kitchen, bathroom (H & C) and toilet. *Attractive private grounds in peaceful surroundings. Famous village inns, two beautiful Coarse Fishing Lakes and farm shop.* Small private camping site. Pony trekking available. Special welcome to less experienced riders.

Pets Welcome ● Open all year ● Enquiries to D. L. Salter

DRAYDON COTTAGES EXMOOR (Near Dulverton)
6 attractive s/c barn conversion cottages offering outstanding accommodation in a glorious tranquil setting with magnificent views across the Barle Valley between Dulverton and Tarr Steps. Gardens. Parking. Dogs welcome by arrangement. Ideal base for relaxing, walking, riding and exploring Exmoor's beautiful National Park. Holidays/Short breaks. For brochure and tariff please contact:
Katharine Harris Tel: 0392 433524

FOSFELLE Country House Hotel
Hartland, Bideford, Devon EX39 6EF

17th century Manor House set in peaceful surroundings. * Bar ** Excellent Food *
Close to cliff walks and sandy beaches. Trout and coarse fishing available at Hotel.
** Pets Welcome **
Tel: 0237 441273

DEVON *Hope Cove, Ilfracombe, Instow*

HOPE COVE: HOPE BEACH HOUSE

Seven Luxury two and three-bedroomed Apartments, set 50 yards from safe sandy beach, in old-world fishing village nestling under Bolt Tail National Trust headland. All apartments furnished and equipped to a very high standard. Night storage heating, electric fires in all rooms. Colour TV, kitchen with electric cooker, microwave, fridge/freezer, dishwasher, washing machine, dryer etc. Linen and towels supplied FREE. Magnificent coastal walks with golf at nearby Bigbury and Thurlestone. Open all year. Children and pets welcome.

ETB 🐾 🐾 🐾 🐾 Commended. Full details from:
Mr & Mrs P.G. Pedrick, Hope Beach House, Hope Cove, Nr. Kingsbridge,
S. Devon TQ7 3HH
Tel: 0548 560151

TANFIELD HOTEL

Hope Cove, near Kingsbridge, South Devon Tel: 0548 561268

A warm welcome awaits you from John and Pauline Ward at this Ashley Courtenay recommended, licensed hotel overlooking the tiny fishing village of Hope Cove. A peaceful place, quiet and uncrowded, Hope Cove is ideal for a relaxing holiday. The spectacular coastal path over miles of National Trust property offers an ideal situation for dog owners.
All rooms are centrally heated, en suite and all have colour TV, hairdryers, tea and coffee making facilities. Colour brochure available on request. Mid-week bookings accepted. Bargain breaks available.

ILFRACOMBE HOLIDAY PARC
ILFRACOMBE · DEVON

JOHN FOWLER HOLIDAYS

Conveniently set above the town and sea, the Parc commands wonderful views.
Free amenities include
● 56' heated Pool ● crazy golf
● children's play areas ● sauna
● Solarium ● Exmoor Club with regular entertainment ● discos and live bands
● launderette ● latest video games

● pool tables ● take away meals
● Country Kitchen Restaurant Superb range of accommodation in luxury apartments, bungalows for 2-8 persons.

BOOK EARLY FOR GENEROUS DISCOUNTS
0271 866666 FOR COLOUR BROCHURE

Dept 34, Marlborough Road, Ilfracombe, Devon EX34 8PF

DARNLEY HOTEL
Belmont Road, Ilfracombe EX34 8DR   Telephone: (0271) 863955
A small licensed hotel of charm and character, quietly situated yet only 5 mins. walk from the main shopping street and sea front. Friendly personal service and superb food. Central heating, tea-making facilities; most rooms en suite. TV lounge, games room, bar. Ample parking. Bed and Breakfast from £14; Bed, Breakfast and Evening Meal from £22. Entertainment in bar one night per week.   Pets free of charge

Midships, Lane End, Instow Sleeps 6 plus cot
45 yards from sandy beach, pretty cottage with gas central heating. Double bedded room, twin bedded room with washbasin; modern bathroom, lounge with colour TV and convertible sofa, dining room. Fitted kitchen with fridge/freezer, cooker, washing machine and tumble dryer. Children and pets welcome. SAE for brochure of this and two other properties to:
Mrs P. Baxter, Huish Moor Farmhouse, Instow, Bideford, Devon EX39 4LT or phone (0271) 861146.

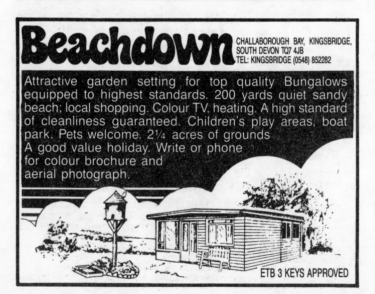

ALL THE CREATURE COMFORTS

You and your Pets can enjoy all the creature comforts of a self catering holiday on Devon's Golden Coast. Saunton Beach Villas sleep from 2 to 8 and are fully equipped to a high standard. Detached bungalows offering every amenity and located adjacent to five miles of golden, unspoilt beach and dunes.
Open from Easter to October they provide the ideal early, late or summer holiday venue particularly for pet owners. There's no bar or disco to keep you up at night, just the sound of the sea. Whilst the grandeur of Exmoor & North Devon's unrivalled coastline provides a superb playground for all the family.

WEEKEND & MIDWEEK BREAKS AVAILABLE

FOR FREE COLOUR BROCHURE AND TARIFFS PLEASE CONTACT: SAUNTON BEACH VILLAS BROADFIELD HOLIDAYS, 1 PARK VILLAS, TAW VALE, BARNSTAPLE, DEVON. EX32 8NJ

TELEPHONE (0271) 22033 24 Hours

DEVON *Salcombe, Seaton, Sidmouth*

Seamark Holiday Apartments

Thurlestone Sands, Near Salcombe, Devon TQ7 3JY

Five lovely apartments adjoining coastal path. Outstanding sea views, spacious grounds. Beach 500 yards–windsurfing; golf course one mile.
56ft Games Room–table tennis, darts, snooker.
Laundry room. Pay phone.
Colour brochure on request

SELF CATERING *HOLIDAYS*

**COTTAGES,
BUNGALOWS,
APARTMENTS**

Coast and Country on
Devon/Dorset border

Free Colour Brochure

English Tourist Board
REGISTERED AGENCY

MILKBERE
HOLIDAYS

WEST COUNTRY TOURIST BOARD
MEMBER

**Milkbere House, 14 Fore Street,
Seaton Devon EX12 2LA.   Tel: (0297) 22925**

---

* SEATON *

Bed & Breakfast, Evening Meal optional. Children & pets welcome.
**R. Hallett, Borolands Farm, Axmouth, Seaton, Devon
Tel: (0297) 552680**

Lower Knapp Farm

Sidbury, Sidmouth, Devon EX10 0QN

Luxury self-catering cottages, sleeping 2-8, set in 16 acres of accessible East Devon. Sidmouth 5 miles. Seaton, Lyme Regis & Exmouth 30 mins. Delightful walking country, the farm being on the East Devon Way. Pets welcome. Indoor heated swimming pool, sauna, solarium, children's play area. All cottages fully fitted kitchens, microwaves, some dishwashers. Colour TV, central heating, cots, high chairs, video players available. Some four-poster beds. Linen supplied, laundry room. Fishing, golf, riding available locally. Open all year. Prices from £168 to £650 per week. For free colour brochure, telephone **Farway (040487) 438.**

FREE and REDUCED RATE Holiday Visits!
Don't miss our Readers' Offer Vouchers on pages 5 to 20.

Appledore

Unspoilt resort and small port on estuaries of Taw and Torridge. Sandy beach, good bathing. Bideford 3 miles.

MARINERS COTTAGE, IRSHA STREET, APPLEDORE. Elizabethan fisherman's Cottage at sea edge. Extensive views of sea and boats. Enclosed garden. Sleeps 6: three bedrooms, lounge, dining room, children's play house. Good fishing, coastal walks. SAE please to MRS P. A. BARNES, BOAT HYDE, NORTHAM, BIDEFORD EX39 1NX or phone 0237 473801 for prices and vacancies. *[pw! £5 per week.]*

TIDES END, APPLEDORE. Seaside thatched cottage, by the beach. Listed fisherman's cottage. Restored. Three double rooms, cot. Terrace with picnic table. Dogs welcome. Lively area, places of interest. APPLY: MRS P. T. BARNES, BOAT HYDE, NORTHAM, BIDEFORD EX39 1NX (0237 473801). *[£5 per week.]*

OTTER COTTAGE. Traditional fisherman's cottage. Totally equipped – 2 TVs, VCR, microwave, autowasher etc. Also unique harbourside apartments and bungalow. Brochure from B. H. SMITH, 26 MARKET STREET, APPLEDORE EX39 1PP (0237 476154). *[£8 per week.]*

Ashburton

Delightful little town on southern fringe of Dartmoor. Centrally placed for touring and the Torbay resorts. Plymouth 24 miles, Exeter 20, Kingsbridge 20, Tavistock 20, Teignmouth 14, Torquay 14, Totnes 8, Newton Abbot 7.

MRS R. PARKER, HIGHER MEAD FARM, ASHBURTON TQ13 7LJ (0364 652598). Family-run site. 6-Berth Caravans. Showers. One third mile from A38 Plymouth/ Exeter Road, central for Devon and Cornwall. Touring and Tents. Any pets accepted. *[pw! £11 per week.]*

MRS A. BELL, WOODER MANOR, WIDECOMBE-IN-THE-MOOR, NEAR ASHBUR-TON TQ13 7TR (036 42 391). Cottages on family farm. Surrounded by unspoilt woodland and moors. Clean and well equipped, colour TV, central heating, laundry room. One property suitable for disabled visitors. Brochure available. 4 Keys Commended. *[🐕]*

Aveton Gifford

Village on River Avon, 3 miles from lovely Bigbury Bay. Good fishing. Salcombe 8 miles, Kingsbridge 4.

MISS E. M. BALKWILL, LITTLECOURT, AVETON GIFFORD, KINGSBRIDGE TQ7 4LE (0548 550362). Guest House, opposite family farm, 3 miles from sea. Television lounge. Car space. Dogs welcome. Tea making facilities.

Axminster

Agricultural town in the Axe river valley, famous for carpets. Cattle and street market.

LILAC COTTAGE. A beautifully renovated cottage. Oil-fired central heating. All electric kitchen. Inglenook fireplace; beamed ceiling. Sleeps six plus cot. Colour TV. Garden. Garage. SAE please. APPLY – MRS J. M. STUART, HUNSCOTE HOUSE, WELLESBOURNE, WARWICKSHIRE CV35 9EX (Tel/Fax: 0789 840228) or Mrs Young (0769 573788). *[£5 per week.]*

Barnstaple

The largest town in Devon, once an important centre for the wool trade, now a lively shopping centre with thrice-weekly market, modern leisure centre etc.

BEACH AND BRACKEN EXMOOR HOLIDAYS, BRATTON FLEMING, BARNSTA-PLE EX31 4TJ (0598 710702). Comfortable self-catering cottages; farmhouse accommodation with food. Short notice all-season breaks. Telephone anytime.

NORTH DEVON HOLIDAY HOMES, 19 CROSS STREET, BARNSTAPLE EX31 1BD (0271 76322 24 hours). Send for guide to 500 of best value Cottages around Devon's National Trust coast. All regularly inspected and guaranteed to offer first class value.

MRS V. M. CHUGG, VALLEY VIEW, MARWOOD, BARNSTAPLE EX31 4EA (0271 43458). Bungalow on 300 acre farm. Bed and Breakfast accommodation. Near Marwood Hill Gardens and Arlington Court. Children most welcome, free baby-sitting. Dogs by arrangement. Terms from £11. *[pw!]*

Berrynarbor

Pretty coastal village with thatched cottages and church. Ilfracombe 3 miles.

DAWN AND RICHARD GILSON, SANDY COVE HOTEL, BERRYNARBOR EX34 9SR (0271 882243 or 882888). Hotel set amidst acres of gardens and woods. Heated swimming pool. Children and pets welcome. A la carte restaurant. All rooms en-suite with colour TV, tea-making. Free colour brochure on application. *[🐕]*

Bideford

Neat port and resort on River Torridge. Attractive, many-arched stone bridge, wooded hills. Boat trips from quay. The sea is 3 miles distant at Westward Ho! Exeter 43 miles, Launceston 32, Bude 26, Ilfracombe 21, Barnstaple 9, Torrington 7.

MRS D. DOUGHTY, KUMBA, CHUDLEIGH ROAD, EAST THE WATER, BIDEFORD EX39 4AR (0237 471526). Peaceful Edwardian detached house. Licensed. Parking. Spacious rooms; en suite available. "Tarka Trail" 50 yards for walking, cycling. All water-based activities nearby. WCTB 2 Crowns, AA Listed Q. *[🐕]*

Bigbury-on-Sea

A scattered village overlooking superb coastal scenery and wide expanses of sand.

PAT CHADWICK, 'MARINERS', RINGMORE DRIVE, BIGBURY-ON-SEA, KINGS-BRIDGE TQ7 4AU (0548 810454). 2 large flats with extensive sea views. Sandy beaches within yards. Golf nearby. Dogs welcome. *[🐕]*

MR SCARTERFIELD, HENLEY HOTEL, FOLLY HILL, BIGBURY-ON-SEA TQ7 4AR (0548 810240). Edwardian cottage-style hotel, spectacular sea views. Near good beach, dog walking. En-suite rooms with telephone, tea making, TV etc. Home cooking. No smoking establishment. Licensed. 3 Crowns Commended. AA 1 Star. *[🐕]*

Bolberry

South Hams village within strolling distance of beautiful National Trust coastline. Kingsbridge 6 miles, Hope Cove 1.

PORT LIGHT HOTEL AND INN, BOLBERRY DOWN, SALCOMBE TQ7 3DY (0548 561384). Former golf clubhouse set in acres of National Trust countryside. Homecooked fayre. En suite rooms. Full licence. Panoramic views. Bargain Breaks. *[🐕]*

Bovey Tracey

Little town nestling on southern fringe of Dartmoor. Fine scenery including Haytor Rocks (4 miles) and Becky Falls (3½ miles). The 14th cent. Church is of interest. Exeter 14 miles, Torquay 13, Teignmouth 12, Ashburton 8, Newton Abbot 6, Chudleigh 4.

SELF CATERING. Large, modern three-bedroomed detached traditionally built holiday bungalows; fenced gardens. Linen provided. Children and pets welcome. 3 Keys. ENQUIRIES: MRS J. R. MOUNTFORD, CHURCH MEADOW, COOMBE CROSS, BOVEY TRACEY, NEWTON ABBOT TQ13 9EP (0626 832824). *[🐕]*

BLENHEIM COUNTRY HOUSE HOTEL, BOVEY TRACEY TQ13 9DH (0626 832422). Family Hotel on edge of Dartmoor National Park. RSPCA member. Open all year. All pets free. 2 Crowns. [🐾]

Brixham

Lively resort and fishing port, with quaint houses and narrow winding streets. Ample opportunities for fishing and boat trips.

MR & MRS COUSINS, BLACK COTTAGE GUEST HOUSE, 17 MILTON STREET, BRIXHAM TQ5 0BX (0803 853752). Delightful 15th century guest house with olde worlde charm. All bedrooms have central heating, washbasins, colour TV, and tea making facilities. Specialist home cooking. Pub nearby welcomes dogs. Patio garden. [£1 per night.]

DEVONCOURT HOLIDAY FLATS, BERRYHEAD ROAD, BRIXHAM TQ5 9AB (0803 853748 24 hours). 24 self-contained flats with private balcony, colour television, heating, private car park, all-electric kitchenette, separate bathroom and toilet. Open all year. [pw! £10 per week.]

Buckfastleigh

Market and manufacturing town five miles from Totnes. Close to Buckfast Abbey where monks make and sell honey and wine.

JOHN & EVELYN FLACH, WOODHOLME GUEST HOUSE, 113 PLYMOUTH ROAD, BUCKFASTLEIGH TQ11 0DB (0364 643350). Spacious Victorian house offers twin, double and luxury en suite double; colour TV, tea/coffee making. Evening Meal if pre-booked. Bed and Breakfast from £15.50 daily, £95 weekly. Two Crowns. Dogs welcome.

Chagford

Unspoilt little town on the edge of Dartmoor in an area rich in prehistoric remains. Noted for 16th century bridge, and Tudor and Georgian houses.

A wonderful variety of over 450 cottages, houses and apartments all over the West Country, ideal for self-catering holidays. Many accept pets. Free colour brochure from: HELPFUL HOLIDAYS, COOMBE 49, CHAGFORD, DEVON TQ13 8DF (0647 433593) (Fax: 0647 433694).

Chittlehamholt

Standing in beautiful countryside in the Taw Valley and just off the B3227. Barnstaple 9 miles, South Molton 5.

SNAPDOWN FARM CARAVANS, CHITTLEHAMHOLT, UMBERLEIGH, NORTH DEVON EX37 9PF (0769 540708). 12 only – 6 berth caravans with flush toilets, showers, colour TV, fridges, cookers and fires. Laundry room. Picnic tables. Unspoilt countryside – field and woodland walks. Terms (2 types) £70–£180 or £75–£195 inc. gas and electricity in caravans. [£7 per week.]

Chulmleigh

Mid-Devon village set in lovely countryside, just off A377 Exeter to Barnstaple road. Exeter 23 miles, Tiverton 19, Barnstaple 18.

THE FOX AND HOUNDS, EGGESFORD HOUSE HOTEL, EGGESFORD, NEAR CHULMLEIGH EX18 7JZ (0769 80345). 30 acres of countryside and forest. 7 miles River Taw salmon/trout fishing. Ideal touring centre for Dartmoor, Exmoor and coasts. 20 en-suite bedrooms. B&B from £31.50. [£2.50 per night.]

Combe Martin

Coastal village with harbour set in sandy bay. Good cliff and rock scenery. Of interest is the Church and 'Pack of Cards' Inn. Barnstaple 14 miles, Lynton 12, Ilfracombe 6.

MIKE AND PAM CARTER, MIRAMAR HOTEL, COMBE MARTIN (0271 883558). Homely Hotel with relaxed, friendly atmosphere. Licensed residents' bar, large heated swimming pool, children's playground. Good varied menu. Children at reduced rates. *[pw!]*

SAFFRON HOUSE HOTEL, KING STREET, COMBE MARTIN, NORTH DEVON EX34 0BX (0271 883521). Charming farmhouse hotel in picturesque coastal village on Exmoor. Ideal for touring, lovely views. Heated swimming pool and pretty gardens. *[🐕pw!]*

RONE HOUSE HOTEL, KING STREET, COMBE MARTIN EX34 0AD (027 188 3428). Small, comfortable, family-run Hotel, close to sea. Central heating. TV in all bedrooms, private facilities in most. Heated swimming pool. Children and dogs welcome.

MR M. J. HUGHES, MANLEIGH HOLIDAY PARK, RECTORY ROAD, COMBE MARTIN EX34 0NS (0271 883353). Holiday Chalets, accommodate 4/6 persons. In 6 acres. Free use of swimming pool. Dogs and cats welcome provided they are kept under control. Also 12 Caravans to let. Graded 4 ticks *[£14 per week.]*

Crediton

Ancient small town. Chapter house with Cromwellian relics. Cider-making. Cathedral type church. 7 miles from Exeter.

WEST AISH FARM, MORCHARD BISHOP, NEAR CREDITON EX17 6RX (0363 877427). Relax by a log fire after a day's touring, walking or riding. Self catering cottages situated in the peaceful setting of a former cobbled farmyard. Two cottages, sleep 5. £110–£250.

Croyde Bay

Charming village nestling in a sheltered combe behind Croyde Bay.

MRS S. SULLIVAN, MIDDLEBOROUGH HOUSE, BAGGY POINT, CROYDE EX33 1PA (0271 890285). Very comfortable bungalow. Sleeps 4/5. Enclosed garden. Garage. Easy walking distance to beach and village. Coastal footpath and golf nearby. Available all year.

MRS JENNIFER PENNY, CROYDE BAY HOUSE HOTEL, CROYDE BAY, NORTH DEVON EX33 1PA (0271 890270). Small hotel beside beach at Croyde Bay. All rooms en-suite with tea/coffee making facilities. Good food and friendly atmosphere. AA & RAC 2 Star. 3 Crowns Highly Commended. *[🐕]*

Cullompton

Small market town off the main A38 Taunton–Exeter road. Good touring centre. Noted for apple orchards which supply the local cider industry. Taunton 19 miles, Exeter 13, Honiton 11, Tiverton 9.

FOREST GLADE HOLIDAY PARK (PW), KENTISBEARE, CULLOMPTON EX15 2DT (0404 841381). Country estate with deluxe 2/4/6 berth caravans. All superbly equipped. Many amenities on site. Mother and Baby Room. Campers and tourers welcome. SAE for free colour brochure.

Dartmoor

365 square miles of National Park, with spectacular unspoiled scenery and fringed by picturesque villages.

MAGPIE LEISURE PARK, DEPT PW, BEDFORD BRIDGE, HORRABRIDGE, YELVERTON PL20 7RY (0822 852651). Purpose-built lodges in peaceful woodland setting. Sleep 2–7. Furnished to very high standard (microwave, dishwasher etc). Easy walk to village and shops. Launderette. Dogs accepted (max. 2 per property). *[£12.50 per week.]*

MOORLAND HALL HOTEL, BRENTOR ROAD, MARY TAVY, NEAR TAVISTOCK PL19 9PY (0822 810466). Small Victorian country house hotel in 5 acres of grounds, with direct access onto Dartmoor. All rooms en suite. Children and pets welcome. Riding, fishing, golf nearby. *[£1.50 per night.]*

TWO BRIDGES HOTEL, TWO BRIDGES, DARTMOOR PL20 6SN (082-289 581; Fax: 082-289 575). Famous Olde Worlde riverside inn. Centre Dartmoor. Log fires, gleaming copper antiques. Ideal walking. Pets very welcome. Hotel owners are dog lovers. Open all year. ETB 3 Crowns. [🐕]

P. WILKENS, POLTIMORE, RAMSLEY, SOUTH ZEAL EX20 2PD (0837 840209). Dartmoor National Park. Self catering accommodation consisting of summer chalet, granite barn conversion and superb detached bungalow. Also pretty thatched hotel. All with direct access to the Moor. Write or phone for details. *[1st pet free, 2nd or more £7.50 each per week.]*

CHERRYBROOK HOTEL, TWO BRIDGES, YELVERTON PL20 6SP (0822 88260). Set in the heart of Dartmoor National Park. Seven comfortably furnished en suite bedrooms. Good quality home-cooked food with menu choice. Ideal for touring.

MISS P. NEAL, MIDDLE STOKE FARM, HOLNE, NEAR ASHBURTON TQ13 7SS (036-43 444). Warm welcome for adults, children, horses, dogs. Stud (thorough-breds) on Dartmoor. All rooms with washbasins. Bed and Breakfast £14.50 to £16.50. Excellent evening meals obtainable locally. *[pw! £1.50 nightly.]*

MRS SUSAN BOOTY, 'ROGUES ROOST', POUNDSGATE, ASHBURTON TQ13 7PS (03643 223). Dartmoor National Park. Two self-catering moorland properties sleeping 4 and 8. Children and dogs welcome. Off beaten track. *[🐕]*

Dartmouth

Historic and picturesque port and resort on the estuary of the lovely River Dart. Sandy coves; pleasure boat trips up river. Car ferry to Kingswear. Of interest are St. Saviour's Church (14th cent.); old houses and Butterwalk; Tudor Castle; Royal Naval College.

MRS S. R. RIDALLS, THE OLD BAKEHOUSE, 4 BROADSTONE, DARTMOUTH TQ6 9NR (0803 832109). 2 Cottages (one with four-poster bed) and one apartment. Sleep 2–6. Near river, shops, restaurants. Blackpool Sands 15 minutes' drive. TV, linen hire, baby-sitting. Open all year. ETB 3 Keys up to Commended. *[🐕]*

Dawlish

Bright resort with sandy beach and sandstone cliffs. Lovely gardens with streams, waterfalls and famous black swans. Exeter 13 miles, Torquay 12, Newton Abbot 9, Teignmouth 3.

MRS P. KITSON, "THE COBBLES", 9 HIGH STREET, DAWLISH EX7 9HP (0626 865053). Period "Listed" Town House. Seven bedrooms, two bathrooms (one ground floor). Three minutes' walk beaches. Parking. Colour TV, microwave oven, cot. Accommodates 2-10 in comfort.

MRS F. E. WINSTON, "STURWOOD", 1 OAK PARK VILLAS, DAWLISH EX7 0DE (0626 862660). Holiday Flats. Comfortable, self-contained, accommodating 2-6. Own bathroom, 1/2 bedrooms. Colour television. Garden. Parking. Pets welcome. [pw!]

MR AND MRS L. F. PAPWORTH, 5 BROOKDALE TERRACE, DAWLISH EX7 9PF (0626 865111). Flats accommodating 2/8 people. Central prime position. No hills to climb. Dogs accepted by arrangement. [£4 per week]. Self-catering.

Dunsford

Attractive village in Upper Teign Valley with Dartmoor to the west. Plymouth 35 miles, Okehampton 16, Newton Abbot 13, Crediton 9, Exeter 8.

MR C. J. BRIMBLECOMBE, HAZARD, FARRANTS CROSS, DUNSFORD, EXETER EX6 7BA (0392 811456). Mid-Devon. Detached stream-side cottage 'twixt Dartmoor/ Exeter. Sleeps 4–6; reduction for two people; ideal wheelchairs & pets. ETB 3 Keys. Central heating, linen, colour TV, WASHING MACHINE, fitted oak kitchen, beamed sitting room, log effect gas fire, garden.

ROYAL OAK INN, DUNSFORD, NEAR EXETER EX6 7DA (0647 52256). Welcome to our Victorian country inn. We specialise in real ales and home-made food. All en suite rooms are in a 300-year-old converted barn. Each room has its own front door opening into a beautiful walled courtyard. [🐾]

East Allington

South Hams village hidden away down leafy lanes yet within easy reach of numerous beaches. Kingsbridge 5 miles S.W.

Farm Cottages within easy reach of coast and moors. Pets welcome. APPLY – MR R. C. MATTHEWS, LOWER COMBE FARM, EAST ALLINGTON, TOTNES TQ9 7PQ (054 852 348). [🐾]

Delightfully modernised end terrace cottage in good touring location. Double and twin bedrooms. Sleeps 4. Well equipped, linen, parking. Attended by owners. Apply: MRS BARBARA BOWHAY, TIVOLI, HIGHER WESTONFIELDS, TOTNES TQ9 5RB (0803 862781). [🐾]

Eastleigh Barton

Small village near to Bideford. Ideal for touring this lovely area.

MRS F. E. MAY, EASTLEIGH BARTON, EASTLEIGH, NEAR BIDEFORD (0271 860536). Fully modernised, three-bedroomed cottage sleeps 6/8, all modern facilities, log fires, part double glazing, garage, small enclosed garden. Near moors and beaches. SAE please.

Exeter

Chief city of the South-West, Exeter, with its Cathedral and University, has a long and glorious history. Ample shopping, sports and leisure facilities.

MRS D. L. SALTER, HALDON LODGE FARM, KENNFORD, NEAR EXETER EX6 7YG (0392 832312). Modern 40ft Holiday Caravan. Two bedrooms, kitchen, lounge, bathroom/toilet, TV. Farm shop, famous village Inns. Sea short distance. Private grounds near Teign Valley Forest with two Coarse Fishing lakes. Pets welcome. [pw!]

CLOCK TOWER HOTEL, 16 NEW NORTH ROAD, EXETER EX4 4HF (0392 52493). Listed building of character, 10 minutes' level walk Cathedral and all major stores. Comfortable, all modern facilities. Private bathrooms. Easy distrance rail/ coach stations. B&B £15 single, £25 twin/double; en suite room £2.50 extra per person.

MRS SALLY GLANVILL, RYDON FARM, WOODBURY, EXETER EX5 1LB (0395 232341). 16th Century Devon Longhouse on working dairy farm. Washbasins, hair-dryers, tea/coffee facilities. En-suite available. Central heating. Open all year. Colour brochure available. B&B from £16. ETB 2 Crowns. [🐕]

Exmoor

265 square miles of unspoiled heather moorland with deep wooded valleys and rivers, ideal for a walking, pony trekking or fishing holiday.

Draydon Cottages, Exmoor. 6 attractive s/c barn conversion cottages situated 2 miles north-west of Dulverton. Well equipped and maintained with heating throughout. Excellent base for exploring Exmoor. KATHARINE HARRIS, 6 CRABB LANE, ALPHINGTON, EXETER EX2 9JD (0392 433524).

MRS C. M. WRIGHT, FRIENDSHIP FARM, BRATTON FLEMING, BARNSTAPLE EX31 4SQ (059 83 291 evenings). Comfortable three-bedroom Bungalow, sleeps 6 plus cot. Linen provided. Situated on edge of Exmoor, near coast (Combe Martin). From £95 Low Season, £200 High Season. [pw!]

MRS T. H. FARTHING, BRENDON HOUSE HOTEL, BRENDON, LYNTON EX35 6PS (05987 206). Small comfortable country hotel. Licensed. Good food. Fishing permits sold. Dogs very welcome. Dinner, Bed and Breakfast from £27. [🐕]

Galmpton

Quiet village just outside Torbay. Brixham 3 miles, Paignton 4.

HOLIDAY BUNGALOWS at Galmpton Holiday Park, near Brixham, in lovely peaceful countryside above the River Dart. Sea 10 minutes away. Two bedrooms, colour TV, own parking. APPLY: B. C. AND MRS L. H. BOWERMAN, 29 CROKERS MEADOW, BOVEY TRACEY, NEWTON ABBOT TQ13 9HL (0626 832496). [£10 weekly.]

Harberton

Small picturesque village two miles from Totnes.

M. H. & J. S. GRIFFITHS, "OLD HAZARD", HIGHER PLYMOUTH ROAD, HARBERTON, TOTNES TQ9 7LN (0803 862495). 3 miles Totnes. Attractive well-equipped self catering cottages and farmhouse flat. Convenient rural location. Open all year. Dogs welcome. Brochure on request. [£7.00 per week.]

Hartland

Pretty village with stone and slate cottages. Clovelly 4 miles.

FOSFELLE COUNTRY HOUSE HOTEL, HARTLAND, BIDEFORD EX39 6EF (0237 441273). 17th century manor house set in peaceful surroundings. Bar; excellent food. Close to cliff walks and sandy beaches. Trout and coarse fishing available at hotel.

Honiton

Busy south Devon town now happily by-passed. Noted for lace and pottery. Excellent touring centre. Newton Abbot 31 miles, Exmouth 18, Taunton 18, Exeter 17, Budleigh Salterton 16, Lyme Regis 15, Chard 13, Sidmouth 10.

MRS E. TUCKER, LOWER LUXTON FARM, UPOTTERY, HONITON EX14 9PB (082-360 269). Olde worlde Farmhouse in an area of outstanding natural beauty. Ideal for touring. Good home cooking. Children welcome. B&B or D,B&B.

Hope Cove

Attractive fishing village, flat sandy beach and safe bathing. Fine views towards Rame Head; cliffs. Kingsbridge 6 miles.

Seven luxury 2 and 3 bedroom Apartments, all facilities, equipped to highest standards: ETB 4 Keys Commended. Linen supplied free. Open all year. Children/pets welcome. Apply: MR AND MRS P. G. PEDRICK, HOPE BEACH HOUSE, HOPE COVE, NEAR KINGSBRIDGE TQ7 3HH (0548 560151). *[£11 weekly.]*

BLUE BAY APARTMENTS, GRANDVIEW ROAD, HOPE COVE TQ7 3HD (0548 561676). Four fully equipped Apartments 300 yards from safe sandy beach. Personally supervised; cleanliness assured. Write or phone for brochure. *[pw!]*

TANFIELD HOTEL, HOPE COVE, NEAR KINGSBRIDGE TQ7 3HF (0548 561268). A warm welcome awaits you at this Ashley Courtenay recommended, licensed Hotel. Ideal for a relaxing holiday. All rooms have central heating, en suite facilities, hairdryers, colour TV, tea/coffee making. Colour brochure. Bargain breaks available. *[£1.50 per night.]*

CHRIS AND JO MOON, SUN BAY HOTEL, INNER HOPE COVE, NEAR SALCOMBE TQ7 3HH (0548 561371). Licensed hotel overlooking sandy beach. Television lounge. Magnificent coastal walks. Children and pets welcome. *[£2 per night.]*

Ilfracombe

This popular seaside resort clusters round a busy harbour. The surrounding area is ideal for coastal walks.

COMBE LODGE HOTEL, CHAMBERCOMBE PARK, ILFRACOMBE EX34 9QW (0271 864518). Pets and their owners will enjoy holidays at our licensed Hotel. En-suite rooms available, good food, total freedom and walks galore. Dogs sleep in your bedroom. *[🐕]*

JOHN FOWLER HOLIDAYS, DEPARTMENT 34, MARLBOROUGH ROAD, ILFRACOMBE EX34 8PF (0271 866666). Modern Bungalows to sleep 2, 4, 6 or 8 people. Lounge with free colour television. Heated swimming pool, crazy golf course. Free entertainment and dancing. Sea and shops are close.

THE OLD COACH HOUSE, WATERMOUTH, ILFRACOMBE EX34 9SJ (0271 867340). Accommodation for 2 to 6 persons in converted courtyard complex. Fully equipped, colour TV etc. Terms from £80 to £310. Colour brochure from **Peggy Dobson.**

THE DARNLEY HOTEL, BELMONT ROAD, ILFRACOMBE EX34 8DR (0271 863955). Small licensed Hotel in beautiful garden. Renowned for superb food and personal service. Bed and breakfast from £14. With Evening Meal from £22.00. Pets free of charge. Open all year. *[pw!]*

ST. BRANNOCKS HOUSE HOTEL, ST. BRANNOCKS ROAD, ILFRACOMBE EX34 8EQ (0271 863873). Good food and excellent accommodation guaranteed at this friendly seaside Hotel. All rooms TV, tea making; en-suite available. Licensed bar. Parking. Children and pets welcome. 3 Crowns. *[🐕]*

Instow

On estuaries of Taw and Torridge, very popular with boating enthusiasts. Barnstaple 6 miles, Bideford 3.

Modern cottage-style house next to beach. Excellent views. Sleeps six people plus cot. Full central heating. Pets and children welcome. For brochure APPLY – MRS P. BAXTER, HUISH MOOR FARMHOUSE, INSTOW, BIDEFORD EX39 4LT (0271 861146). [🐾]

Kingsbridge

Pleasant town at head of picturesque Kingsbridge estuary. Centre for South Hams district with its lush scenery and quiet coves. Plymouth 21 miles, Dartmouth 15, Totnes 13.

HALLSANDS HOTEL, NORTH HALLSANDS, KINGSBRIDGE (054-851 264). Fully licensed family Hotel offering Bed, Breakfast and Evening Meal. Good food. Fishing, bathing and compressed air available.

TOAD HALL COTTAGES, UNION ROAD, KINGSBRIDGE TQ7 1EF (0548 853089 24 hrs). For a wonderful selection of waterside and rural cottages and farmhouses in South Devon, some with swimming pools, games rooms etc. All chosen for their individuality. Telephone for brochure.

ODDICOMBE HOUSE HOTEL, CHILLINGTON, KINGSBRIDGE TQ7 2JD (0548 531234). Set in three acres of grounds, convenient for all South Devon. Eight bedrooms, all en suite. Noted for good food and wines. Outdoor swimming pool. 3 Crowns Commended. [£2.50 per day.]

WOODLAND VIEW GUEST HOUSE, KILN LANE, STOKENHAM, KINGSBRIDGE TQ7 2SQ (0548 580542). In picturesque village one mile sea. Superb walking. Comfortable rooms. Pets very welcome. No guard dogs. [95p nightly.]

MRS J. TUCKER, MOUNT FOLLY FARM, BIGBURY-ON-SEA, KINGSBRIDGE TQ7 4AR (0548 810267). Spacious, self catering wing of farmhouse, overlooking the sea and sandy beaches of Bigbury Bay. Ideal for coastal walks and fishing. Situated beside golf course.

MRS B. KELLY, BLACKWELL PARK, LODDISWELL, KINGSBRIDGE TQ7 4EA (0548 821230). 17th century Farmhouse, 5 miles from Kingsbridge. Ideal centre for Dartmoor, Plymouth, Torbay, Dartmouth and many beaches. Some bedrooms en-suite. Bed, Breakfast and Evening Meal or Bed and Breakfast. Pets welcome free of charge. ETB 2 Crowns. [🐾]

BEACHDOWN, CHALLABOROUGH BAY, KINGSBRIDGE TQ7 4JB (0548 852282). Seaside bungalows 200 yards from quiet, sandy beach. Children's playground. Local shopping. Pets welcome. Fully furnished and equipped. ETB Approved 3 Keys. [pw! £16 per week.]

Lamerton

Rural village to west of Dartmoor, close to Cornish border, Tavistock 3 miles S.E.

Country Cottages in pleasant, peaceful position north-west of Tavistock. Fully equipped except linen. Easy reach Dartmoor. Stamp please for details. MRS T. DENLEY, 10 ST. GABRIELS LEA, CHINEHAM, BASINGSTOKE, HAMPSHIRE (0256 23388). [🐾]

Lewdown

With Dartmoor to the west and the lovely Lyd Valley to the south, Lewdown is a fine touring centre on the A30 for Cornwall and Devon. Okehampton 11 miles, Launceston 8.

THE HORSE HOTEL, LOBHILL FARM, LEWDOWN, OKEHAMPTON EX20 4DT (Tel and Fax: 056-683 248). Set in 35 acres of pasture and woodlands in beautiful countryside close to Dartmoor and Roadford Lake. All facilities; ideal for dog walkers, fishing; stabling for horses. Open all year. *[pw!]*

UNA CORNTHWAITE, HAYNE MILL, LEWDOWN, NEAR OKEHAMPTON EX20 4DD (056 683 342). Come and live 'en famille' with us, the Braddabrook Bearded Collies and Cavaliers, and enjoy our lovely home, in 3 acres of garden. Fishing. Excellent cuisine, 4-course evening meal. Bathroom en suite.

Little Torrington

Picturesque village eight miles inland from the north Devon coast. Excellent centre for touring both coast and inland. Bideford 7 miles.

ELAINE JOY & BARBARA TERRY, TORRIDGE HOUSE, LITTLE TORRINGTON EX38 8PS (0805 22542). Delightfully situated cottages, centrally heated, warm and comfortable. Microwave, fridge/freezer, colour TV etc. 2-5 bedrooms. Farm setting – cows, pigs, poultry, rabbits, lambs and kids. Outdoor heated pool, playroom, tennis, putting. Beautiful countryside with sandy beaches, moors and good attractions nearby. *[pw! First pet free, others £15 per week.]*

Lynton/Lynmouth

Picturesque twin villages joined by a unique cliff railway (vertical height 500ft). Lynmouth has a quaint harbour and Lynton enjoys superb views over the rugged coastline.

COUNTISBURY LODGE HOTEL, TORS PARK, LYNMOUTH EX35 6NB (0598 52388). Former Victorian vicarage, peacefully secluded yet only 5 minutes to Lynmouth village. En suite rooms with tea/coffee facilities, central heating, and choice of menu. Self catering cottage also available. *[🐕]*

MR AND MRS P. MURPHY, NEUBIA HOUSE HOTEL, LYNTON (0598 52309). Family-run Hotel set in old Lynton. All 12 rooms have private bath. Cordon Bleu cuisine. Proprietor chef. Large private car park. Off-season breaks. Colour brochure on application. Sorry – NO GUARD DOGS. *[🐕]*

MRS W. PRYOR, STATION HOUSE, LYNTON (0598 52275/52381). Holiday Flat situated in the former narrow gauge railway station closed in 1935, overlooking the West Lyn Valley. Centrally placed for Doone Valley and Exmoor. Parking available. *[🐕]*

THE EXMOOR SANDPIPER INN, COUNTISBURY, NEAR LYNMOUTH EX35 6NE (05987 263). This fine old coaching inn is in a beautiful setting with good food and hotel facilities for complete comfort. All 16 rooms en-suite with colour TV, tea/coffee making.

MRS BOYCE, DEAN STEEP, BARBROOK, LYNTON EX35 6JS (0598 53272). Peacefully situated in a uniquely beautiful setting of 17 acres of EXMOOR NATIONAL PARK. 12 comfortable two-bedroomed stone bungalows. Spectacular scenery, wildlife abounds. Ideal for moorland and coastal walking. Brochure with pleasure.

R. S. BINGHAM, NEW MILL FARM, BARBROOK, LYNTON EX35 6JR (Lynton [0598] 53341). Exmoor Valley. Two cottages by stream and modern Bungalow with panoramic views of Exmoor on 86-acre farm with Ponies Association Approved riding stables. Free fishing. SAE for brochure. *[pw! £15 per week.]*

SILVER HORSESHOE HOLIDAY BUNGALOWS, HIGH BULLEN FARM, ILKERTON, LYNTON (0598 53318). Self catering holidays in good accommodation - well equipped, carpeted throughout. Sleep up to 7. Games room, restaurant, licensed bar in farmhouse. Full details from Mrs Dyer.

CASTLE HILL HOUSE HOTEL, LYNTON (0598 52291). Delightful family-run hotel, all en suite rooms; colour TV, tea and coffee facilities. Lovely scenery, coastal walks and beaches. Children and pets most welcome.

DAVID BARNES AND JOHN WALLEY, COMBE PARK HOTEL, HILLSFORD BRIDGES, LYNTON EX35 6LE (0598 52356). Exmoor. Comfortable exquisite Country House Hotel near Lynton within National Trust parkland. Bedrooms with all facilities. Licensed. Dogs welcome. Bargain breaks. [pw! £1 per night.]

SHELLEY'S COTTAGE HOTEL, WATERSMEET ROAD, LYNMOUTH EX35 6EP (0598 53219). Small family-run hotel, overlooking village and sea. Some en suite and family rooms. All rooms have colour TV and tea/coffee facilities. Write or phone for brochure.

Mortehoe

Adjoining Woolacombe with cliffs and wide sands. Interesting rock scenery beyond Morte Point. Barnstaple 15 miles, Ilfracombe 6.

LUNDY HOUSE HOTEL, MORTEHOE, WOOLACOMBE EX34 7DZ (Woolacombe [0271] 870372). Lovely views over Mortehoe Bay. En-suite bedrooms; central heating; bar lounge and TV lounge. Traditional home cooking; friendly atmosphere. Pets welcome free of charge. Parking. Bargain Breaks available. [🐾 pw!]

Newton Abbot

Known as the gateway to Dartmoor and the coast, this lively market town has many fine buildings, parks and a racecourse.

ROSELANDS HOLIDAY CHALETS, TOTNES ROAD, IPPLEPEN, NEWTON ABBOT TQ12 5TD (0803 812701). Three detached self-contained chalets in private garden. Personally supervised. Easy reach of beaches, Dartmoor and South Devon attractions. Walking distance of pay/play golf course. Pets very welcome. Safe parking. [pw! First pet free, others £5 per week each.]

Ottery St. Mary

Pleasant little town in East Devon, within easy reach of the sea. Many interesting buildings including 11th century Parish Church. Birthplace of the poet, Coleridge.

Delightful thatched holiday cottages, near Sandy Bay, Exmouth; all within easy reach of beaches. Ideal touring areas. Sleep 4/6/8. Well equipped. Pets and children welcome. Brochure: D. MARRIOTT, BRAMLEYS, WEST HILL, OTTERY ST MARY EX11 1UX (0404 813286). [£15 weekly.]

MR AND MRS M. FORTH, FLUXTON FARM HOTEL, OTTERY ST MARY EX11 1RJ (0404 812818). Charming 16th century farmhouse with large garden. Good food superbly cooked, log fires, Teasmaids. Licensed. [🐾 pw!]

Paignton

Popular family resort on Torbay with long, safe, sandy beaches and small harbour. Exeter 25 miles, Newton Abbot 9, Dartmouth 8, Brixham 6, Totnes 6, Torquay 3.

J. AND E. BALL, DEPARTMENT P.W., HIGHER WELL FARM HOLIDAY PARK, STOKE GABRIEL, TOTNES TQ9 6RN (0803 782289). Within 4 miles Torbay beaches and 1 mile of River Dart. Central for touring. Dogs on leads. Tourist Board graded park, 3 ticks. [pw! £8 per week.]

AMBER HOUSE HOTEL, 6 ROUNDHAM ROAD, PAIGNTON TQ4 6EZ (0803 558372). Family-run licensed hotel. En-suite facilities and ground floor rooms. Good food. Highly recommended. A warm welcome assured to pets and their families. 3 Crowns. [🐕pw!]

Parracombe

Attractive North Devon village encompassed by steep hills. Good touring centre for sea and Exmoor. Lynton 5 miles.

COASTAL EXMOOR HIDEAWAYS. Holiday cottages including secluded Saxon millhouse; luxury house on beach; picturesque 300 year old cottage. Pets welcome and free. Breaks from £98. TELEPHONE 05983 339. [🐕]

Plymouth

Famous and historical port and resort, impressively rebuilt after severe war damage. Large naval docks at Devonport. Beach of pebble and sand. Of particular interest is the Hoe, overlooking the Sound, old and new lighthouses and Barbican.

HEADLAND HOTEL, RADFORD ROAD, WEST HOE, PLYMOUTH PL1 3BY (0752 660866). Licensed. Very friendly atmosphere. Pets welcome. Rooms with bath en suite. Two lounges. Spacious restaurant. 150 yards sea-front.

CHURCHWOOD VALLEY, DEPT PW, WEMBURY BAY, NEAR PLYMOUTH PL9 0DZ (0752 862382). Quality holiday Cabins in peaceful wooded valley, 500 metres from beach. Licensed shop, launderette, riding stables. Near Plymouth and Dartmoor. Family pets welcome free. √√√√ [🐕]

Poundsgate

Village surrounded by the rugged grandeur of Dartmoor, on B3357. Ashburton 5 miles S.E.

IVOR AND MIRANDA RUSSELL, LEUSDON LODGE, POUNDSGATE TQ13 7PE (Poundsgate [036 43] 304). Dartmoor National Park, near Widecombe. Friendly, family-run country Hotel. Newly refurbished. Off the beaten track. Panoramic views. Good food and wine. Children and dogs welcome. Winter Breaks. Bed and Breakfast with Evening Meal. [🐕]

Salcombe

Fishing and sailing centre in a sheltered position. Fine beaches and coastal walks nearby.

GRAFTON TOWERS HOTEL, MOULT ROAD, SALCOMBE TQ8 8LG (0548 842882). Small luxury Hotel with wonderful views. Convenient for ferry, town. Magnificent walks. Speciality local seafood. Homemade desserts. 2 stars AA, RAC. [pw! £2.00 per night.]

HERON HOUSE, THURLESTONE SANDS, NEAR SALCOMBE, DEVON (0548 561308). Idyllic location at sea's edge. En-suite rooms, splendid views, exceptional cuisine using Devon seafood and produce. Fully licensed. Heated outdoor pool. Open all year. ETB 4 Crowns Commended, Ashley Courtenay.

MRS E. J. LONSDALE, FERN LODGE, HOPE COVE, KINGSBRIDGE TQ7 3HF (0548 561326). Fern Lodge offers comfort, good food and personal attention. Five rooms en-suite. Three minutes from sea. All pets accepted. ETB Two Crowns. [£1.75 per day.]

A. R. AND J. A. FERRIS, ROCK HOUSE MARINE, THURLESTONE SANDS, NEAR SALCOMBE TQ17 3JY (0548 561285). Sample a touch of luxury in Hotel apartments in secluded bay. Heated pool, games rooms, waterside bar. Full Hotel facilities except Breakfast. Restaurant serves fresh food, bar snacks.

THE SALCOMBE BOAT COMPANY, WHITESTRAND, SALCOMBE TQ8 8ET (0548 843730). A holiday with a difference. Unwind with a houseboat holiday on Salcombe's tranquil estuary. Write or phone for brochure. *[£15 weekly.]*

SEAMARK HOLIDAY APARTMENTS, THURLESTONE SANDS, NEAR SALCOMBE TQ7 3JY (0548 561300). 5 lovely apartments adjoining coastal path. Beach 500 yards, golf one mile. Games room with darts, table tennis, snooker. Laundry room. Pay phone. Colour brochure. *[£10 per week.]*

Saunton Sands

Excellent sands, about 4 km long. Barnstaple 8 miles, Croyde 3.

SAUNTON BEACH VILLAS sleep 2-8 and are fully equipped. Every amenity nearby; adjacent to unspoilt beach. Open Easter to October. Weekend and Midweek breaks available *[£12 per week]*. APPLY – SAUNTON BEACH VILLAS, BROADFIELD HOLIDAYS, 1 PARK VILLAS, TAW VALE, BARNSTAPLE EX32 8NJ (0271 22033; 24 hours).

Seaton

Sheltered little resort at seaward end of a wooded valley. Beach is of sand and rocks. Plymouth 13 miles, Looe 5.

MILKBERE HOLIDAYS, MILKBERE HOUSE, 14 FORE STREET, SEATON EX12 2LA (0297 22925). Attractive self-catering Cottages, Bungalows, Apartments. Coast and Country on Devon/Dorset border. Free colour brochure. Pets welcome. *[pw! £12 per week.]*

SEATON. Self-contained Holiday Bungalows, ETB 2 Keys Approved, rural site. Fully equipped, accommodate six plus cot. Optional linen hire. Parking. Adjacent filling station and shop. Pets, children welcome. Contact: NETHERHAY HOLIDAYS, NETHERHAY, NEAR BEAMINSTER, DORSET DT8 3RH (Tel and Fax: 0308 868872 [24 hours]). *[£8 per week.]*

R. HALLETT, BOROLANDS FARM, AXMOUTH, SEATON (0297 552680). Bed and Breakfast, Evening Meal optional. Children and pets welcome. *[pw!]*

Shaldon

Delightful little resort facing Teignmouth across the Teign estuary. Sheltered by the lofty prominence of Shaldon Ness, beach-side activities are largely concerned with boats and sailing; beaches are mainly of sand. Mini-golf course. The attractions of Teignmouth are reached by a long road bridge.

EAST CLIFF HOLIDAY APARTMENTS, MARINE PARADE, SHALDON TQ14 0DP (0626 872334). Situated on Shaldon's lovely beach will superb views over sea, river and picturesque harbour. Each beautifully furnished, self-contained Apartment with modern kitchen and bathroom. Our prices include bed linen, colour television, central heating, car parking. Laundry facilities, telephone. No smoking. *[pw! £5 weekly.]*

Sidmouth

Charming and sheltered resort, winner of many awards for its floral displays. Good sands at Jacob's Ladder beach.

OAKDOWN CARAVAN PARKS, WESTON, SIDMOUTH EX10 0PH (029780 387; Fax: 0395 513731). Two privately owned parks set in the East Devon Heritage Coast. Level, well drained and closely mown. Luxury Holiday Homes for hire, pitches for touring units. Colour brochure. AA Three Pennants; BGHP Five Ticks. *[pw! from 70p per night.]*

LOWER KNAPP FARM, SIDBURY, SIDMOUTH EX10 0QN (040-487 438). Luxury self catering cottages sleeping 2/8 set in 16 acres. Indoor heated pool, sauna, solarium. All cottages with fully fitted kitchens; colour TV etc. Linen supplied. Colour brochure on request. Three Keys. *[£15 per week]*

SWEETCOMBE COTTAGE HOLIDAYS, HIGHER SWEETCOMBE, SIDBURY, SIDMOUTH EX10 0QR (0395 597343; Fax: 0395 597660). Selection Cottages, Farmhouses and Flats in Devon and Cornwall. Televisions, gardens. Pets welcome. SAE please.

GEOFF AND JOY STONE, CRANMERE HOUSE, 2 FORTFIELD PLACE, STATION ROAD, SIDMOUTH EX10 8NX (0395 513933). Discover lovely Sidmouth from Cranmere House. A stone's throw from sea front, town, buses and eating out. Rooms have colour TV, tea-making and winter heating. Own keys to room and house. Laundered sheets. B&B £12–£15, special weekly and family rates. *[pw!]*

Stoke-in-Teignhead

Quiet village, 4 miles East of Newton Abbot. 6 miles Torquay and close to sandy beaches.

Charming character cottage and barn conversion for 3/5 persons. Both provide every facility for comfort/convenience. TV, dishwasher, microwave, games room, linen. Delightful quiet village. Six miles Torquay/Teignmouth. Ideal base whether touring/walking or just resting. Beaches two miles. Moors 20 miles. MRS J. A. REES, 52 VICTORIA ROAD, PENARTH, SOUTH GLAMORGAN CF64 3HZ (0222 701115). [🐾]

South Brent

Just off the busy A38 Plymouth to Exeter Road, this is a good centre on the River Avon for Dartmoor and the South Devon resorts. Plymouth 15 miles, Ashburton 8.

EDESWELL FARM CARAVAN AND CAMPING PARK, RATTERY, SOUTH BRENT TQ10 9LN (0364 72177). Picturesque Park in quiet rural setting. Two/three bedroomed luxury units with every facility. Tourers and tents welcome. Showers, shop, TV lounge, bar, launderette; indoor heated pool. *[pw! £7.00 weekly static, £1 per night touring.]*

Enchanting, select site for those seeking a quiet restful holiday amidst beautiful surroundings, overlooking the Dartmoor Hills. Fully serviced luxury caravans, with colour TV, fridge, heater and shower. Separate low density site for tents/tourers. Several acres for carefree exercising. 3 ticks. APPLY – TREVOR AND JILL HORNE, WEBLAND FARM HOLIDAY PARK, AVONWICK, NEAR SOUTH BRENT TQ10 9EX (0364 73273) *[pw! £1 nightly]*

Southleigh

Village situated 3 miles north-west of Seaton.

WISCOMBE PARK, SOUTHLEIGH, NEAR COLYTON EX13 6JE (040 487 474). Nature lovers' and children's paradise. Working farm. Beautiful walks. Trout and coarse fishing. Near Coast. Comfortable self-contained accommodation. Free brochure. *[🐾]*

Tavistock

Birthplace of Sir Francis Drake, and site of a fine ruined Benedictine Abbey. On edge of Dartmoor, 13 miles north of Plymouth.

MRS P. G. C. QUINTON, HIGHER QUITHER, MILTON ABBOT, TAVISTOCK PL19 0PZ (082 286 284). Modern self-contained barn conversion, sleeps 4. Terms from £160 inc. linen, coal and logs. Electricity metered. *[🐕]*

Teignmouth

Resort at mouth of River Teign. Bridge connects with Shaldon on the other side of the estuary.

LYME BAY HOUSE HOTEL, DEN PROMENADE, TEIGNMOUTH TQ14 8SZ (0626 772953). Near rail and coach stations and shops. En suite facilities. Lift – no steps. Bed and Breakfast. *[🐕]*

Thurlestone

Picturesque South Hams village near the glorious sands of Bigbury Bay. Famous golf course, delightful cliff scenery. Plymouth 20 miles, Kingsbridge 4.

LA MER, THURLESTONE SANDS TQ7 3JY (0548 561207). Country Hotel on water's edge. Ten bedrooms with washbasins, several with showers en-suite. Residential licence. Children and pets most welcome. Please phone for details. *[£0.80 per night.]*

Tiverton

Market town on River Exe 12 miles north of Exeter, centrally located for touring both North and South coasts.

MRS PRATT, MOOR BARTON, NOMANSLAND, TIVERTON EX16 8NN (0884 860325). 18th century superior farmhouse on a 250-acre mixed farm, situated equidistant from the North and South coast. Four double, four family and one twin-bedded rooms. Children welcome. B&B from £14 per night; DB&B £120 per week inclusive.

SWALLOWFIELD, HORNHILL FARM, EXETER HILL, TIVERTON EX16 4PL. Luxury 5-bedroomed house (sleeps 8 + cot) in idyllic position. Perfect for children and pets. Swimming, tennis, riding, country walks nearby. Games room. Linen provided. For details contact BARBARA PUGSLEY (0884 253352). *[🐕]*

Torbay

The bay which extends from Hope's Nose in the north to Berry Head in the south and the location of three of Devon's most popular resorts: Torquay, Paignton, and Brixham.

Holiday bungalows on beautiful park. APPLY – JAMES AND ANN BOASE, CHURSCOMBE HOUSE, VICARAGE ROAD, MARLDON, PAIGNTON TQ3 1NN (0803 558707). *[£10 weekly.]*

Torquay

Premier resort on the English Riviera with a wide range of attractions and entertainments. Yachting and watersports centre with 10 superb beaches and coves.

MARGARET AND TERRY SKINNER, PINELEIGH GUEST HOUSE, 20 QUINTA ROAD, BABBACOMBE, TORQUAY TQ1 3RN (0803 324714). Friendly, comfortable Guest House, convenient beaches, shops, theatres. Central heating. Colour television. Children and pets welcome. Doggie sitting available; large exercise field nearby. *[pw!]*

MR AND MRS D. G. MAISEY, CROSSWAYS AND SEA VIEW HOLIDAY FLATS, MAIDENCOMBE, TORQUAY TQ1 4TH (0803 328369). Modern self-contained flats set in one-acre grounds. Sleep 2/5. Colour TV. Pets welcome – exercise field adjacent. Fishing, golf, sailing etc within easy reach. *[🐕]*

ANSTEY'S COVE HOTEL, 327 BABBACOMBE ROAD, TORQUAY TQ1 3TB (0803 293674). The Torquay official guide mentions 4 walks, 3 of which pass Anstey's Cove, so that exercising one's pet presents no difficulty here.

VILLA ST CHRISTOPHER HOLIDAY FLATLETS, HESKETH ROAD, TORQUAY TQ1 2LN. 300 yards beach/coastal walks. Convenient town/harbour. Sleep 2/5. Free parking. Colour TV. Own keys. Dogs welcome. Send SAE for brochure or telephone 0803 294252. *[£7 weekly.]*

MRS M. A. TOLKIEN, FAIRMOUNT HOUSE HOTEL, HERBERT ROAD, CHELSTON, TORQUAY TQ2 6RW (0803 605446). Small licensed Hotel with en suite bedrooms, central heating. Peaceful setting; excellent coast and country walking. One mile town centre. DB&B from £36.50 per person. Bargain Breaks available. *[🐕]*

COTTAGE AND DETACHED BUNGALOWS. All ideally located for a family holiday close to Torbay's beaches and all its amenities or the peaceful tranquillity of Devon's lovely villages and moors. MR AND MRS CANN, "KINGSHILL", CHURCH END ROAD, KINGSKERSWELL, NEAR NEWTON ABBOT TQ12 5DS (0803 873957).

SOUTH SANDS APARTMENTS, TORBAY ROAD, LIVERMEAD, TORQUAY TQ2 6RG (0803 293521). 18 superior self-contained ground and first floor Apartments for 1–5 persons. Central heating. Open all year. Parking. Beach 100 yards. Convenient Riviera Centre, theatre, marina. *[pw! £1 per night.]*

LORNA DOONE APARTMENTS, TORWOOD GARDENS ROAD, TORQUAY (RESERVATIONS: 0694 722244). Situated 500 yards from town centre shops and seafront. Luxury apartments with colour TV, microwave, modern bathroom and kitchen. Families and dogs welcome. From £172 per week for 2 persons. *[£15 per week.]*

MR AND MRS T. H. FISH, FAIRLAWNS HALL, ST. MICHAEL'S ROAD, TORQUAY TQ1 4DD (0803 328904). Delightful self-contained holiday apartments and mews cottages. Central heating available. Pets welcome. Large woods nearby, gardens and parking. Stamp for brochure. *[£10 weekly.]*

RED HOUSE HOTEL AND MAXTON LODGE HOLIDAY APARTMENTS, ROUSDOWN ROAD, CHELSTON, TORQUAY TQ2 6PB (0803 607811). Choose either the friendly service and facilities of an hotel or the privacy and freedom of self-catering apartments. The best of both worlds! 4 Keys/3 Crowns Commended. *[🐕]*

Torrington

Pleasant market town on River Torridge. Good centre for moors and sea. Exeter 36 miles, Okehampton 20, Barnstaple 12, Bideford 7.

SMYTHAM MANOR HOLIDAYS, LITTLE TORRINGTON, TORRINGTON EX38 8PU (0805 622110). 17th Century Manor House in 15 acres of parkland. Close to Coast and Moors. We offer both Guest House and Self-Catering accommodation. Bar. Restaurant. Heated outdoor pool. 3 Crowns. *[£2 per night in Manor, £1 per night self catering.]*

SALLY MILSOM, STOWFORD LODGE, LANGTREE, NEAR TORRINGTON EX38 8NU (08055 540). Away from the crowds. Four luxury cottages in peaceful countryside. Sleep 4/6. Heated indoor pool. Magnificent views and walks. Phone for brochure. *[pw! £10 per week.]*

Westward Ho!

Charming village named after the novel by Charles Kingsley. Good sands; two-mile long pebble ridge to the north-west.

For the very best in self catering. 11 cottages in idyllic position one mile from coast. Sleep 2–8 persons. Heated pool, licensed restaurant and bar, children's play area, laundry, etc. Full colour brochure. WEST PUSEHILL FARM COTTAGES, WEST-WARD HO! DEVON (0237 475638 or 474622).

2/6-berth seaside holiday Bungalows adjoining sandy beach. Also at Ilfracombe. Fully equipped. Colour television. Kitchen. Refrigerator. Bathroom. Toilet. H & C. Dogs welcome. March 1st to November 1st. From £99 per week. SAE. APPLY – MRS D. SMITH, 8 DAISY BANK CLOSE, HIGH HEATH, PELSALL, WALSALL, WEST MIDLANDS WS3 4BL (0922 684742).

BROCKENHURST, 11 ATLANTIC WAY, WESTWARD HO! EX39 1HX (0237 423346). Warm, clean and comfortable en suite bedrooms. Close to village centre and seafront. Ideal for walking. Brochure on request. Acess/Visa welcome.

Self-catering Bungalows, almost adjoining three miles of glorious sand. Fully carpeted, with free colour TV, bathroom, WC, H&C, electric cooker, fridge. Free colour brochure on request. APPLY – JOHN FOWLER HOLIDAYS, DEPARTMENT 36, MARLBOROUGH ROAD, ILFRACOMBE EX34 8PF (0271 866666).

Woody Bay

A beautiful little spot on the northern edge of the National Trust property of the same name. Ilfracombe 12 miles, Lynton 4.

GORDON AND BARBARA MCKAY, MARTINHOE MANOR, WOODY BAY, NEAR LYNTON EX31 4QX (059-83 424). 'Where Exmoor meets the sea'. Self-catering apartments sleeping from one to eight, with superb facilities. Residents' lounge bar. Open all year. From £90 per week.

Woolacombe

A favourite resort for children, with long, wide stretches of sand. Barnstaple 15 miles, Ilfracombe 6.

PEBBLES HOTEL, COMBESGATE BEACH, WOOLACOMBE EX34 7EA (0271 870426). Family-run Hotel overlooking sea and beaches. All rooms en suite, with colour TV, tea/coffee making etc. Special Short Break packages. Write or phone for colour brochure. *[🐕]*

DEVON

CROSSWAYS HOTEL, SEAFRONT, WOOLACOMBE EX34 7DJ (0271 870395). Homely, family-run licensed Hotel surrounded by National Trust land. Children and pets welcome. [🐕]

JOHN AND JOSE ROLFE, COMBE RIDGE HOTEL, THE SEA FRONT, WOOLACOMBE EX34 7DJ (0271 870321). Small, family Hotel facing Combesgate Beach. Excellent cuisine. Bathing and surfing from the Hotel. Children and pets welcome. Senior Citizens' discount early/late season. Free car park. 3 Crowns. [£1 per night.]

EUROPA PARK, STATION ROAD, WOOLACOMBE (0271 870159/870772). Luxury bungalows, superb views. Touring caravans and tents. Full facilities. Pets welcome, 6-acre dog park. Indoor heated swimming pool.

LITTLE BEACH HOTEL, THE ESPLANADE, WOOLACOMBE EX34 7DJ (0271 870398). Elegant, spacious and friendly family-run hotel. Superb seafront location with magnificent views of sea and countryside. Early and late season breaks. ETB 3 Crowns Commended [🐕]

MRS JOYCE BAGNALL, CHICHESTER HOUSE, THE ESPLANADE, WOOLACOMBE EX34 7DJ (0271 870761). Holiday apartments on sea front. Fully furnished, sea and coastal views. Watch the sun go down from your balcony. Open all year. SAE Resident Proprietors. [£8 per week.]

DORSET

127

DORSET *Bournemouth*

SYMBOLS
🐕 Indicates no charge for pets.
£ Indicates a charge for pets: nightly or weekly.
pw! Indicates some special provision for pets: exercise, feeding etc.

SYMBOLS
🐕 Indicates no charge for pets.
£ Indicates a charge for pets: nightly or weekly.
pw! Indicates some special provision for pets: exercise, feeding etc.

For a super selection of self catering properties in all the best areas either by the coast or in the countryside call SUMMER COTTAGES LTD, 1 WEST WALKS, DORCHESTER, Dorset DT1 1RE. (0305) 268988.

Abbotsbury

Village of thatched cottages in sheltered green valley. Benedictine monks created the famous Abbotsbury Swannery.

MRS JOSEPHINE PEARSE, TAMARISK FARM, WEST BEXINGTON, DORCHESTER DT2 9DF (0308 897784). Self Catering. On Chesil Beach: two secluded Chalets and one large and two smaller Bungalows on farm with various animals and organic market garden. Good centre for touring, sightseeing, all sports. Pets and children welcome. Terms from £75.

Bishop's Down

Farming community, 5 miles south of Sherborne.

MRS R.A. DARKNELL, THE BUNGALOW, WILLOW TREE FARM, BISHOP'S DOWN, NEAR SHERBORNE DT9 5PN (0963 210400). Bed, Breakfast and Evening Meal, £55-£60 per week. Good food. Quiet. Children and dogs welcome. Senior Citizens. *[🐕]*

Readers are requested to mention this guidebook when seeking accommodation (and please enclose a stamped addressed envelope).

Bournemouth

One of Britain's premier holiday resorts with miles of golden sand, excellent shopping and leisure facilities. Lively entertainments include Festival of Lights at the beginning of September.

3 self-contained apartments in quiet avenue, one minute from clean, sandy beaches and 5 minutes from shops. Sleep 3/6. Fully equipped including linen. All have fridge, toilet and shower room, fitted carpets, colour TV, central heating, electric meter. Parking. Terms from £75. Contact: MRS HAMMOND, STOURCLIFFE COURT, 56 STOURCLIFFE AVENUE, SOUTHBOURNE, BOURNEMOUTH BH6 3PX (0202 420698). *[£5 weekly.]*

MR AND MRS E. A. MURRAY AND MRS B. ECTOR, 'SURREY DENE', 33 SURREY ROAD, BOURNEMOUTH BH4 9HR (0202 763950). Comfortable self-contained Flats, beautifully situated adjoining Bournemouth Upper Gardens. Free private parking. SAE for brochure. *[🐶]*

CRAVEN GRANGE HOLIDAY FLATS, 17 BODORGAN ROAD, BOURNEMOUTH BH2 6JY (0202 296234). Self-contained flats and cottage, 2-6 persons. Town centre, golf and parks nearby. Car parking. Free Welcome Pack. Pets welcome. Telephone or SAE for details. *[🐶]*

THE EMBASSY HOTEL, MEYRICK ROAD, EAST CLIFF, BOURNEMOUTH BH1 3DW (0202 290751; Fax: 0202 557459). Privately owned Hotel within walking distance of town centre and amenities. En suite bedrooms; heated outdoor pool and games room. Superb service and excellent cuisine. B&B from £25 per night. ETB 4 Crowns. *[£3.50 per night.]*

St George's Holiday Flats are near sea and shops; Questors overlooks quiet, wooded Pleasure Gardens; superb for you and your dog. Both have good car parks; pay-phones, laundry, TV, fridges in all units. Clean and fully equipped. We like dogs. Apply: SANDRA & BARRY GLENARD, 45 BRANKSOME WOOD ROAD, BOURNE-MOUTH BH4 9JT (0202 763262). *[£12 per week.]*

SUE AND CLIFF LOGGEY, ASHDALE HOTEL, 35 BEAULIEU ROAD, ALUM CHINE, BOURNEMOUTH BH14 8HY (0202 761947). Recommended for our warm, friendly atmosphere and good, plentiful food. Delightful situation by Alum Chine. Clean, well-equipped bedrooms. Licensed. [🐶]

FIELDEN COURT, 20 SOUTHERN ROAD, SOUTHBOURNE, BOURNEMOUTH BH6 3SR (0202 427459). Licensed Hotel. All rooms toilet en-suite. Three minutes' walk to shops/sandy beach. Parking. Small pets welcome. SAE for brochure. *[🐶]*

Country Holiday Chalet near woods and sea. Dogs welcome. SAE. APPLY - MRS L. M. BOWLING, OWLPEN, 148 BURLEY ROAD, BRANSGORE, DORSET BH23 8DB (0425 672875). *[pw!]*

CAIRNSMORE PRIVATE HOTEL, 37 BEAULIEU ROAD, BOURNEMOUTH BH4 8HY (0202 763705). 4 minutes' walk through wooded glades to sea. Colour TV in all bedrooms, all en suite. Parking. BB & ED from £123 per person per week. Residential licence. Special diets catered for. No charge for pets. 3 Crowns Commended. *[🐶pw!]*

JUNE HOATH, ALUM GRANGE HOTEL, 1 BURNABY ROAD, ALUM CHINE, BOURNEMOUTH BH4 8JF (0202 761195). Pets and owners are assured of a warm welcome at this superbly furnished hotel, 250 yards from the beach. All rooms with colour TV and tea/coffee making.

BILL AND MARJORIE TITCHEN, WHITE TOPPS HOTEL, 4 CHURCH ROAD, SOUTHBOURNE, BOURNEMOUTH BH6 4BB (Bournemouth [0202] 428868). Situated in quiet position close to lovely walks on the beach. Dogs welcome. Free parking. Residential licence. *[pw!]*

MR AND MRS R. LAMBERT, LYTTELTON LODGE, 16 FLORENCE ROAD, BOURNEMOUTH BH5 1HF (0202) 304925/(0425) 474007). Modern Holiday Apartments sleeping one to 10 persons, close to sea and shops. Recently extensively renovated with new kitchens and bathrooms. Clean, well-equipped flats. Car park and garages. Write or phone for colour brochure and terms. *[£14 weekly.]*

MRS E. DORAN, "CORRA LINN", 13 KNYVETON ROAD, BOURNEMOUTH BH1 3QG (0202 558003). Self-catering holiday Flatlets. Television. Linen. Free car parking. Children and dogs welcome. SAE stating number in party. *[£5 per week.]*

OVERCLIFF HOTEL, 29 BEAULIEU ROAD, ALUM CHINE, BOURNEMOUTH BH4 8HY (0202 761030). Small comfortable licensed Hotel; en suite available. Home cooking, TV lounge. Three minutes to beach. B&B from £15, BB&EM from £90–£140 weekly. Open all year. *[ ]*

THE COUNTRY HOTEL, WESTOVER ROAD, BOURNEMOUTH (0202 552385). 50 bedroomed Hotel situated in the heart of Bournemouth; en suite rooms with colour TV, central heating etc. Pets and guests can look forward to excellent attention from a well-trained staff.

Self contained holiday flats with exercise area in garden. Three minutes' level walk between shops and cliffs, with lift to fine, sandy "Pets Allowed" beach. Most reasonable terms early and late season. EATON HOUSE, 41 GRAND AVENUE, SOUTHBOURNE, BOURNEMOUTH BH6 3SY (0202 300351). *[pw!]*

THE STUDLAND DENE HOTEL, ALUM CHINE, WEST CLIFF, BOURNEMOUTH BH4 8JA (0202 765445). Overlooking the beach, marvellous walks. All rooms with TV, direct-dial phone; all en-suite. A la carte restaurant, carvery. *[ ]*

MRS W. HOLLAND, 12 AVONCLIFF ROAD, SOUTHBOURNE, BOURNEMOUTH BH6 3NR (0202 426650). Self catering flatlet on Southbourne cliff top. Fully equipped, close shops, buses; car parking available. Small dogs welcome. Open all year. SAE Mrs W. Holland. *[ ]*

SEA BREEZE, 32 ST. CATHERINE'S ROAD, SOUTHBOURNE, BOURNEMOUTH BH6 4AB (0202 433888). Small peaceful Hotel, opposite beach. Most rooms en suite, TV, teamakers. Parking. Generous home cooking. Pets welcome. B&B from £15; Evening Meal £6. *[£1 per night, £5 per week.]*

DAVID & CHRISTINE TROMAN, 52 STOURCLIFFE AVENUE, SOUTHBOURNE, BOURNEMOUTH BH6 3PX (0202 425235). Two self contained one-bedroomed flats, sleep 2–6. 5 minutes' walk from sea/shops. Lounge, kitchen, bathroom. Linen supplied. Forecourt parking. Terms from £120–£295 weekly. SAE brochure. *[ ]*

EAST CLIFF COURT, EAST OVERCLIFF DRIVE, BOURNEMOUTH (0202 554545; Fax 0202 557456). Luxury seafront Hotel, all bedrooms en suite. Games room, outdoor pool, sauna, solarium. Pets welcome. Send for colour brochure and menus. AA** RAC** *[£5 per day.]*

MR AND MRS J. JENKINS, THE VINE HOTEL, 22 SOUTHERN ROAD, SOUTH-BOURNE, BOURNEMOUTH BA6 3SR (0202 428309). Small family Hotel only 3 minutes' walk from sea and shops. All rooms en-suite. Residential licence. Pets welcome. No smoking in bedrooms and dining room. *[£5 per week.]*

Bridport

Market town of Saxon origin, noted for rope and net making. Harbour at West Bay has sheer cliffs rising from the beach.

MR AND MRS HADDON AND MR AND MRS RICE, DURBEYFIELD GUEST HOUSE, WEST BAY, BRIDPORT DT6 4EL (0308 23307). 2 minutes from Chesil Beach. Near small harbour. Home cooking. Washbasins all rooms. Colour television. Prices from £14–£17.50. Free parking. Dogs welcome. ETB Listed.

Super Self Catering Bungalows in old smugglers' haunt of Eype, near market town of Bridport. Beach 5 minutes' walk. Accommodation suitable for the wheelchair user. No club or disco. CONTACT: MR SPEED, GOLDEN ACRE, EYPE, NEAR BRIDPORT DT6 6AL (0308 863434).

MRS S. NORMAN, FROGMORE FARM, CHIDEOCK, BRIDPORT DT6 6HT (0308 456159). The choice is yours – Bed and Breakfast, optional Evening Meal, in charming farmhouse, OR self-catering Cottage equipped for six plus cot, pets welcome. Brochure and terms free on request. [🛏pw!]

Thatched Cottages on beach. Sleep 6 to 8. Sea view Flat. Children, dogs welcome. Winter breaks. APPLY: MRS I. FORBES, FOURFOOT HOUSE, EYPE, BRIDPORT DT6 6AL (0308 25600). [🛏]

BRIDPORT ARMS HOTEL, WEST BAY, BRIDPORT DT6 4EN (0308 22994). Thatched Hotel on edge of beach in picturesque West Bay. Two character bars, real ale, wide range bar meals. A la carte Restaurant featuring local fish. 2 Crowns Approved. AA/RAC one star. [🛏]

Charmouth

Small resort on Lyme Bay, 3 miles Lyme Regis. Sandy beach backed by undulating cliffs where many fossils are found. Good walks.

DOLPHINS RIVER PARK, BERNE LANE, CHARMOUTH DT6 6RD (0297 60022). Luxury 4 and 6 berth Caravans on small, peaceful park. Licensed shop, coin-op laundry; children's play area. One mile from beach. Colour brochure available. [pw! £1.20 per night.]

MR F. LOOSMORE, MANOR FARM HOLIDAY CENTRE, CHARMOUTH, BRIDPORT DT6 6QL (Charmouth [0297] 60226). All units for 6 people. 10 minutes level walk to beach, many fine local walks. Swimming pools, licensed bar with family room, shops, launderette. Sporting facilities nearby. Children and pets welcome. SAE. [£15 per week.]

Chideock

Village near coast 3 miles west of Bridport.

MRS M. CHATTIN, DOGHOUSE FARM, CHIDEOCK, BRIDPORT DT6 6HY (0297 89208). 17th-century farmhouse, comfortable and welcoming. TV lounge. Tea/coffee making facilities. Two twin rooms, one double en suite. Terms from £15. Footpath, sea and village 10 minutes. Adjoining National Trust.

Eype

A lane leads from the village to a small pebble beach. Good sea views from the cliffs. Bridport 2 mills.

MR MUNDY, EYPE HOUSE, EYPE, BRIDPORT DT6 6AC (0308 24903). A small quiet family-run park in area of outstanding natural beauty just 200 yards from the beach. Ideal for walkers and the less energetic.

Piddletrenthide

Village 6 miles north of Dorchester.

THE POACHERS INN, PIDDLETRENTHIDE DT2 7QX (0300 348358). On B3143 in lovely Piddle Valley, this delightful Inn offers en-suite rooms with colour TV, tea/coffee making, phones. Swimming pool; residents' lounge. Restaurant or Bar meals available. Garden – good dog walks! B&B £23. 3 Crowns. AA/RAC QQQ. [🐕]

Poole

Popular resort, yachting and watersports centre with large harbour and many creeks. Sand and shingle beaches. Salisbury 30 miles, Dorchester 23, Blandford 14, Wareham 9, Bournemouth 5.

D. R. SHAW, THE WHITE HOUSE, 10 TOWER ROAD WEST, BRANKSOME PARK, POOLE BH13 6LA (0202 763559). Self-contained holiday Flats, 5 minutes beach. Colour television, garden, parking. Children/dogs accepted.

WHISPERING PINES. Self-contained holiday flat. Fully equipped except linen. Colour TV. Within easy reach of beaches and entertainments. SAE for brochure to: MRS H. LEE, 9 SPUR HILL AVENUE, LOWER PARKSTONE, POOLE BH14 9PH (0202 740585). [🐕]

TWIN CEDARS HOTEL, 2 PINEWOOD ROAD, BRANKSOME PARK, POOLE BH13 6JS (0202 761339). All dogs welcome. Marvellous freshly prepared food; licensed bar, table tennis. Own grounds. Bed and Breakfast from £19.00, Evening Meal £9.00 p.p. Bathrooms/WCs en-suite. Accommodation also available in Cottage adjoining.

"SEA-WITCH", 47 HAVEN ROAD, CANFORD CLIFFS, POOLE BH13 7LH (0202 707697). Small licensed Hotel, clean, comfortable, fully en suite. B&B from £20; Evening Meals. Convenient for ferries. Own car park. Open all year round. [🐕]

Studland

Unspoilt seaside village at south-western end of Poole Bay, 3 miles north of Swanage.

FAIRFIELDS HOTEL, SWANAGE ROAD, STUDLAND BAY BH19 3AE (0929 44224). In a rural setting, with extensive views of Purbeck Hills and across to the Isle of Wight. All rooms en suite. Residential licence. B&B from £23; DB&B £33. Good food, a warm welcome and friendly service in comfortable surroundings. Call Matt and Niki.

THE MANOR HOUSE, STUDLAND BAY (0929 44288). An 18th century Manor House, nestling in 20 acres of secluded grounds. All bedrooms en suite with central heating, colour TV, direct dial telephone, tea/coffee making facilities. *[£2.50 per night.]*

KNOLL HOUSE HOTEL, STUDLAND BN19 3AW (092 944 251; Fax: 092 944 423). Country House Hotel within National Trust reserve. Golden beach. 100 acre grounds. Family suites, six lounges. Tennis, golf, swimming, games rooms, health spa. Full board terms £53–£78 daily. See also our full page advertisement under Studland Bay. *[£3.50 nightly.]*

Swanage

Traditional family holiday resort set in a sheltered bay ideal for water sports. Good base for a walking holiday.

MRS M. STOCKLEY, SWANAGE CARAVAN SITE, 17 MOOR ROAD, SWANAGE BH19 1RG (0929 424154). 4/5/6-berth Caravans. Pets welcome. Easter to October. Colour TV. Shop. Parking space. Rose Award Park. √ √ √ √ /ᐧ⊤ᐧ/

MRS GILLIAN MACDERMOTT, THE LITTLE MANOR, 389 HIGH STREET, SWAN-AGE BH19 2NP (0929 422948). A friendly small Guest House open all year round, where pets and children are welcome. Tea and coffee making facilities in all rooms.

MRS M. SMITH, 35 PROSPECT CRESCENT, SWANAGE BH19 1BD (0929 423441). Comfortable Guest House in quiet, level position. Good food. Bed and Breakfast. TV Lounge. Pets welcome. Parking. /ᐧ⊤ᐧ/

LIMES HOTEL, 48 PARK ROAD, SWANAGE BH19 2AE (0929 422664). Small friendly Hotel. En suite rooms; tea/coffee facilities. Licensed bar. Central heating. Children and pets welcome. Telephone or SAE for brochure.

Sydling St. Nicholas

Village two miles from Cerne Abbas with its 180 foot Chalk Giant on the hillside.

MRS BOWN, 11 DORCHESTER ROAD, SYDLING ST NICHOLAS, DORCHESTER DT1 9NU (0300 341790). Lamperts Farmhouse is a 17th century thatched Listed farmhouse in a peaceful unspoilt village nestling in Dorset's beautiful Sydling valley. Self Catering in one-bedroom farm cottage or B&B in prettily decorated en suite bedrooms. Guests' own sitting room.

Wareham

Picturesque riverside town, almost surrounded by earth works, considered pre-Roman. Nature reserves of great beauty nearby. Weymouth 19 miles, Dorchester 17, Bournemouth 14, Swanage 10, Poole 6.

GLEBE COTTAGES. Thatched farmhouse and three adjoining thatched cottages sleeping 5/7 respectively. All furnished to high standard, fully equipped except linen and towels. Coin meter. Open all year. Dogs welcome. SAE to: MR & MRS P. G. MacDONALD-SMITH, PEAK'S COPSE, BLOXWORTH ESTATE, NEAR WAREHAM BH20 7EF (0929 459442).

MRS L. S. BARNES, LUCKFORD WOOD HOUSE, EAST STOKE, WAREHAM BH20 6AW (Tel and Fax: 0929 463098). Spacious, peaceful surroundings. Bed and Breakfast available in luxurious farmhouse. Camping facilities include showers and toilets. Near Lulworth Cove, Tank Museum and Corfe Castle. Open all year. Listed. AA QQ. /ᐧ⊤ᐧ/

West Bexington

Seaside village with pebble beach. Chesil Beach stretches eastwards. Nearby is Abbotsbury with its Benedictine Abbey, Chapel and famous Swannery. Dorchester 13 miles, Weymouth 13, Bridport 6.

GORSELANDS CARAVAN PARK, WEST BEXINGTON-ON-SEA DT2 9DJ (0308 897232 or 0305 871457). All amenities, fully equipped 4/6 berth caravans. Personal attention. Attractive park; glorious sea views. Two minutes by car to sea. Shop and Launderette on site. Holiday flats with sea views to let nearby. Send for brochure: Dept. P.W. /ᐧ⊤ᐧ/

Weymouth

Set in a beautiful bay, with fine beaches and a picturesque 17th century harbour, Weymouth has a wide range of entertainment and leisure amenities.

WEYMOUTH BAY HOLIDAY PARK, PRESTON. 1 6-berth Caravan. Near sea. Dogs welcome. APPLY – MRS D. W. CANNON, 151 SANDSTONE ROAD, GROVE PARK, LONDON SE12 0UT (081-857 7586). *[🐕]*

MR P. COOPER, 'BUCKLANDS', 22 BUXTON ROAD, WEYMOUTH DT4 9PJ (0305 785014). Holiday Flats Flatlets. Fully equipped. Television. Children and pets welcome. SAE for details. *[🐕]*

ACE HOLIDAY FLATS, 48 50 SPA ROAD, WEYMOUTH DT3 5EW (0305 779393). Clean, comfy self-contained Flats. 2–8 persons and dogs. Ample car park and garden. Near local shops, pub, Radipole Lake. Easy access town and sea. *[£12 weekly.]*

CO. DURHAM

Barnard Castle

Situated on River Tees, ideal for touring Teesdale. Bowes Museum has large collection of art treasures. Darlington 15 miles.

MRS J. DIXON, EAST HOUSE, LANGLEYDALE, BARNARD CASTLE, DURHAM DL12 8SL (0833 37225). 28ft Caravan with WC, shower; television and fridge. Short distance to Lake District, sea-side, Beamish Museum, Hadrian's Wall, Durham Cathedral, Bowes Museum, Raby Castle, golf, fishing and horse-riding.

Consett

Town lying 12 miles south-west of Newcastle-upon-Tyne.

MRS LAWSON, BEE COTTAGE FARM, CASTLESIDE, CONSETT DH8 9HW (0207 508224). Working farm in lovely surroundings. Visitors welcome to participate in all farm activities. Ideal for Metro Centre, Durham Cathedral etc. Bed and Breakfast; Evening Meal available. ETB 2 Crowns Highly Commended. *[🐕]*

ESSEX

Colchester

Fascinating town which retains many traces of its rich history. First Roman capital of Britain. Lively shopping centre with medieval lanes and alleys, and bustling street market.

MRS C. A. SOMERVILLE, ROSEBANK, LOWER STREET, STRATFORD ST MARY, COLCHESTER CO7 6JS (0206 322259). Attractive 14th century part Manor House, with river frontage and fishing rights in peaceful Dedham Vale. Comfortable bedrooms have TV and tea/coffee facilities; two double rooms and two twin, some en suite including a family room. Terms from £15.50 for Bed and Breakfast.

Saffron Walden

Unspoilt town dominated by 193' spire of Essex's largest church. Timber-framed 15th and 16th century buildings with elaborate plasterwork.

MRS D. FORSTER, PARSONAGE FARM, ARKESDEN, SAFFRON WALDEN CB11 4HB (0799 550306). Lovely Victorian farmhouse on busy arable farm with some resident pets; lots of "walkies" on "set aside" and footpaths for pets. For owners, en-suite facilities available; coffee/tea making and TV in rooms. Tennis, swimming and relaxing in large garden. Bed and Breakfast from £16 per person. 2 Crowns. [🐕]

GLOUCESTERSHIRE

CHESTER HOUSE
—Hotel—

Bourton-on-the-Water

*A haven of genuine peace and comfort tucked away
in a backwater of this famous village.
We welcome dogs & well behaved owners.*

- 23 tastefully furnished rooms
- All with bathroom or shower room
- 4 poster beds
- Family rooms
- Ground floor rooms wheelchair friendly
- Information centre
- Enclosed parking
- Colour TV and radio
- Tea & Coffee facilities
- Fully licensed
- Central Heating

- The Old Well restaurant
- Creative, imaginative cooking
- Comprehensive wine list
- Separate Breakfast room with garden
- Friendly helpful staff
- Central base for touring the Cotswolds
- Quiet walled garden
- Dogs Free

Julian & Susan Davies
Welcome You to Chester House & The Cotswolds

Chester House Hotel, Victoria Street,
Bourton-on-the-Water, Gloucestershire, GL54 2BU
Telephone (0451) 820286. Fax (0451) 820471

RAC AA
★ ★

GLOUCESTERSHIRE *Cirencester, Painswick, Slimbridge, Stow-on-the-Wold, Stroud, Symonds Yat (East)*

Old Mill Farm, Poole Keynes, Cirencester

Four superior barn conversions situated on tranquil farm four miles from Cirencester. Extremely well equipped, full central heating, colour TV. Ample parking. Ideal for touring Cotswolds, Stratford-upon-Avon, Bath etc. Terms include heating, electricity, bed linen, use of laundry room. Children and pets welcome. Terms from £125 to £425. Details from **G.E. & C. Hazell, Ermin House Farm, Syde, Cheltenham GL53 9PN (0285 821255).**　　4 Keys Commended

---

HAMBUTTS MYND, EDGE ROAD, PAINSWICK GL6 6UP.
Tel: (0452) 812352

Bed and Breakfast. Old Cotswold house, superb views, very quiet. Close to village. Near M4 and M5. Many walks. Bell House and Garden, Westbury (as seen on Gardeners' World), Bath, Stratford-upon-Avon and many more places of interest within easy reach. Car parking. Central heating and open fire in winter months. One double room, one twin, one single, all with colour TV. Two bathrooms. From £18 to £35 per night. RAC Acclaimed.

"STILL MEADOWS" Moorend Lane, Slimbridge

De Luxe, well appointed bungalow set in quarter acre garden. Accommodation for four to nine people (ideal for two families holidaying together). Full central heating. Two bathrooms. Children and pets welcome. Ideal holiday centre, close to Cotswolds, Forest of Dean, Gloucester, Cheltenham, Bath etc. Brochure available from **MRS P. M. ABBOTT, LORD'S RAKE, MOOREND LANE, SLIMBRIDGE G12 7DG TEL: (0453 890322)**

Established 19 years　　　　　　　　　AA and RAC Listed

Large Country House with attractive garden, overlooking fields. Four minutes to town centre. One four poster bedroom, double, twin or family rooms; some en suite. Tea/coffee making facilities, colour TV in all rooms. TV lounge. Central heating. Children and pets welcome. Car park. Bed and Full English Breakfast from £15.00.

THE LIMES
Tewkesbury Road, Stow-on-the-Wold
GL54 1EN Tel: 0451 830034

DOWNFIELD HOTEL

134 CAINSCROSS RD, STROUD GL5 4HN
(0453-764496)

Bed and Breakfast, Evening Meal optional. Hot and cold all rooms, some with private baths. Central heating. TV lounge. Colour TV in most rooms, tea/coffee facilities all rooms. Some with telephones. Residents' bar. Ideal for touring Cotswolds and as stopover for travel to Devon/Cornwall. 5 miles from Junction 13, M5. Ample parking. Families and pets welcome. Personal supervision by proprietors. AA. RAC Acclaimed. Access and Visa accepted. ETB.

SYMONDS YAT ROCK MOTEL
Hillersland, Near Coleford GL16 7NY
Telephone: Dean (0594) 836191

Small family run Motel. All rooms en suite with colour TV and central heating. Licensed restaurant. Situated near Symonds Yat East and the Wye Valley in a beautiful area of the Royal Forest of Dean. Dogs welcome. Brochure on request. Tourist Board Listed.

POWELLS COTTAGE HOLIDAYS, 61 HIGH STREET, SAUNDERSFOOT, PEMBROKESHIRE, DYFED SA69 9EJ (0834 813232). Cottages along the coasts of Pembrokeshire, The Gower, and West of England. Also inland riverside and the countryside. Well equipped; some with swimming pool. Jacuzzi baths. Pets welcome.

Bourton-on-the-Water

Delightfully situated on the River Windrush, which is crossed by miniature stone bridges. Stow-on-the-Wold 4 miles.

CHESTER HOUSE HOTEL, VICTORIA STREET, BOURTON-ON-THE WATER GL54 2BU (0451 820286). Personally supervised by proprietor Mr Julian Davies. All rooms en-suite, all with central heating, colour TV, radio, phone, tea/coffee making facilities. Ideal for touring Cotswolds. *[£1.50 per night.]*

Cirencester

Country town on site of Roman Corinium. Situated 14 miles north-west of Swindon.

OLD MILL FARM, POOLE KEYNES, CIRENCESTER. Four superior barn conversions, extremely well equipped, full central heating, colour TV. Ideal for touring Cotswolds, Stratford, Bath. Children and pets welcome. 4 Keys Commended. Details from G. E. & C. HAZELL, ERMIN HOUSE FARM, SYDE, CHELTENHAM GL53 9PN (0285 821255).

Mitcheldean

Village 3 miles north of Cinderford. Noted for 14th/15th century church with 12th century font with the Twelve Apostles.

MRS M. FIELDER, ABENHALL HOUSE, ABENHALL ROAD, MITCHELDEAN GL17 0DT (0594 544201). Family-run period Guest House on edge of village in the Royal Forest of Dean. Bed and Breakfast from £13 daily. Parking. Washbasins and tea-making all bedrooms. Pets and children welcome. Ideal for walking, touring and birdwatching in the Severn and Wye Valleys. *[🐾]*

Painswick

Beautiful little Cotswold town with characteristic stone-built houses.

MISS E. COLLETT, HAMBUTTS MYND, EDGE ROAD, PAINSWICK GL6 6UP (0452 812352). Bed and Breakfast. Old Cotswold house, very quiet. Close to village. Central heating and open fire in winter months. One double room, one twin, one single, all with TV. From £18 to £35 per night. RAC Acclaimed. *[pw!]*

Slimbridge

Village near Severn Estuary with Wildfowl Trust nature reserve. M5 is close by. Gloucester 10 miles, Stroud 10, Wotton-under-Edge 9.

STILL MEADOWS, MOOREND LANE. De luxe, well-appointed bungalow sleeping from four to nine persons. Full central heating. Two bathrooms. Set in quarter acre garden. Children and pets welcome. Ideal holiday centre. Brochure from MRS P. M. ABBOTT, LORD'S RAKE, MOOREND LANE, SLIMBRIDGE GL2 7DG (0453 890322).

Stow-on-the-Wold

Charming Cotswold hill-top market town with several old inns and interesting buildings, including the Church (Perp.) in which hundreds of prisoners were confined after a Civil War battle in 1646. Birmingham 45 miles, Gloucester 26, Stratford-upon-Avon 21, Cheltenham 18, Evesham 16, Chipping Norton 9.

'THE LIMES', TEWKESBURY ROAD, STOW-ON-THE-WOLD GL54 1EN (0451 830034). Large country house. Attractive garden, overlooking fields. 4 minutes town centre. Television lounge. Central heating, Car park. Bed and Breakfast from £14.50. Children and pets welcome. AA, RAC. Twin, double or family, some en suite.

Stroud

Cotswold town on River Frome below picturesque Stroudwater Hills, formerly renowned for cloth-making. Bristol 32 miles, Bath 29, Chippenham 25, Cheltenham 14, Gloucester 9.

DOWNFIELD HOTEL, CAINSCROSS ROAD, STROUD GL5 4HN (0453 764496). Washbasins in all rooms, central heating. Residents' bar. Ideal for touring Cotswolds. Personal supervision, 5 miles M5. Ample parking. Children and pets welcome. Evening Meal optional. ETB 3 Crowns; AA; RAC Acclaimed. [🐾]

Symonds Yat (East)

Famous beauty spot in a richly wooded setting and lying on a loop of the River Wye. High above towers Yat Rock (473 feet) from which there are magnificent views. Accessible by road from the Gloucester side. Ross-on-Wye 10 miles, Monmouth 6.

MR L. E. CAPELL, SYMONDS YAT ROCK MOTEL, HILLERSLAND, NEAR COLEFORD GL16 7NY (0594 836191). Family-run Motel in Royal Forest of Dean near Wye Valley. All rooms en suite, colour TV, central heating. Licensed restaurant. Dogs welcome. Brochure on request. [🐾 pw!]

Uley

Village 2 miles east of Dursley. Convenient for M5, Bristol, Bath etc.

MRS C. C. COBHAM, 61A THE STREET, ULEY, DURSLEY GL11 5SL (0453 860313). Large bungalow in pleasant garden. Ample parking. Trays and washbasins in bedrooms. Guest bathroom. Within easy reach of Slimbridge Wildfowl Trust, Berkeley Castle and many places of interest. [🐾]

HAMPSHIRE

HAMPSHIRE *Ashurst*

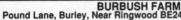

AA★★ RAC★★
ETB 👑👑👑👑
COMMENDED

Busketts Lawn Hotel New Forest

Woodlands, Nr Southampton, Hampshire SO4 2QL

Delightful family-run Country House Hotel in quiet forest surroundings. • Excellent food, service and comfort. All rooms en suite, colour TV, direct dial telephone, tea-making facilities, hairdryer, trouser press • Licensed; Dancing some weekends • 2 acre safe and sheltered garden, Putting, Croquet, Swimming pool heated in Season, Mini Football Pitch.

CHILDREN AND PETS MOST WELCOME • COLOUR BROCHURE ON REQUEST
Tel: 0703 292272/292077 Fax: 0703 292487

OPEN ALL YEAR   ESTABLISHED 1968

Ashurst

Three miles north-east of Lyndhurst.

WOODLANDS LODGE HOTEL, BARTLEY ROAD, WOODLANDS, NEW FOREST SO4 2GN (0703 292257). Luxury Hotel offering peace and tranquillity. 18 bedrooms, all en suite, with TV, hairdryer, telephone etc. Modestly priced dinner menu and wine list offering excellent value. ETB 4 Crowns Highly Commended.

Bramshaw

New Forest village surrounded by National Trust land. Golf course nearby. Southampton 10 miles, Lyndhurst 6.

BRAMBLE HILL HOTEL, BRAMSHAW, NEAR LYNDHURST SO43 7JG (0703 813165). Fully licensed country house hotel with adjacent livery stables. Unique seclusion amidst glorious surroundings. Unlimited riding and walking territory. Horses and dogs welcome. DIY livery. *[£4 per night.]*

Hayling Island

Family resort with sandy beaches. Ferry to Portsmouth and Southsea. Linked by bridge to Havant (5 miles).

HAYLING HOLIDAYS LTD, 44A EASTOKE AVENUE, HAYLING ISLAND PO11 9QP (0705 467271). Book with confidence. Holiday homes and caravans all close to sea. Superbly equipped and very clean. Personal service. Telephone now for free colour brochure. *[£10 per week.]*

Lyndhurst

Good base for exploring the fascinating New Forest as well as the Hampshire coast resorts. Facilities for golf and riding exist. Bournemouth 20 miles, Salisbury 19, Winchester 19, Ringwood 12, Lymington 9, Southampton 9.

EVERGREENS HOTEL, LYNDHURST SO43 7AR (0703 282175). Lovely country house Hotel in New Forest. Excellent food and service. We love children and pets. RAC** *[£2 per night.]*

New Forest

Area of heath and woodland of nearly 150 square miles, formerly Royal hunting grounds. Home of ponies which roam freely through unspoilt countryside.

WHITLEY RIDGE COUNTRY HOUSE HOTEL, BEAULIEU ROAD, BROCK-ENHURST SO42 7QL (0590 22354; Fax: 0590 22856). Georgian Hotel set in 5 acres of secluded grounds. Twelve bedrooms, all en-suite, cosy bar and splendid dining room. Superb cuisine, friendly and efficient service. Ideally located for the New Forest. *[🐾]*

BALMER LAWN HOTEL, LYNDHURST ROAD, BROCKENHURST SO42 7ZB (0590
23116; Fax: 0590 23864). Country House Hotel set in the heart of the New Forest.
Ideal for country walking. Indoor and outdoor leisure facilities. 58 Bedrooms, all en
suite. Excellent cuisine. AA***, RAC. [🐾]

Portsmouth

*Port and naval base with rich maritime heritage. Nelson's flagship HMS Victory lies in the harbour;
of interest too are HMS Warrior and the Mary Rose.*

MAYVILLE HOTEL, WAVERLEY ROAD, SOUTHSEA PO5 2PN (Portsmouth [0705]
732461). Dogs. Car park for 20 cars on premises. Good food. Families catered for.
Near beach. [🐾]

Ringwood

*Busy market town on the River Avon, and a centre for trout fishing, trekking and rambling. There
are some attractive old houses and inns, and a pretty Early English church. Bournemouth 13
miles, Lyndhurst 12.*

MR AND MRS D. C. HAYLES, BURBUSH FARM, POUND LANE, BURLEY, NEAR
RINGWOOD BE24 4EF (0425 403238). Character cottages delightfully situated in
the heart of the New Forest close to Burley village. Equipped to highest standard with
central heating. Each sleeps five. From £150 per week.

MS S. P. STREET AND MS M. D. JENKINS, SUNEST PARK, 126 RINGWOOD
ROAD, ST. IVES, RINGWOOD BH24 2NT (0425 473750). New Forest: Bungalow/
Chalets, fully equipped, sleep 2/8. Small park, fenced gardens. Pets welcome. Local
fishing, riding, walking, golf, sailing, coast 8 miles. [pw! £8.00 per week.]

Sway

Village in southern part of New Forest and within easy reach of sea. Lymington 4 miles SE.

THE NURSE'S COTTAGE, STATION ROAD, SWAY, LYMINGTON SO41 6BA
(Tel/Fax: 0590 683402). Obedient pets and owners welcome! This popular licensed
guest house, once home of the District Nurse, provides every possible comfort in a
cosy cottage environment. [🐾]

MRS THELMA ROWE, 9 CRUSE CLOSE, SWAY, HANTS SO41 6AY (0590
683092). Ground floor accommodation. Bedroom, private bathroom and sitting room.
Tea making facilities. TV. 3 minutes from open Forest. 4 miles from coast. Bed and
Breakfast from £13.50. [🐾]

Woodlands

Village on fringe of New Forest. Delightful scenery. Southampton 7 miles, Lyndhurst 4½.

BUSKETTS LAWN HOTEL, WOODLANDS, ASHURST, NEAR SOUTHAMPTON
SO4 2GL (0703 292272 or 292077; Fax: 0703 292487). Comfortable Country House
Hotel. Quiet surroundings, heated swimming pool, mini football/cricket pitch, putting
and croquet lawns. All rooms en suite. Open all year.

HEREFORDSHIRE

HEREFORDSHIRE   *Hereford, Ledbury, Leominster, Much Birch*

FELTON HOUSE
FELTON, NEAR HEREFORD HR1 3PH
Tel: (0432) 820366

Romantic, old, stone-built former rectory in 3 acres of beautiful grounds in a tiny hamlet in the heart of rural England. The house combines the very best of modern, centrally heated facilities with period furnishings including four-poster and half-tester beds, superb dining room, drawing room, library and garden room. All bedrooms have washbasins and tea/coffee making facilities. Wide choice of traditional English and vegetarian breakfasts. Local inns serve excellent evening meals. Just off the A417 between Ledbury and Leominster, 8 miles north of Hereford. Open January to November. Children and pets welcome. B&B from £14. ETB 2 Crowns Highly Commended.

NEW PRIORY HOTEL
STRETTON SUGWAS, HEREFORD Tel & Fax: 0432 760264

This friendly family-run Hotel is situated just a short distance from the Hereford city limits. Set in its own 3½ acres of beautiful Herefordshire with a large car park, lawned gardens and terraces. 10 Bedrooms all with private bath or shower except for single rooms which have an adjacent shower. All rooms have central heating, TV and tea making facilities. Write or telephone for terms.

FARMHOUSE   LEDBURY

Black and white 16th century Farmhouse on working farm close to Malvern Hills. Equidistant Hereford, Worcester, Gloucester and Ross-on-Wye. Three double bedrooms. Warm welcome assured, excellent home cooking. Tourist Board Listed.

SAE to Mrs Jane West, Church Farm, Coddington, Ledbury HR8 1JJ.
Tel: 0531 640271.

LEOMINSTER–Farm Cottage/Bungalows

17th century farm in peaceful location. Four cottages
(1 suitable for disabled) and bungalows. Storage heating in all.
Terms £72–£186 weekly. Children welcome.
One dog permitted. Lovely walks and carp fishing lake on farm.
Personal management.
Mrs P. W. Brooke, Nicholson Farm, Leominster HR6 0SL
Tel: 056-882-269

Poolspringe Farm Cottages
Much Birch, Near Hereford. Cottages sleep 2/7

Delightfully converted cottages and a bungalow on secluded 17th-century, 50-acre farm, amongst the orchards of South Hereford. Ideal for touring the Wye Valley, the Forest of Dean and mid-Wales. Visitors have the use of covered swimming pool, sauna and solarium; large garden, games and coarse fishing available. Fully equipped and furnished including colour TV; kitchens with fridges etc.; everything supplied for your holiday needs. Linen may be hired at extra charge. Children and pets welcome. Ample parking. Terms from £80 per week. Available all year. ETB and HETB registered.
David and Val Beaumont, Poolspringe Farm, Much Birch, Hereford HR2 8JJ Tel: 0981 540355

Readers are requested to mention this guidebook when seeking accommodation (and please enclose a stamped addressed envelope).

Country Guest House

Glewstone, Ross-on-Wye, Herefordshire HR9 6AZ

Tel: 0989 770456

Comfortable old farmhouse, 3 miles from Ross, set in an acre of garden and orchards, with views to the Black Mountains. Stone walls, exposed beams, and a massive open fireplace combine with well equipped bedrooms (some en suite), and freshly cooked meals for the perfect holiday atmosphere. Ideal base to explore the Forest of Dean and Wye Valley. B&B from £15.00.

THE ARCHES COUNTRY HOUSE HOTEL
Walford Road, Ross-on-Wye, Herefordshire HR9 5PT

Attractive Georgian-style building set in half acre of lawns, only ten minutes' walk from town centre. All rooms are furnished and decorated to a high standard and have views of the lawned garden, together with tea-making facilities and TV. Renowned for good food, a warm and friendly atmosphere with personal service. Pets made welcome. Ample parking.

Bed and Breakfast £15; en suite room £20; luxury ground floor en suite available. Generous weekly reductions.

AA Listed   RAC Acclaimed   Routiers Award   ETB ♕♕♕
For details please telephone or send SAE

JEAN & JAMES JONES (0989) 63348

BROOKFIELD HOUSE

AA & RAC
Listed

♕♕

Ledbury Road, Ross-on-Wye HR9 7AT

Geoffrey and Josephine Baker extend a warm welcome to guests and their pets at this early 18th century Listed house only five minutes' walk from the centre of lovely Ross-on-Wye. All the comfortable bedrooms have TV and tea-making facilities. Licensed. An ideal centre for golfers and walkers in an area famed for scenic beauty, with easy access to the Welsh Borders and the Cathedral towns of Gloucester, Hereford and Worcester.   **Tel: 0989 62188**

OAKLANDS, LLANGARRON, ROSS-ON-WYE HR9 6NZ
Tel: 0989 770277 Mrs Pauline Amos

4 country Cottages in idyllic surroundings. Fully equipped to a high standard: central heating, colour TV, microwaves: cots, highchairs. Modern kitchens and bathrooms. Parking. Sleep 2/7 people. Two of the cottages have large enclosed private lawns. The one in the picture has a view of five counties. Beautiful countryside. Terms from £95 weekly.

3 Keys Approved

FREE and REDUCED RATE Holiday Visits!
Don't miss our Readers' Offer Vouchers on pages 5 to 20.

Ye Hostelrie

GOODRICH, ROSS-ON-WYE, HEREFORDSHIRE HR9 6HX
TEL: 0600 890241

Enjoy seclusion, comfort, and good food at this fully centrally heated 17th Century Inn. Sited near to Goodrich Castle in a beautiful part of the Wye Valley, it affords easy access to the Forest of Dean, rural Herefordshire and Wales; although it is in a very quiet village it is only a mile from the A40. We have a reputation for quality food at a reasonable price. We offer salmon straight from the Wye, and use fresh vegetables (some from our own garden) whenever possible. We are proud of our list of fine wines.

Prices: Bed and Breakfast double or twin bedded room with
bathroom or shower room and lavatory en suite.
Single £30, Double £44 (two nights or more £40)
Dinner : TABLE D'HOTE £14 or A LA CARTE
(minimum charge £12)

Restaurant closed Monday and Tuesday, but substantial bar meals available every morning and evening.

Hereford

Well-known touring centre on River Wye with several interesting old buildings, including Cathedral (Norm. and Dec.). Good sport and entertainment facilities including steeple-chasing. Cheltenham 37 miles, Gloucester 28, Worcester 26, Ludlow 24, Malvern 21, Monmouth 18, Ross-on-Wye 15.

NEW PRIORY HOTEL, STRETTON SUGWAS, HEREFORD (Tel and Fax: 0432 760264). The New Priory Hotel is situated just a short distance from the Hereford city limits in 3½ acre grounds. 10 bedrooms all with private bath or shower except for single rooms which have an adjacent shower. 3 Crowns. *[★]*

MARJORIE AND BRIAN ROBY, FELTON HOUSE, FELTON, NEAR HEREFORD HR1 3PH (0432 820366). Period-furnished stone-built Rectory in charming rural area. Double, single, twin-bedded rooms. Bed and Breakfast from £14.00. Vegetarian choice. Good Inns nearby for evening meals. Ideal locality for touring. *[★]*

Huntington

Remote village on Welsh border. Views from Hergest Ridge. Kington 4 miles.

MRS C. D. WILLIAMS, RADNOR'S END, HUNTINGTON, KINGTON HR5 3NZ (Gladestry [054-422] 289). Detached cottage sleeping 5. Quiet, peaceful, four miles from Kington. Scenic walks over Hergest Ridge, Radnor Forest, Glascwm Hills. Golfing, trekking in area. Ideal birdwatching. *[★]*

Ledbury

Pleasant town ideally situated for Ledbury Park, Market Hall, Cotswolds and Wye Valley. Buildings of note include Almshouses, Black and White Houses and Church (Norman to Perp.). Good centre for bowls, fishing, riding and tennis. Monmouth 23 miles, Leominster 22, Gloucester 17, Tewkesbury 14, Malvern 8.

MRS JANE WEST, CHURCH FARM, CODDINGTON, LEDBURY HR8 1JJ (0531 640271). Black and white 16th-century Farmhouse close to the Malvern Hills – ideal for touring. Three double bedrooms. Excellent home cooking. Bed and Breakfast from £17. Open all year. SAE for details. [★]

Leominster

Old wool town among rivers, hop-yards and orchards. Many lovely timbered buildings. Five miles north-west is Croft Castle. Birmingham 45 miles, Gloucester 37, Hereford 13, Ludlow 11.

MRS P. W. BROOKE, NICHOLSON FARM, LEOMINSTER HR6 0SL (056 882 269). 17th century working farm in peaceful location. Cottage sleeps 2/3; bungalows sleep 2/6 (two suitable for wheelchairs). Children welcome. One dog permitted. Bed and Breakfast available in farmhouse. Fishing on farm. Lovely walks in beautiful Teme and Wye valleys.

Much Birch

Village six miles south of Hereford.

POOLSPRINGE FARM COTTAGES. 5 delightfully converted cottages and a bungalow on secluded farm. Ideal for touring. Use of swimming pool, sauna and solarium. Fully equipped incl. colour TV. Linen for hire on request. APPLY: DAVID AND VAL BEAUMONT, POOLSPRINGE FARM, MUCH BIRCH, HEREFORD HR2 8JJ (0981 540355). [£15 weekly.]

Pembridge

Tiny medieval village surrounded by orchards and meadows. Set on a hill above 16th cent. Market Hall; remains of motte-and-bailey castle adjoins churchyard.

NORTHWOOD COTTAGE. Three miles from Pembridge village in quiet country lane. Sleeps 4. Double and two singles in twin room. Dining area, lounge; shower, toilet. Electricity on 50p meter. Two Economy 7 heaters included in rent. Linen included. Open all year. MR AND MRS L. MORGAN, NORTHWOOD FARM, PEMBRIDGE, LEOMINSTER HR6 9HP (054-47 368).

Ross-on-Wye

An attractive town standing on a hill rising from the left bank on the Wye. Cardiff 47 miles, Gloucester 17.

THE ARCHES COUNTRY HOUSE HOTEL, WALFORD ROAD, ROSS-ON-WYE HR9 5PT (0989 63348). Georgian Country House. Comfortable rooms with all facilities; en-suite available. Centrally heated. Pets welcome. Bed and Breakfast or Half Board, weekly reductions available. AA, RAC, Les Routiers, Three Crowns.

GRAHAM WILLIAMS, THE SKAKES, GLEWSTONE, ROSS-ON-WYE HR9 6AZ (0989 770456). 18th century farmhouse, orchard and garden setting, with superb views. Stone walls, open fireplace, licensed barn restaurant; well-equipped rooms, central heating. Parking. Bed and Breakfast from £15.00. [★]

YE HOSTELRIE, GOODRICH, ROSS-ON-WYE HR9 6HX (0600 890241). Enjoy seclusion, comfort and good food at this fully centrally heated 17th Century Inn. We have a reputation for quality food at a reasonable price. [★]

BROOKFIELD HOUSE, LEDBURY ROAD, OVERROSS, ROSS-ON-WYE HR9 7AT (0989 62188). Guests and their pets are warmly welcomed by Geoffrey and Josephine Baker at Brookfield House. Licensed. All rooms TV and tea-making facility. ETB 2 Crowns, AA/RAC Listed. [★]

MRS PAULINE AMOS, OAKLANDS, LLANGARRON, ROSS-ON-WYE HR9 6NZ (0989 770277). Four cottages in countryside setting; all fully equipped, sleep up to seven. Modern bathrooms, kitchens with all facilities. Personally supervised. Lots to do in the area. Terms from £95 weekly. Details on request. 3 Keys Approved. *[One pet free; others £15 weekly.]*

LANGSTONE COURT FARM, LLANGARRON, ROSS-ON-WYE. Three self contained units sleeping 2/8. Near Forest of Dean and Black Mountains. Each has electric cooker, microwave, dishwasher etc. Up to 4 Keys Commended. Colour brochure contact: DORIS WILDING, LINDEN HOUSE, VOWCHURCH COMMON HR2 0RL (0981 550360 or 0989 770217). *[pw! £15 per week.]*

ISLES OF SCILLY

St Mary's

Largest of group of granite islands and islets off Cornish Coast. Terminus for air and sea services from mainland. Main income from flower-growing. Seabirds, dolphins and seals abound.

PAMELA MUMFORD, SALLAKEE FARM, ST MARY'S TR21 0NZ (0720 22391). Self catering cottage, sleeps 5. Open all year. Write or phone for details. *[🐕]*

ISLE OF WIGHT

ISLE OF WIGHT   *Chale, Colwell Bay*

ISLE OF WIGHT *Alum Bay, Cowes, Freshwater*

Holiday Apartments
In acres of National Trust land with breathtaking
views over the Needles. Immaculate 2 bedroom
luxury Flats—fully equipped for 4 including
colour television.

Open all year. Short breaks available
October–May (except Easter)
Dogs welcome by arrangement

Colour brochure: **Marion Smith, Headon Hall, Alum Bay, Isle of Wight
PO39 0JD
Tel: (0983) 752123**

SUNNYCOTT CARAVAN PARK
COWES • ISLE OF WIGHT

20 Deluxe and Luxury 4 and 6 berth Caravans on quiet country Park in rural surroundings close to Cowes. All Caravans are fully self-contained and are connected
to all main services. There is a Laundry Room on the Park and a Shop which can
cater for all your daily needs. We are open from March to January: why not come
for an extra holiday over the Christmas and New Year period? Bring your pets for a
holiday too! Phone: 0983 292859 for brochure. Member of B.H. & H.P.A. & S.T.B.

MOUNTFIELD HOLIDAY PARK
BHHPA STB
FRESHWATER, ISLE OF WIGHT
Telephone: Freshwater (0983) 752993
Set in four acres of beautiful countryside, 2/6 berth Bungalows, 2/6 berth Chalets,
2/6 berth Caravans all with own toilet, bath or shower, TV. Licensed bar and club
room with pool table. Good food. Table tennis room. Heated swimming pool. Play
area for children with swings, etc. SAE please.
Proprietors: **The Roberts Family, Mountfield Holiday Park,
Norton Green, Freshwater, Isle of Wight.**

FRESHWATER, ISLE OF WIGHT
Cottage and flat at the pleasant resort of Freshwater on Freshwater Bay. Each is
fully equipped for 5 people. Colour television. Large garden and swimming
pool. Pets welcome. SAE, please, for details, to: **Mr D. Venables, Afton Bank,
Manor Road, Freshwater PO40 9UB. Telephone: (0983) 754938**

* WHITECLIFF HOUSE *
Holiday Flats in quiet country setting, close to sea and downs.
Dogs welcome.
**Apply: Victoria Road, Freshwater Bay, Isle of Wight PO40 9PX
Tel: 0983 753731**

Country Garden Hotel

'A Peaceful Retreat'

Church Hill, Totland Bay
Isle of Wight PO39 0ET

RAC ★★★   Ashley Courtenay

Tucked away behind the gentle curve of Totland's golden sands and lovely walks, yet overlooking the sea, this really does offer the best of both worlds. Ashley Courtenay sums it up perfectly as "…A really superb hotel set in beautiful gardens", adding that here too "you will relish the superb cuisine" in one of the island's finest restaurants. All rooms have bath AND shower, TV, radio, fridge, phone, hairdryer and hospitality tray.

ANY DAY TO ANY DAY
B&B HALF BOARD
FULL BOARD
Doubles ★ Twins
★ Singles ★ Suites
SPECIAL SPRING AND
AUTUMN RATES

Tel: (0983) 754521
Fax: (0983) 754421

For brochure, tariff and sample menu.

4 CROWN	1 - 12	12
27.00		240.00
45.00		290.00

The Nodes Country Hotel

★ Glorious walks to safe beaches
★ Riding, fishing, sailing and golf nearby
★ Rooms with shower and toilet en suite
★ Table tennis, darts and badminton
★ Children at reduced rates
★ Country cooking
★ Colour television
★ Parking in grounds
★ Central heating
★ Courtyard bar

ISLE OF WIGHT   **AA, RAC APPROVED**

A lovely Country House in extensive grounds overlooking Tennyson Downs
Alum Bay Old Road, Totland Bay PO39 0HZ. Tel: 0983 752859

RAVENSCOURT
HOLIDAY BUNGALOWS

PETS ARE WELCOME
For self catering holidays for you and your pet on England's Sunshine Isle.

Ocean View Road, Ventnor, Isle of Wight PO38 1AA

These attractive bungalows are in the woodland grounds of Ravenscourt, a large old private house which adjoins the National Trust downland overlooking Ventnor. There are some superb panoramic views over the picturesque town and the sea from this small quiet site. Each bungalow will accommodate up to six people. From £70 per bungalow per week.

SAE or phone for brochure **Tel: 0983 852555**

Alum Bay

In extreme west of island, one mile from the Needles and lighthouse. Cliffs and multicoloured sands. Newport 13 miles, Yarmouth 5.

MARION SMITH, HEADON HALL, ALUM BAY PO39 0LD (0983 752123). Immaculate 2-bedroom luxury Flats, fully equipped for 4/6, including colour television. Breathtaking views. Dogs welcome by arrangement. [£10 per week.]

Chale

Pleasant village with sand and shingle beach. Several picturesque chines in the vicinity. Freshwater 11 miles, Newport 9, Ventnor 7.

JOHN AND JEAN BRADSHAW, THE CLARENDON HOTEL, CHALE PO38 2HA (Isle of Wight [0983] 730431). 17th Century Coaching Inn, overlooking magnificent West Wight coast. Television lounge. First-class restaurant. [pw! £3 per night, £15 per week.]

Colwell Bay

Small resort at western extremity of the island, excellent sands, cliff walks. Totland 2 miles, Yarmouth 2.

ONTARIO PRIVATE HOTEL, COLWELL COMMON ROAD, COLWELL BAY (0983 753237). Family-run Hotel. Home cooking. En-suite bedrooms, licensed bar, private parking. Only four minutes' walk to the beach. Two Crowns. [🐶]

Cowes

Yachting centre with yearly regatta since 1814. Home of Royal Yacht Squadron. Victorian and Edwardian shops line narrow streets behind wide esplanade. 4 miles Newport.

SUNNYCOTT CARAVAN PARK, COWES PO31 8NN (0983 292859). 20 Deluxe and Luxury 4 and 6 berth caravans on quiet country park in rural surroundings. Laundry room and shop on site. Open from March to January. [🐕]

Freshwater

Pleasant and quiet resort on Freshwater Bay near the start of the Tennyson Trail. Sandown 20 miles, Cowes 15, Newport 11, Yarmouth 4.

WHITECLIFF HOUSE, VICTORIA ROAD, FRESHWATER BAY PO40 9PX (0983 753731). Holiday Flats close to sea and downs. Dogs welcome. [🐕]

FARRINGFORD HOTEL, BEDBURY LANE, FRESHWATER BAY PO40 9PE (0983 752500 and 752700; Fax: 0983 756515). Hotel bedrooms with en suite bathrooms, ground floor cottage bedrooms. Also self catering cottages, bar, restaurant, snacks etc. Free 9-hole golf course, swimming pool, croquet and putting. Baby listening. ETB 4 Crowns Commended. /pw £1.50 per night./

THE ROBERTS FAMILY, MOUNTFIELD HOLIDAY PARK, NORTON GREEN, FRESHWATER (0983 752993). 2/6-berth Bungalows, Chalets and Caravans, all set in beautiful countryside. Licensed bar. Television. Good food. ETB 3 ticks. /£10 per week./

MR D. VENABLES, AFTON BANK, MANOR ROAD, FRESHWATER PO40 9UB (0983 754938). Freshwater Bay. Cottage and Flat. Each fully equipped for five people. Colour television. Large garden and swimming pool. Pets welcome. SAE for details. /pw!/

Niton

Delightful village near sea at the southernmost part of the island. Several secluded chines nearby, cliff walks. Ventnor 5 miles.

MR AND MRS D. A. HERON, WINDCLIFFE MANOR, SANDROCK ROAD, NITON UNDERCLIFF PO38 2NG (0983 730215). Bed, Breakfast and Evening Meal in a historic Manor House set in wooded gardens. Heated pool. Colour television. Games room. Children and dogs welcome. 3 Crowns. /pw!/

Ryde

Popular resort and yachting centre, fine sands, pier. Shanklin 9 miles, Newport 7, Sandown 6.

HILLGROVE PARK, ST HELENS, NEAR RYDE PO33 1UT (0983 872802). Select site 10 minutes sea, 3 minutes bus stop. Self-service shop, heated swimming pool. Pets welcome. SAE brochure.

Shanklin

Safe sandy beaches and traditional entertainments make this a family favourite. Cliff lift connects the beach to the cliff top.

MRS JANET POULTON, THE CRESCENT HOTEL, 21 HOPE ROAD, SHANKLIN PO37 6EA (0983 863140). Family Hotel, en-suite rooms with colour TV and tea-making. Beautiful coastline and country walks. Two minutes from beach. Parking. Short Breaks arranged. "Crescent Strollers" walkers' planning pack available. /pw! £1.50 nightly, £9 weekly./

SORABA PRIVATE HOTEL, 2 PADDOCK ROAD, SHANKLIN PO37 6NZ (0983 862367). Excellent home cooking in a small, friendly hotel in old village. En suite available. Open green spaces nearby. Car ferry reductions. RAC Acclaimed. AA Listed QQQ. 2 Crowns Commended. Bed and Breakfast from £14.50, BB & EM from £118 per week. *[pw! £1 per night, £5 per week.]*

Totland

Little resort with good sands, safe bathing and high cliffs. Newport 13 miles, Yarmouth 3, Freshwater 2.

COUNTRY GARDEN HOTEL, CHURCH HILL, TOTLAND BAY PO39 0ET (0983 754521; Fax: 0983 754421). Overlooking the sea, superb hotel; all rooms with bath and shower, TV, telephone, fridge, hairdryer etc. Telephone for brochure, tariff. Special spring and autumn rates.

SENTRY MEAD HOTEL, MADEIRA ROAD, TOTLAND BAY PO39 0BJ (0983 753212). Get away from it all at this friendly and comfortable haven, just two minutes from sandy beach. Bedrooms have en suite bath or shower, colour TV and radio. Delicious table d'hôte dinners; lunchtime bar menu.

THE NODES COUNTRY HOTEL, TOTLAND BAY PO39 0HZ (0983 752859). Lovely Country House in extensive grounds. Children at reduced rates. Country cooking. Riding, fishing, sailing and golf nearby. *[pw!]*

Ventnor

Well-known resort with good sands, downs, popular as a winter holiday resort. Nearby is St. Boniface Down, the highest point on the island. Ryde 13 miles, Newport 12, Sandown 7, Shanklin 4.

RAVENSCOURT HOLIDAY BUNGALOWS, OCEAN VIEW ROAD, VENTNOR PO38 1AA (0983 852555). For self catering holidays for you and your pet on England's Sunshine Isle. Attractive bungalows, each accommodates up to six. Adjoins National Trust downland overlooking Ventnor. SAE or phone for brochure.

A. EVANS, "THE WATERFALL", SHORE ROAD, BONCHURCH, VENTNOR PO38 1RN (0983 852246). Spacious, self-contained Flats. The beach, the sea and the downs nearby. *[🐶]*

Comfortable self-contained holiday apartments in picturesque seaside village from £70 per week. Pleasant seaside and country walks, gardens and private parking. Dogs welcome. Tourist Board Member. Please write or phone for brochure and tariff. WOODLYNCH HOLIDAY APARTMENTS, SHORE ROAD, BONCHURCH, VENTNOR PO38 1RF (0983 852513). *[🐶]*

KINGS BAY CHALETS. 4 self-contained chalets in cliff top position, fully equipped for 2–5 people, well maintained. ETB One Key Commended. Apply – MRS A. H. GILES, KINGS BAY HOUSE, KINGS BAY ROAD, VENTNOR, ISLE OF WIGHT PO38 1QR (0983 853718). *[🐶]*

Yarmouth

Coastal resort situated 9 miles west of Newport. Castle built by Henry VIII for coastal defence.

'TUCKAWAY' – Holiday Chalet in private, secluded position. Sleeps six. Swimming pool. Dogs welcome. Large grassed area. Tourist Board Approved. APPLY – MR R. STEDMAN, FURZEBREAK, CRANMORE AVENUE, YARMOUTH PO41 0XR (0983 760082).

KENT

HANSON HOTEL Licensed

Belvedere Road, Broadstairs. Tel: Thanet (0843) 868936

A small friendly Georgian hotel with relaxed atmosphere, centrally
situated for beach, shops and transport.
Renowned for excellent food, we offer a 5-course Evening Dinner with choice
of menu prepared by Chef/Proprietor.
* TV Lounge * Attractive Bar * Reading Room * Private Showers
**Babies, children and pets welcome. Children reduced rates—one child
per family free when sharing parents' room on weekly stays. High tea,
baby-sitting etc.**
OPEN ALL YEAR INCLUDING CHRISTMAS   SPRING AND WINTER BREAKS
S.A.E. or telephone for brochure to Trevor and Jean Webb

Broadstairs

Quiet resort, once a favourite of Charles Dickens. Good sands and promenades.

CASTLEMERE HOTEL, WESTERN ESPLANADE, BROADSTAIRS CT10 1TD (0843
861566; Fax: 0843 866379). 40 bedrooms, 31 with private bathrooms. Telephone
and colour television in bedrooms. Television lounge. Licensed. Selective menus.
Near beach, on seafront. Diets and children catered for. Dogs welcome. ETB 3
Crowns. *[£1.00 per night.]*

TREVOR AND JEAN WEBB, HANSON HOTEL, BELVEDERE ROAD, BROAD-
STAIRS (Thanet [0843] 868936). Small, friendly, licensed Georgian Hotel. Home
comforts; babies, children and pets welcome. Baby-sitting. SAE. *[pw! 50p per night.]*

Folkestone

*Important cross-Channel port with good sandy beach and narrow old streets winding down to the
harbour.*

THE HORSESHOE HOTEL, 29 WESTBOURNE GARDENS, FOLKESTONE CT20
2HY (0303 243433). Spacious Private Hotel close Promenade and town centre. All
rooms colour TV, washbasins, tea/coffee making facilities; some en suite. Parking.
Friendly hospitality and good home cooking. Mini Breaks. Details on request.

Herne Bay

*Homely family resort on North Kent coast. Shingle beach with sand at low tide. Maidstone 32
miles, Faversham 13, Canterbury 9, Whitstable 5.*

MR & MRS N. EVANS, 156 BELTINGE ROAD, HERNE BAY CT6 6JE (Herne Bay
[0227] 375750). Semi-detached House for 5 adults (East Cliff). Also Cottage and
Bungalow (Beltinge) sleeping 2 and 3 adults respectively. Pets welcome. *[🐕]*

Margate

*Most popular family resort with sands and harbour. Numerous attractions and entertainments.
Maidstone 44 miles, Dover 22, Canterbury 16, Herne Bay 13, Sandwich 9, Ramsgate 5.*

THE RAMBLERS, 19 ROYAL ESPLANADE, WESTBROOK, MARGATE CT9 5DX
(0843 227306). Family-run licensed guest house overlooking the sea. All rooms have
TV and tea making facilities. Open all year. Short breaks. Telephone for brochure.
[🐕]

LANCASHIRE

LANCASHIRE   *Ashton-under-Lyne, Blackpool*

AA
**

LANCASTER HOTEL
17 RICHMOND STREET, ASHTON-UNDER-LYNE
TEL: 061-330 1350

This small licensed hotel is situated on the borders of Cheshire, Yorkshire and Derbyshire. Double, single and family rooms, all with showers, colour TV etc.

Continental breakfast inclusive; English breakfast £6.50 extra.

Pets free of charge. Open all year.

SELECT HOLIDAY FLATLETS, ADJOINING QUEENS PROMENADE
COTSWOLD HOLIDAY FLAT/FLATLETS, 2A HADDON ROAD, NORBRECK, BLACKPOOL FY2 9AH Tel: (0253) 52227
• Fully equipped including colour television and fridge • Select area North Shore
• Cross road to beach and trams • Short breaks early season and illuminations
• Sleep up to seven. Rates from £53 per week. Details from Mrs C. Moore.
Open all year • S.A.E. for brochure stating dates plus number in party. Pets free

---

ASH-LEA GUEST HOUSE
76 LORD STREET, BLACKPOOL FY1 2DG TEL: 0253 28161

Good food and comfort assured. Tea making facilities in all rooms. Some rooms with TV; some rooms with toilet en suite. Large TV lounge. Free showers. Close to all amenities. B&B £10, BB&EM £13.50. Open all year. Special rates for Senior Citizens, children and weekly bookings.

---

9 Pleasant Street,   *IT'S SERVICE WITH A SMILE*   (OFF DICKSON ROAD)
North Shore,   *AT THE*   RESIDENTIAL LICENCE
Blackpool FY1 2 JA **New Osborne Private Hotel**   Tel: 0253 24578
★ Excellent central position only one minute walk to promenade.
★ Short walk along seafront to North Pier, town centre, railway and bus stations.
★ Close to local clubs with entertainment.
★ Open all year ★ Bar lounge (organ) ★ Television lounge (colour).
★ Families welcome. Children all ages ★All bedrooms have colour TV and tea/coffee
   making facilities ★ Central heating–free showers.
★ Bed and Breakfast from £10.50 per night. Evening Meal, Bed and Breakfast from £12.50.
★ **Home cooking our speciality. Special rates for children and Senior Citizens early season.**
* Bar lunches and packed lunches always available ★Pets are very welcome—but not allowed in public rooms.
WHY NOT JOIN US FOR CHRISTMAS?
Registered with ETB. Please write or telephone Resident Proprietress **Mrs B. READ**

SYMBOLS
🐕 Indicates no charge for pets.
£ Indicates a charge for pets: nightly or weekly.
pw! Indicates some special provision for pets: exercise, feeding etc.

164

ETB Registered

"NORMANDY"
278 Queens Promenade
Bispham, Blackpool FY2 9AX
Telephone: (0253) 52160

The NORMANDY is a family-run Hotel on the Queens Promenade with panoramic views of the Irish Sea, situated on the quiet side of town away from hustle and bustle.

All rooms are double or twin with tea/coffee making facilities, colour TV, full central heating and en suite. Cleanliness and high standards assured. Excellent home cooking, with choice of menu. Regretfully, no facilities for children.

PETS WELCOME—LOVELY GRASSY WALKS ALONG THE SEA FRONT.

* Guest Lounge   * Open all year   * Free Car Park

★ Christmas House Party & ★ New Year Special
Bed and Breakfast per day — from £19.00 per person
Bed, Breakfast & Evening Dinner — from £24.00 per person
FOR FURTHER INFORMATION PLEASE PHONE
(0253) 52160

Mrs E.R. Green, Tebnor, 59 St Andrews Road North, St Annes-on-Sea
Telephone: 0253 724024

A spacious self contained Flat sleeping 2-6 people, situated near shops, park and amenities. The rear of the house overlooks lovely Ashton gardens. The Flat has fitted carpets, shower, refrigerator, cooker, colour TV, cot and high chair, and bed linen is supplied at no extra cost. The Flat is thoroughly cleaned between tenancies by pet owning proprietor.

Own keys   SAE FOR LEAFLET   Parking opposite
            P E T S W E L C O M E

Ashton-under-Lyne

Town lying 6 miles east of Manchester.

LANCASTER HOTEL, 17 RICHMOND STREET, ASHTON-UNDER-LYNE (061-330 1350). Small licensed hotel on borders of Cheshire, Yorkshire and Derbyshire. Double, single and family rooms, all with showers, colour TV etc. Continental breakfast incl; English breakfast £6.50 extra. Pets free of charge. Open all year. AA 2 Stars. [🐕]

Blackpool

Famous resort with fine sands and many attractions and vast variety of entertainments. Blackpool Tower (500ft). Three piers. Manchester 47 miles, Lancaster 26, Preston 17, Fleetwood 9.

ASH-LEA GUEST HOUSE, 76 LORD STREET, BLACKPOOL FY1 2DG (0253 28161). Good food and comfort assured. Some rooms TV, some rooms toilet en suite. Free showers. Close to all amenities. B&B £10, BB&EM £13.50. [🐕]

MRS B. READ, NEW OSBORNE PRIVATE HOTEL, 9 PLEASANT STREET, NORTH SHORE, BLACKPOOL FY1 2JA (0253 24578). Residential licence. Home cooking. Colour television lounge. Central heating. Pets very welcome. [🐕]

MRS C. MOORE, COTSWOLD HOLIDAY FLAT/FLATLETS, 2A HADDON ROAD, NORBRECK, BLACKPOOL FY2 9AH (0253 52227). Holiday Flatlets fully equipped. Cross road to beach and trams. Select area. Open all year. Short Breaks early season and illuminations. SAE. [🐕]

NORMANDY HOTEL, 278 QUEENS PROMENADE, BISPHAM, BLACKPOOL FY2 9AX (0253 52160). Family-run Hotel on quiet side of town away from crowds. Panoramic sea views. Double/twin rooms with en-suite. Guest lounge. Own keys. Free parking. Choice of menu. Bed and Breakfast, Dinner optional. Open all year. [🐕]

Clitheroe

Pleasant market town, with ruined Norman keep standing on limestone cliff above grey roofs. Pendle Hill 4 miles to the east, from where there are spectacular views of the Forest of Bowland.

MRS FRANCES OLIVER, WYTHA FARM, RIMINGTON, CLITHEROE BB7 4EQ (Gisburn [0200] 445295). Farmhouse accommodation in heart of countryside. Panoramic views. Warm welcome. Double and family rooms. Ideal touring centre. Bed and Breakfast from £13.50. Evening Meal £7. ETB Listed. [pw! £1 per day.]

THE INN AT WHITEWELL, FOREST OF BOWLAND, NEAR CLITHEROE BB7 3AT (02008 222). Beautiful riverside setting. Log fires and antique furniture throughout. Six miles of salmon and trout fishing. Shooting by arrangement. [pw!]

Southport

Coastal resort 16 miles north of Liverpool. Long sandy beaches.

THE AMBASSADOR PRIVATE HOTEL, 13 BATH STREET, SOUTHPORT PR9 0DP (0704 543998 or 530459). Delightful small Hotel centrally situated between Promenade and Lord Street. Noted for warm welcome, good food and hospitality. Bedrooms en suite with colour TV and all facilities. Comfortable bar where lunchtime/late night snacks are available. Choice of menu; children's menu. Central heating. Car park. ETB 3 Crowns Commended, AA QQQQ.

St Annes-on-Sea

Popular family resort with good sands. Preston 15 miles, Blackpool 5.

MRS E. R. GREEN, TEBNOR, 59 ST. ANDREWS ROAD NORTH, ST. ANNE'S-ON-SEA FY8 2JF (0253 724024). Clean, comfortable Flat, personally supervised. Three rooms, sleep 6. Everything provided including linen. Near shops/park. 5 minutes sea. SAE for leaflet. Seasonal rates. [🐕]

LEICESTERSHIRE

LEICESTERSHIRE   *Melton Mowbray*

**SYSONBY KNOLL HOTEL
ASFORDBY ROAD
MELTON MOWBRAY
LEICESTERSHIRE LE13 0HP
TEL: 0664-63563**

Traditional family-run Hotel with 24 bedrooms, all en-suite. All have TV, tea/coffee facilities and telephone. Restaurant serving à la carte menu, also set meals. Bar snacks served until 9pm. Large enclosed car park. Lovely gardens; outdoor swimming pool.

4 Crowns Commended RAC/AA 2 stars Les Routiers

Melton Mowbray

Old market town, centre of hunting country. Noted for Stilton cheese and pork pies. Large cattle market. Church (E.E. and Perp.) and Anne of Cleve's House are of interest. Kettering 29 miles, Market Harborough 22, Nottingham 18, Grantham 16, Leicester 15.

MRS S. BOOTH, SYSONBY KNOLL HOTEL, ASFORDBY ROAD, MELTON MOWBRAY LE13 0HP (0664 63563). Set in two acres of grounds with outdoor swimming pool. Emphasis upon good food and the comfort of our guests. Central heating. TV and tea/coffee facilities in all our en-suite rooms. 2 lounges, cosy bar. [🛏]

LINCOLNSHIRE

LINCOLNSHIRE   *Rippingale, Skegness*

TWO COTTAGES IN BEAUTIFUL LINCOLNSHIRE COUNTRYSIDE
LARGE COTTAGE sleeps 8 in 4 bedrooms; sitting room, dining room, kitchen, toilet, bathroom. Comfortably furnished. 400-YEAR-OLD COTTAGE sleeps 4; open fires, dining room, sitting room, kitchen, bathroom. Both properties have fridge, colour TV, washing machine; linen supplied. £100 to £225 weekly. Apply: **Mrs V. Sanders, Barn Farm House, Station Street, Rippingale, Near Bourne, Lincs. PE10 0TD, or telephone (0778 440 666).**

SOUTH LODGE 147 Drummond Road, Skegness PE25 3BT
A warm welcome awaits you at South Lodge. All rooms have colour TV and teamaking facilities. All are en-suite. Golf course 600 yards. Miles of beach, a Dog's Paradise in fact. There is a walled-in garden where you can relax while your pet can play in safety. RAC Acclaimed. **Tel: 0754 765057**

Bucknall

Village 3 miles east of Bardney.

Lincolnshire, in the heart of the countryside: Self-catering cottages, fully equipped, bed linen provided. Children and pets welcome. ETB Registered. [🛏pw!] APPLY MRS R. ALLEN (0526 388328).

Rippingale

Interesting Lincolnshire village 5 miles north of Bourne; Bourne noted as home town of Saxon hero Hereward the Wake, whose manor house stood in park where earthworks of 11th century castle remain.

Two delightful holiday cottages in rural situation. 400-year-old Cottage sleeps 4, larger Cottage sleeps 8. Both comfortably furnished, colour TV, fridge, washer, linen. From £100 to £225 weekly. Apply: MRS V. SANDERS, BARN FARM HOUSE, STATION STREET, RIPPINGALE, NEAR BOURNE PE10 0TD (0778 440 666).

Skegness

Bright family resort with fine sands. Lincoln 42 miles, Grimsby 40, Boston 23, Mablethorpe 18.

MR AND MRS R. HOWKINS, SOUTH LODGE, 147 DRUMMOND ROAD, SKEGNESS PE25 3BT (0754 765057). Comfortable Guest House near beach and golf course. All rooms have colour TV, tea making facilities, all en suite. Relax in walled garden for pets' safety. RAC Acclaimed. *[🐾]*

Woodhall Spa

Spa town 6 miles south-west of Horncastle.

KIRKSTEAD MILL OLD COTTAGE, WOODHALL SPA. Sleeps 7–10 plus baby. Non-smokers only. Very well equipped - colour TV, washing machine, fridge/freezer, microwave etc. 4 Keys Highly Commended. £99–£350 per week. Membership of local leisure club. Beside river; rowing boat provided. Apply: MRS HODGKINSON, 'BAILE GATE HOUSE', 52 KELSO CLOSE, WORTH, CRAWLEY, WEST SUSSEX RH10 7XH (0293 882008; Fax: 0293 883352). *[£10 per week.]*

LONDON

LONDON   *Kingston-upon-Thames, London*

Kingston-upon-Thames

Market town, Royal borough, and administrative centre of Surrey. Kingston is ideally placed for London and environs.

CHASE LODGE GUEST HOUSE, 10 PARK ROAD, HAMPTON WICK, KINGSTON-UPON-THAMES KT1 4AS (081-943 1862). Charming Guest House, recently refurbished, situated in a quiet area close to Hampton Court and Bushy Park. All rooms have telephone, TV, fridge, teamaking. Some four-poster rooms. Bed & Breakfast, Evening Meals, Supper Trays. 4 Crowns.

London

Legislative Capital of UK and major port. Theatres, shops, museums, places of historic interest. Airports at Heathrow and Gatwick.

ST ATHAN'S HOTEL, 20 TAVISTOCK PLACE, RUSSELL SQUARE, LONDON WC1H 9RE (071-837 9140). Family Bed and Breakfast near British Museum, shops, parks and theatres. Russell Square two blocks away; Euston and King's Cross stations ten minutes. LTB Listed. [🐕]

NORFOLK

NORFOLK   *Bacton-on-Sea, Brooke*

Bacton-on-Sea

Village on coast, 5 miles from North Walsham.

CASTAWAYS HOLIDAY PARK, PASTON ROAD, BACTON-ON-SEA, NORFOLK NR12 0JB (0692 650436). In peaceful village with direct access to sandy beach. Modern caravans with all amenities. Licensed club, entertainment, children's play area. Ideal for touring. *[£12 per week.]*

RED HOUSE CHALET AND CARAVAN PARK, PASTON ROAD, BACTON-ON-SEA NR12 0JB (0692 650815). Small family-run site, ideal for touring Broads. Chalets, caravans and flats, all with showers, fridges and colour TV. Some with sea views. Licensed. SAE for details, please. Open March–January. *[£10 weekly.]*

Brooke

Small, pretty village seven miles N.E. of Norwich.

WELBECK HOUSE, BROOKE, NEAR NORWICH NR15 1AT (0508 550292). 300-year-old Farmhouse; double, twin and single bedrooms, all with CH, tea/coffee making etc. Within easy reach of many places of interest, nature reserves etc. B&B from £16–£20. *[£1 per night.]*

Burnham Market

Village five miles west of Wells-next-the-Sea.

THE HOSTE ARMS, THE GREEN, BURNHAM MARKET PE31 8HD (0328 738257). 17th century Hotel overlooking village green. 12 bedrooms, elegantly furnished, all en suite with colour TV and telephone. Bar and restaurant menus. B&B £32 pp per night. Special 2-day breaks. *[🐕]*

California

Small coastal resort five miles from Great Yarmouth. Close to Caister Castle.

SOMBRERO HOLIDAY CHALETS, AT SANDS ESTATE, CALIFORNIA, NEAR GREAT YARMOUTH. Only 500 yards from beach. We welcome well-behaved pets and children in our self catering Chalet/Bungalows. All amenities on site including licensed club, swimming pools etc. Details from MR & MRS D. GUNN, 43 MERLIN MEWS, SPROWSTON, NORWICH NR7 8BZ (0603 412896).

Cromer

Attractive resort built round old fishing village. Norwich 21 miles.

ROSEACRE COUNTRY HOUSE, WEST RUNTON, CROMER. Apartments and one chalet sleeping 2-8. Colour TV. Large grounds and car park. Sea, shops, golf and riding facilities nearby. Beautiful woodland walks. *[£5 weekly.]*. Joan and Rodney Sanders (0263 837221).

All-electric Holiday Cottages accommodating 4 to 7 persons in beautiful surroundings. Sandy beaches, sports facilities, Cinema and Pier (live shows). Parking. Children and pets welcome. *[pw! £12 weekly.]* Brochure: NORTHREPPS HOLIDAY PROPERTIES, CROMER, NORFOLK NR27 0JW (0263 512236).

Diss

Twisting streets with Tudor, Georgian and Victorian architecture. 12th century St. Mary's Church and 6 acre mere, haven for wildfowl.

MRS BRENDA WEBB, "THE STRENNETH", THE OLD FARMHOUSE, OLD AIRFIELD ROAD, FERSFIELD, NEAR DISS IP22 2BP (Tel 037988 8182). 17th century former farmhouse, recently renovated. Most rooms en-suite. Separate lounge for non-smokers. Bed and Breakfast, optional three-course Evening Meal. Special diets catered for. 3 Crowns Commended. *[🐕]*

Foxley

Village 6 miles east of East Dereham.

Self Catering Chalets (2/3 bedrooms) on working farm. All fully equipped, with central heating. 20 miles from coast, 15 from Broads. Mature woodland nearby – ideal for walking. MOOR FARM HOLIDAYS, FOXLEY NR20 4QN (036-288 523). *[🐕]*

Great Yarmouth

Traditional lively seaside resort with a wide range of amusements, including the Marina Centre and Sealife Centre. Once one of Britain's wealthiest medieval towns, its buildings and walls retain many traces of the past.

BLUE RIBAND HOLIDAYS, HEMSBY, GREAT YARMOUTH NR29 4HA (0493 730445). Brick-built Bungalows with colour television. Modern holiday Chalets. All mains Caravans with showers and hot water. Dogs welcome. Free colour brochure on request. *[pw! £6 per week.]*

MRS PAULINE SMITH, "ANCHOR", 21 NORTH DENES ROAD, GREAT YARMOUTH NR30 4LW (0493 844339). Completely self-contained Flats with own shower and toilet. Fully equipped at no extra cost. Reduced terms early and late season. Close by public amenities. Children and pets welcome. *[pw!]*

MRS J. S. COOPER, SILVERLEA, MILE ROAD, CARLETON RODE, NORWICH NR16 1NE (0953 789 407). Modern holiday chalets at Winterton-on-Sea. Sleep six. Grassed site close to beach with heated indoor pool, snack bar, shop, club bar. Ideal for pets. *[pw! £5 per week.]*

SOMBRERO HOLIDAY CHALETS AT SUNDOWNER HOLIDAY PARK, NEWPORT, NEAR HEMSBY (0603 412896). We welcome well-behaved pets & children in our self catering Holiday Chalet/Bungalows. All amenities. For free brochure: MR & MRS D. GUNN, 43 MERLIN MEWS, SPROWSTON, NORWICH NR7 8BZ (0603 412896). *[£10 per week.]*

CAREFREE HOLIDAYS, SOLITAIRE, PARKLAND ESTATE, NORTH ROAD, HEMSBY, GREAT YARMOUTH NR29 4HE (0493 732176). A wide selection of superior chalets for live-as-you-please holidays near Great Yarmouth and Norfolk Broads. All amenities on site. Sports facilities, parking. Children and pets welcome. *[pw! £10 weekly.]*

Horning

Lovely riverside village ideally placed for exploring the Broads. In the vicinity are the remains of St. Benet's Abbey. Cromer 19 miles, Great Yarmouth 17, Norwich 10, Wroxham 3.

RIVERSIDE COTTAGE – "a very special place". Utterly delightful; near village centre but secluded. Lawn to river's edge; fishing. Sleeps 5/6. APPLY – Mr & Mrs P. H. H. Rhodes, Rope's Hill Cottage, Horning NR12 8LD (0692 630402). *[£12 per week.]*

SILVER BIRCHES HOLIDAYS, GREBE ISLAND, LOWER STREET, HORNING, NORFOLK NR12 8PF (Horning [0692] 630858). Five well-equipped houseboats and six all-weather motor day launches. All the comforts of a caravan afloat! Surrounded by lawns, adjacent parking. Ideal for families, fishermen and their pets. *[pw! £15 per week.]*

Hunstanton

Neat little resort which faces west across The Wash. Good sands, cliffs, play-green overlooking the sea. Norwich 47 miles, Cromer 38, Wells-next-the-Sea 17, King's Lynn 16.

MR AND MRS BROWN, MARINE HOTEL, HUNSTANTON PE36 5EH (0485 533310). Overlooking sea and green. Pets welcome, free of charge. Colour television lounge. Open all year except Christmas period. SAE for terms and brochure. *[ᛉ]*

King's Lynn

Ancient market town and port on the Wash with many beautiful medieval and Georgian buildings.

MRS JOAN BASTONE, MARANATHA GUEST HOUSE, 115 GAYWOOD ROAD, KING'S LYNN PE30 2PU (0553 774596). Large house 10 minutes' walk from town centre. Direct road to Sandringham and the coast. Animal lovers and their pets welcomed. B&B from £12 per person. 1 Crown, AA, RAC. [🐕pw!]

Mundesley-on-Sea

Small resort of character backed by low cliffs. Good sands and bathing. Norwich 20 miles, Cromer 7, North Walsham 5.

"WHINCLIFF", CROMER ROAD, MUNDESLEY NR11 8DU (0263 720961). Clifftop house, sea views and sandy beaches. Rooms with colour TV and tea-making. En suite family/twin room. Evening Meal optional. An abundance of coastal and woodland walks; many places of interest and local crafts. Well-behaved dogs welcome. [🐕]

Neatishead

Ideal for touring East Anglia. Close to Norwich. Lovely area. Aylsham 14 miles. Norwich 10, Wroxham 3.

ALAN AND SUE WRIGLEY, REGENCY GUEST HOUSE, THE STREET, NEATIS-HEAD, NORFOLK BROADS NR12 8AD (0692 630233). 17th century 5 bedroom Guest House. Established name for very generous English breakfasts. Many good eating places nearby. Ideal East Anglia touring base. Holder of Broadlands 'Good Care' award – high quality service. Tourist Board 2 Crowns. [£1 per night.]

Norwich

County town and Cathedral city with a daily open air market, medieval streets, a Norman castle and good shopping and leisure facilities.

ALBION ROSE PROPERTIES, 94 SOUTHWOLD ROAD, WRENTHAM, SUFFOLK NR34 7JF (0502 75757; Fax: 0502 75462). A range of self catering holiday houses, cottages and flats at affordable prices in Norwich, Norfolk and Suffolk. Many properties welcome pets. Cleanliness, good service and a friendly welcome. [🐕]

THE GEORGIAN HOUSE HOTEL, 32/34 UNTHANK ROAD, NORWICH NR2 2RB (Norwich [0603] 615655 – 4 lines: Fax: 0603 765689). Ideal for sightseeing in Norwich or touring East Anglia. 27 bedrooms, all en-suite, with colour TV, radio, tea/coffee making facilities. Licensed. ETB 3 Crowns Commended. [🐕]

North Walsham

Market town 14 miles north of Norwich, traditional centre of the Norfolk reed thatching industry.

TOLL BARN, OFF NORWICH ROAD (B1150), ONE MILE SOUTH OF NORTH WALSHAM (0692 403063). Charming converted 18th-century barn. All rooms en-suite, tea/coffee, colour TV, fridge, hairdryer. Choice of Continental breakfast in your room or traditional English breakfast in the dining-room. Norwich 12 miles, coast 6 miles, the Broads 5 miles. [pw! £1 per night.]

Sheringham

Small, traditional resort which has grown around a flint-built fishing village. Sandy beaches and amusements.

ACHIMOTA, 31 NORTH STREET, SHERINGHAM NR26 8LW (0263 822379). Small friendly guest house in peaceful surroundings yet within short stroll of town centre and beach. Superb cliff and woodland walks encourage you to do justice to our Evening Meals. NO SMOKING. Brochure on request. ETB Two Crowns Commended. *[🅣]*

Swaffham

Old market town. 15th century church with angel carved roof. Palladian market cross. Norwich 28 miles, King's Lynn 15.

MRS GREEN, PAGET, LYNN ROAD, NARBOROUGH, KING'S LYNN PE32 1TE (0760 337734). Private house offering B&B. Lounge available, log fire. Ample parking. Pleasant local river, lakes and rural walks. Situated between the old market town of Swaffham and King's Lynn. SAE please. *[🅣]*

Nar Valley Holiday Cottages, Norfolk. Choice of two charming cottages in the unspoilt Nar Valley. Winter weekends or Summer holidays. Telephone for brochure. NAR VALLEY HOLIDAYS, ESTATE OFFICE, WESTACRE, KING'S LYNN PE32 1UB (0760 755254; Fax: 0760 755444). *[🅣]*

Trimingham

Norfolk coastal village situated 4 miles south of Cromer.

TRIMINGHAM HOUSE CARAVAN PARK, TRIMINGHAM NR11 8DX (0263 720421). Luxury holiday homes with all amenities on cliff-top site. Heated swimming pool, club, entertainment, etc. *[pw! £15 per week.]*

Wells-next-the-Sea

Lovely little resort with interesting harbour, famous for its cockles, whelks and shrimps. A winding creek leads to a beach of fine sands with dunes. Salt marshes: bird-watchers' paradise. Norwich 31 miles, King's Lynn 27, Cromer 19, Fakenham 10.

MRS J. M. COURT, EASTDENE, NORTHFIELD LANE, WELLS-NEXT-THE-SEA NR23 1LH (0328 710381). Homely Guest House offers warm welcome. Bed and Breakfast, Evening Meal optional. One double, two twin rooms, one single, all en-suite; colour television lounge. Private parking. Les Routiers recommended. Tourist Board 2 Crowns. *[£1 per night.]*

Winterton-on-Sea

Good sands and bathing. Great Yarmouth 8 miles.

Self-contained ground floor of cottage in quiet seaside village. Broad sandy beach and pleasant walks. Close to Norfolk Broads. Secluded garden. Double, twin and single bedroom, sleeps 5 plus cot. Bed linen provided. Fully equipped for self-catering family holiday. £140-£300 per week. Full details from Mr M. J. ISHERWOOD, 79 OAKLEIGH AVENUE, LONDON N20 9JG (081-445 2192). *[£5 per week.]*

Wroxham

Noted yachting centre on the River Bure. 7 miles north-east of Norwich.

THE BROADS HOTEL, STATION ROAD, WROXHAM, NORWICH NR12 8UR (0603 782869; Fax: 0603 784066). Comfortable hotel renowned for its high standard cuisine. Owned and run by dog loving family. Ideally situated for boating, fishing and exploring the beautiful Norfolk countryside and coastline. All rooms fully en suite with tea/coffee making, colour TV, etc. For brochure please telephone. ***[pw! £1 per night.]***

NORTHUMBERLAND

NORTHUMBERLAND *Corbridge, Cornhill-on-Tweed, Kirkwhelpington, Wooler*

LOVELY NORTHUMBERLAND – CORBRIDGE

MATTHEWS, HAYES HOUSE, NEWCASTLE ROAD, CORBRIDGE NE45 5LP (0434 632010)

B&B Self Catering. Spacious, attractive, stone-built Guest House set in seven acres of grounds. Single, Double, Twin, Family bedrooms. Lounge, dining rooms. Open 12 months of the year. B&B £16, children's reductions. Stairlift for disabled. **Self catering**–3 Cottages, Flat, Caravan. Awarded three Farm Holiday Guide Diplomas. Car parking. Brochure/booking send SAE. ETB Registered.

AA *** RAC — Tillmouth Park Hotel — Highly Commended

Cornhill-on-Tweed, Northumberland TD12 4UU

Traditional Country House Hotel. Ideally situated for exploring the Borders. Pets welcome with no charge. Plenty of room to exercise. Ring for brochure

Single £58 Double £86

TEL: 0890 882255

NORTHUMBRIA HOLIDAY COTTAGES

Approx. 200 properties set in beautiful countryside near beaches. Including cosy cottages, farmhouses and luxurious castles.

FREE ILLUSTRATED BROCHURE Telephone: 0668 82040

The Mill Yard, Wooler, Northumberland NE7 6NP

All the advertisers in PETS WELCOME! have an entry in the appropriate classified section and each classified entry may carry one or more of the following symbols:

- 🐕 This symbol indicates that pets are welcome free of charge.
- £ The £ indicates that a charge is made for pets. We quote the amount where possible, either per night or per week.
- pw! This symbol shows that the establishment has some special provision for pets; perhaps an exercise facility or some special feeding or accommodation arrangements.

PLEASE NOTE that all the advertisers in PETS WELCOME! extend a welcome to pets and their owners but they may attach conditions. The interests of other guests have to be considered and it is usually assumed that pets will be well trained, obedient and under the control of their owner.

Alnmouth

Quiet little resort with wide sands. Alnwick with its impressive Norman Castle is 5 miles N.W.

SHEILA AND GORDON INKSTER, MARINE HOUSE PRIVATE HOTEL, 1 MARINE ROAD, ALNMOUTH NE66 2RW (0665 830349). Charming hotel in fine seafront location. Home cooking, cocktail bar, games room. Sea views. Children and pets very welcome. ETB 3 Crowns Commended. AA Listed. RAC Highly Acclaimed. Runners up – Best Family Holiday 1984. Selected Guesthouses 1988. Northumberland TB Holiday Host award. *[🐦]*

MRS CAROL SWEET, THE HOPE & ANCHOR, 44 NORTHUMBERLAND STREET, ALNMOUTH, ALNWICK NE66 2RA (0665 830363). You won't be barking up the wrong tree, when you holiday with Sam the cheeky chihuahua and me; you'll enjoy your stay, that I'll say. *[£2 per night.]*

Belsay

Village five miles north-west of Ponteland. Belsay Hall is a Neo-Classical building resembling a Greek temple, has extensive gardens. 14th century castle.

MRS KATH FEARNS, BOUNDER HOUSE, BELSAY, NEWCASTLE-UPON-TYNE NE20 0JR (0661 881267). Stone farmhouse situated in beautiful Northumbrian countryside off A696 Newcastle/Edinburgh road. Three miles north of Belsay. Two double (en suite), one family and one twin room.

Berwick-upon-Tweed

Historic border town on River Tweed encompassed by massive 13th century walls. Three great bridges span the river on which sailing, canoeing, water ski-ing and fishing are popular pastimes. Castle ruins may be seen adjacent to the railway station. Good resort facilities, fine sandy beaches. North Berwick 42 miles, Alnwick 29, Kelso 23, Wooler 17, Coldstream 14.

MRS H. WIGHT, GAINSLAW HILL FARM, BERWICK-ON-TWEED TD15 1SZ (0289 386210). Well-equipped cottage with own garden 3 miles from Berwick-on-Tweed. Ideal for touring, golf, riding, fishing. Sleeps 6, cot available. Linen provided. Microwave, washing machine etc. Terms from £160. *[🐦]*

JULIE HOLDEN, BEACHCOMBER HOUSE, GOSWICK, BERWICK-UPON-TWEED TD15 2RW (0289 81217). Two fishermen's cottages, each sleeping 6. Also small quiet campsite for tents and tourers. On sand dunes directly overlooking miles of empty beach. Ideal for dogs. Cottages 4 Keys Commended. Campsite 3 Ticks. *[🐦pw!]*

MRS M. MARTIN, FELKINGTON FARM, BERWICK-UPON-TWEED TD15 2NR (0289 87220). Comfortable farm holiday cottages close to coast and countryside. Sleep 6. Colour TV. Electric heaters and log fires, wood provided. Washing machine, playground, games room. Woodland walk. Children and pets welcome. ETB 3 Keys Approved. *[🐦]*

Corbridge

Small town on north bank of River Tyne, 3 miles east of Hexham. Nearby are remains of Roman military town of Corstopitum.

THE HAYES, NEWCASTLE ROAD, CORBRIDGE NE45 5LP (0434 632010). Superior flat for 4/5 and 3 ground floor cottages for 2/5 persons, available all year. Colour TV. Also luxury 6-berth caravan. Children and pets welcome. All properties, except flat, suitable for disabled. For details send SAE (ref FHG). *[🐦]*

Cornhill-on-Tweed

Village situated opposite Coldstream across the river, 12 miles south-west of Berwick-upon-Tweed.

TILLMOUTH PARK HOTEL, CORNHILL-ON-TWEED TD12 4UU (0890 882255). Traditional Country House Hotel. Ideally situated for exploring the Borders. Pets welcome with no charge. Plenty of room to exercise. Single £58, double £86. Ring for brochure. AA/RAC 3 Stars. *[⚑]*

Hexham

Market town on bank of River Tyne, with medieval priory church. Racecourse 2 miles. Newcastle upon Tyne 20 miles.

RYE HILL FARM, SLALEY, NEAR HEXHAM NE47 0AH (0434 673259). Pleasant family atmosphere in cosy farmhouse. Bed and Breakfast and optional Evening Meal. Bedrooms with TV and tea/coffee facilities. Some en-suite. Laundry facilities. Table licence. 3 Crowns Commended. *[pw! £1 per night.]*

Rothbury

Market town on steep bank of River Coquet, 11 miles south-west of Alnwick.

TERRY AND JANET CLUBLEY, WHITTON FARMHOUSE HOTEL, ROTHBURY, MORPETH NE65 7RL (Tel/Fax: 0669 20811). Charming country hotel in open country with en suite rooms (TV and hospitality tray), licensed lounge. Country house style dinners served each evening in attractive dining room. Riding from hotel's stables. Fishing and golf nearby. 14 miles from spectacular beaches.

Wooler

Small town on Harthope Burn, 15 miles north-west of Alnwick, near the north-eastern slopes of the Cheviot Hills.

NORTHUMBRIA HOLIDAY COTTAGES. Approx 200 properties set in beautiful countryside, including farmhouses, cosy cottages and luxurious castles. For illustrated brochure telephone 0668 82040 or write THE MILL YARD, WOOLER, NORTHUMBERLAND NE7 6NP.

NOTE

All the information in this book is given in good faith in the belief that it is correct. However, the publishers cannot guarantee the facts given in these pages, neither are they responsible for changes in policy, ownership or terms that may take place after the date of going to press. Readers should always satisfy themselves that the facilities they require are available and that the terms, if quoted, still apply.

OXFORDSHIRE

EASINGTON HOUSE HOTEL & RESTAURANT

50 Oxford Road
Banbury, Oxon OX16 9AN
Tel (0295) 270181
Fax: (0295) 269527

Beautifully situated in award-winning gardens just 5 minutes' walk from Banbury's famous Cross, Easington Hotel offers modern comfort in a house of exceptional charm and friendliness. There are 12 bedrooms and a beautifully appointed cottage, all decorated and equipped to the very highest standards, and a superb restaurant which is popular with visitors and locals alike. Traditional English breakfasts, including local sausages. Just one mile from the M40, 18 from Stratford, 20 from Oxford – ideal for touring the Cotswolds etc.

RAC Highly Acclaimed, Johansens, Logis of Great Britain

Crown and Cushion Hotel and Leisure Centre   ☻☻☻☻
High Street, Chipping Norton, Near Oxford OX7 5AD   Commended
500-year-old Coaching Inn, tastefully modernised to provide 40 excellent en suite bedrooms; some four-poster suites. "Old World" bar, log fires, real ale, good food, Egon Ronay Recommended. Indoor pool, multi-gym, solarium etc. Modern conference centre. Located in picturesque Cotswolds town midway between Oxford and Stratford-upon-Avon. Convenient London, Heathrow, M40. Blenheim Palace, Bourton-on-the-Water, Stow-on-the-Wold, Shakespeare Country all nearby. Pets welcome.
Price busters start at £19.50; DB&B at just £34.50.
Tel: 0608 642533 Fax: 0608 642926 Colour brochure Free phone 0800 585251

Ascott-under-Wychwood

Village four miles west of Charlbury.

COTSWOLDS. Detached cottage, sleeps 2/4. Central heating, tennis court, garage. Lovely country views. Ideal for Cotswolds, Oxford, Stratford-upon-Avon. ETB recommended. £150–£195 incl. weekly. MRS P. GOODFORD, THE OLD VICARAGE, ASCOTT-UNDER-WYCHWOOD OX7 6AN (0993 830385).

Banbury

Large market town and touring centre in the Oxfordshire Cotswolds. Most famous for its cakes and celebrated cross. Oxford 23 miles, Warwick 20.

EASINGTON HOUSE HOTEL, 50 OXFORD ROAD, BANBURY OX16 9AN (0295 270181/259395). Just 5 minutes from the famous Banbury Cross, Easington House offers modern comfort with exceptional charm and friendliness. One mile from M40, ideal for touring Oxford, Stratford and the Cotswolds. Superb restaurant. ETB 4 Crowns, RAC Highly Acclaimed etc. *[🐕]*

Oxford

Ancient university city on the Thames, here known as the Isis. Apart from the colleges there is a plethora of time-hallowed buildings, particularly churches and inns. Eights Week is a well-known river spectacle held at the end of May. Numerous entertainment and sporting facilities. LONDON 56 miles, Stratford-upon-Avon 39, Windsor 39, Henley-on-Thames 24, Banbury 23, Chipping Norton 20, Burford 19, Wallingford 12.

CROWN & CUSHION HOTEL AND LEISURE CENTRE, HIGH STREET, CHIPPING NORTON, NEAR OXFORD OX7 5AD (0608 642533; Fax: 0608 642926; Colour Brochure Free Phone 0800 585251). 500-year-old coaching inn, tastefully modernised. En suite bedrooms; some four-posters. Old World bar; indoor pool, solarium etc. Convenient Stratford, Oxford, London, Shakespeare Country. Price Busters from £19.50. *[🐕]*

MRS B. A. DOWNES, BRAVALLA GUEST HOUSE, 242 IFFLEY ROAD, OXFORD OX4 1SE (0865 241326 or 250511). Homely Guest House one mile south-east of centre. Majority of rooms en-suite with TV and beverage facilities. Parking. From £16 per person. 2 Crowns, AA/RAC Listed. *[£1 per night.]*

Stanton Harcourt

Delightful village with thatched cottages spread out along winding country road. Parts of ruined manor date back to 12th century.

S. S. CLIFTON, STADDLE STONES, LINCH HILL, STANTON HARCOURT OX8 1BB (0865 882256). A welcome for dogs at the Chalet Bungalow, with four acres of grounds adjoining bridle paths. Bedrooms with en suite or private bathrooms. Disabled persons and children welcome. Bed and Breakfast from £16.

SHROPSHIRE

SHROPSHIRE   *Church Stretton*

The Travellers Rest Inn, Upper Affcot (A49), Church Stretton SY6 6RL
Telephone: (0694) 781275

The Travellers Rest Inn is situated on the main A49 between Church Stretton and Craven Arms. You are assured of a good welcome, good food and good accommodation, and good old fashioned service, plus a smile, at no extra charge. The accommodation is fully centrally heated with four en-suite rooms on the ground floor and six bedrooms on the first floor, all with washbasins and shaver points. Colour TVs in all rooms, together with tea/coffee making facilities. Children and pets welcome. Bed and Breakfast from £20 to £25; Evening Meal from £5.

Bishop's Castle

Small town in hills on Welsh border, eight miles north-west of Craven Arms. Scanty remains of 12th century castle.

MRS P. ALLBUARY, THE GREEN FARM, WENTNOR, BISHOPS CASTLE SY9 5EF (058 861 394). En suite annexe sleeps two–four. B&B from £13. Two inns within 400 yards. Ideal walking country; riding available (extra). [🐾]

Church Stretton

Delightful little town and inland resort in lee of Shropshire Hills. Walking, riding country. Facilities for tennis, bowls, gliding and golf. Knighton 22 miles, Bridgnorth 19, Ludlow 15, Shrewsbury 12.

F. AND M. ALLISON, THE TRAVELLERS REST INN, UPPER AFFCOT, NEAR CHURCH STRETTON SY6 6RL (0694 781275). RAC Inn. Fully licensed Inn on main A49. Good base for touring. Ample parking space. Children and dogs welcome. 2 Crowns Approved. SAE or phone for further details. [pw!]

LONGMYND HOTEL, CHURCH STRETTON, SHROPSHIRE SY6 6AG (0694 722244; Fax: 0694 722718). 3-Star hotel with panoramic views, satellite TV, swimming pool, sauna, solarium. From £36 per person per day for Dinner, Bed and Breakfast. Special Doggy Breaks.

BELVEDERE GUEST HOUSE, BURWAY ROAD, CHURCH STRETTON SY6 6DP (0694 722232). On slopes of Long Mynd, 200 yards from Church Stretton and 6000 acres of National Trust hill country. Central heating. Teasmaids. Two guest lounges. ETB 3 Crowns Commended. Routiers, AA QQQ, RAC Acclaimed. Bed and Breakfast £21. Evening Meal £9.00. Reductions children, party, weekly. [🐕]

Cleobury Mortimer

Charming little town of timbered and Georgian houses, with very little building since the mid-nineteenth century, except Gilbert Scott's restoration of the church. There is fishing on the River Rea, and walking in the Wyre Forest or on Clee Hill, which rises to over 1,600 ft (500m). Mawley Hall, a Georgian house, stands on a hill in a well timbered park, with notable Roman Catholic chapel. Ludlow 10 miles.

THE REDFERN HOTEL, CLEOBURY MORTIMER DY14 8AA (0299 270395). Eleven well-equipped bedrooms, all with private facilities and some on the ground floor. Award-winning restaurant noted for fine food. ETB 4 Crowns. No charge for pets to *PETS WELCOME!* readers. [🐕]

MRS M. B. DAVIES, THE SHOTE FARM, HOPTON WAFERS, CLEOBURY MORTIMER DY14 0ND (0584 890358). Beautiful 17th century farmhouse offers splendid accommodation in single, double and family rooms, some en suite. Ideal for walking and riding, Welsh Borders etc. B&B from £10, Evening Meal available.

Craven Arms

Attractive little town with some interesting old half-timbered houses. Weekly cattle and sheep sales. Nearby is imposing Stokesay Castle (13 cent.) open regularly. Newtown 27 miles, Welshpool 24, Bridgnorth 21, Shrewsbury 20, Ludlow 8.

SUE TRUEMAN'S "B&B AT THE BELL", LEAMOOR COMMON, CRAVEN ARMS SY7 8DN (0694 781231; Fax: 0694 781461). Guests say "home from home". Quality accommodation in 12½ acres of natural beauty. Kids, pets, horses welcome. Exquisite countryside, historic towns. ETB Listed. From £14.50. [🐕]

MRS J. WILLIAMS, HURST MILL FARM, CLUNTON, CRAVEN ARMS SY7 0JA (0588 640224). Comfortable riverside farmhouse. Woodlands, riding ponies. Convenient for Offa's Dyke, Stiperstones. Bed and Breakfast from £14, Dinner, Bed and Breakfast from £22. 2 Crowns. AA Listed, Winner "Shropshire Breakfast Challenge".

Dorrington

Village 6 miles south of Shrewsbury.

RYTON FARM HOLIDAY COTTAGES, RYTON, DORRINGTON, SHREWSBURY SY5 7LY (0743 718449). Traditional country cottage sleeping 6 or converted barn for 2 or 4 persons. Well equipped kitchens, colour TV, fitted carpets, towels and linen. Pets especially welcome. 3 Keys Commended. [£12 per week.]

Ironbridge

Situated on side of River Severn gorge and named after bridge spanning it, which was cast in 1778 and still used by pedestrians.

VIRGINIA AND ROBERT EVANS, CHURCH FARM, ROWTON, WELLINGTON, TELFORD TF6 6QY (0952 770381). Experience a true country holiday on our working farm in scenic Shropshire. En-suite rooms, tea/coffee making, four-poster bed. Also 2 self-catering cottages and 2 caravans for hire. Ideal touring area. 2 Crowns. [🐕]

Ludlow

Lovely and historic town on Rivers Teme and Corve with numerous old half-timbered houses and inns, particularly the 'Feathers', 'Angel' and 'Bull'. Impressive Norman Castle. River and woodland walks. Golf, tennis, bowls, steeplechase course. Worcester 29 miles, Shrewsbury 27, Hereford 24, Bridgnorth 19, Church Stretton 16.

MAURICE & GILLIAN PHILLIPS, THE CECIL GUEST HOUSE, SHEET ROAD, LUDLOW SY8 1LR (0584 872442). Comfortable Guest House offers a relaxing atmosphere, freshly cooked food and spotlessly clean surroundings. Some en suite. All rooms have colour TV and tea makers. Licensed. Parking. ETB Two Crowns Commended, AA QQQ, RAC Acclaimed. *[🐕]*

Oswestry

Borderland Market town. Many old castles and fortifications including 13th century Chirk Castle, Whittington Castle, Oswestry's huge Iron Age hill fort, Offa's Dyke. Wales' highest waterfall close by. Llangollen 10 miles, Shrewsbury 16, Vyrnwy 18, Bala Lake 25.

PEN-Y-DYFFRYN HALL COUNTRY HOUSE HOTEL, NEAR RHYDYCROESAU, OSWESTRY SY10 7DT (0691 653700). Georgian Rectory set in Shropshire/Welsh Hills. Seven en-suite bedrooms, colour TV. Licensed Restaurant. Fishing. Very quiet and relaxed. Dinner, Bed and Breakfast from £39.00 per person. Pets free. 3 Crowns Highly Commended. *[🐕 pw!]*

Shrewsbury

Fine Tudor Town with many beautiful black and white timber buildings, Abbey and Castle. Riverside walks, Quarry Park and Dingle flower garden. 39 miles north-west of Birmingham.

BRENDA AND DAVID COLLINGWOOD, TALBOT HOUSE HOTEL, CROSS HILL, SHREWSBURY SY1 1JH (0743 368889). ETB 3 Crowns Highly Commended. 17th century Grade II Listed. Highly recommended best Town Centre Hotel, but quiet area. See display advert. Everything you could wish for; comfort, relaxation, freedom, extra facilities, with friendly, helpful hosts. *[🐕]*

Stiperstones

Situated beneath Stiperstones Ridge (1700 feet), and near to scenic Shropshire hills and a nature reserve.

ROY AND SYLVIA ANDERSON, TANKERVILLE LODGE, STIPERSTONES, MINSTERLEY, SHREWSBURY SY5 0NB (0743 791401). Country Guest House next to a nature reserve in the dramatic Shropshire hills. Cats and small/medium dogs accepted and may share owners' rooms. Pleasant walks. 1 Crown Commended. AA Listed QQ. *[£1 per night.]*

Telford

New town (1963). Ten miles east of Shrewsbury. Includes the south bank of the River Severn above and below Ironbridge, site of the world's first iron bridge (1777).

BOURTON MANOR, BOURTON, MUCH WENLOCK TF13 6QE (074-636 531). Set in small hamlet nestling close to Wenlock Edge. Single, twin and double luxury bedrooms, each with radio, colour TV etc. Ideal for walking and riding; Telford, Shrewsbury nearby. Dogs welcome.

SOMERSET

SOMERSET   *Brean, Burnham-on-Sea, Crewkerne*

classic cottages

Choose your cottage from 300 of the finest coastal
and country cottages throughout the West Country

Classic Cottages (25) Helston Cornwall TR13 8NA
24 hour dial a brochure 0326 565555

Goose Barn
Watchet Somerset

WESTWARD RISE HOLIDAY PARK
South Road, Brean, Nr Burnham-on-Sea, Somerset TA8 2RD
Tel: 0278 751310
ALL ELECTRIC CHALET BUNGALOWS on small family-owned site adjoining 5 miles of sandy beach.
2 double bedrooms, own shower, toilet. Colour TV, duvets, fridge and cooker. Highly recommended. Shops,
restaurants, clubs and amusements nearby. Dogs welcome. SAE for brochure. Caravan sales available.
Member of the British Holiday and Home Parks Association

Edna & Joe welcome you to
RESTAWAY CARAVAN PARK
SOUTH ROAD, BREAN, BURNHAM-ON-SEA,
SOMERSET TA8 2RD
Tel: 027-875 1283

Pets Welcome FREE on approval

Low-cost caravan holidays at a price to suit your pocket
Open March 1st
Bar – Banks' Beer
50 metres from beach
Caravan and chalet hire
Fully serviced
PLEASE SEND OR PHONE FOR BROCHURE

Embelle Holiday Park   ✓✓✓✓
Coast Road, Brean, Near Burnham-on-Sea TA8 2QZ
Tel: 0278 751346 Fax: 0278 751683
Chalets and caravans on quiet park. Direct access to beach. * Full facilities * Colour television
* Near entertainments * Club and restaurant * Pets welcome
FREE BROCHURE

♚♚♚ De Luxe

Dorset Border. ETB & AA TOP QUALITY AWARDS
Unusual Colonial Bungalow Residence Circa 1926 set in over
an acre of secluded "National Garden Scheme" feature
gardens, many unusual plants. As you enter through the sun
porch, which then opens onto the Dining Hall, you can sense
the Colonial atmosphere, being enhanced by our collection of
furnishings, porcelain & rugs. The guest sitting room is
extremely comfortable & relaxing. 3 carefully furnished en-suite
bedrooms with r.c. col. TV, easy chairs, hair dryer, C/H, tea/coffee. Bed & full English breakfast
£20.00. Quality traditional home cooked dinner £10.00. List provided of 50 varied places to
visit. 1/2 hour Dorset coast. Open all year.
Mrs G. Swann, Broadview, East Street,
Crewkerne (Dorset Border) Somerset TA18 7AG Tel: (0460) 73424

SOMERSET *Dulverton, Exford, Exmoor*

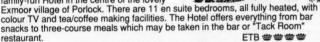

CLASSIC COTTAGES (25), HELSTON, CORNWALL (24 HOUR DIAL-A-BROCHURE 0326 565555). Choose your cottage from 300 of the finest coastal and country cottages throughout the West Country. *[£8 weekly.]*

POWELLS COTTAGE HOLIDAYS, 61 HIGH STREET, SAUNDERSFOOT, PEMBROKESHIRE, DYFED SA69 9EJ (0834 813232). Cottages along the coasts of Pembrokeshire, The Gower, and West of England. Also inland riverside and the countryside. Well equipped; some with swimming pool. Jacuzzi baths. Pets welcome.

Brean

Coastal village with extensive sands. To the north is the promontory of Brean Down. Weston-super-Mare 9 miles, Burnham-on-Sea 5.

WESTWARD RISE HOLIDAY PARK, SOUTH ROAD, BREAN, NEAR BURNHAM-ON-SEA TA8 2RD (0278 751310). All-electric chalet bungalows on small site adjoining beach. 2 double bedrooms, shower, toilet. Colour TV, fridge, cooker. Shops, restaurants, clubs nearby. SAE for brochure. *[£10 per week.]*

Burnham-on-Sea

Resort with sandy beaches and dunes. Bristol 27 miles, Taunton 20, Wells 18, Weston-super-Mare 11, Bridgwater 9.

JAGOVANS HOLIDAYS, RESTAWAY CARAVAN PARK, SOUTH ROAD, BREAN, BURNHAM-ON-SEA TA8 2RD (0278 751283 or 0860 428519). Accommodation designed for family holiday. Electricity, fridges, colour TVs, heaters, hot water, flush toilets and bathroom or shower in all units. Launderette. Supermarket. Pets welcome.

EMBELLE HOLIDAY PARK, COAST ROAD, BREAN, BURNHAM-ON-SEA TA8 2QZ (0278 751346). Chalets and Caravans on quiet park. Direct access to beach. Full facilities. Colour television. Pets welcome. Near entertainments. Club and restaurant. Free brochure. *[£15.00 per week.]*

Crewkerne

Market town on a sheltered slope of the Blackdown Hills.

MRS G. SWANN, BROADVIEW, 43 EAST STREET, CREWKERNE TA18 7AG (0460 73424). Traditionally furnished bungalow in over an acre of gardens. Three en-suite bedrooms with colour TV, central heating etc. Bed and full English Breakfast £20. *[🛏pw!]*

Dulverton

Attractively set between Exmoor and Brendon Hills. Good fishing. In vicinity, prehistoric Tarr Steps (A.M. and N.T.). Exeter 27 miles, Taunton 26, Lynton 23, Minehead 19, Tiverton 13.

MR AND MRS F. A. HEYWOOD, SOUTH GREENSLADE FARMHOUSE, BROMPTON REGIS, DULVERTON TA22 9NU (039 87 207). Two clean and comfortable holiday houses each taking six adults plus one/two children. Reduced terms for fewer occupants. Fully equipped. On eastern side of Exmoor National Park, adjacent to Wimbleball lake. Terms from £185-£270.

MRS STRONG, LOWER CHILCOTT FARM, DULVERTON TA22 9QQ (0398 23439). Excellent base for Exmoor holiday. 25 acres of woods and fields. Children, pets and horses welcome. B&B from £15. DB&B from £23. Self catering cottage (sleeps 6/9) also available. *[🛏]*

Exford

Fine touring centre for Exmoor and North Devon, on River Exe. Dulverton 10 miles.

BEV AND GEOFF DOLMAN, EXMOOR HOUSE HOTEL, CHAPEL STREET, EXFORD TA24 7PY (064-383 304). Situated in picturesque village (middle of Exmoor). Comfortable accommodation, colour TV, private bathroom, beverage facilities available. B&B from £18.00.

MRS P. EDWARDS, WESTERMILL FARM, EXFORD, SOMERSET TA24 7NJ (064383 238; Fax: 064383 660). Delightful Scandinavian pine log Cottages and a Cottage attached to farmhouse. Information centre and small shop. One/Two Keys Commended. *[pw! £6 weekly S/C.]*

THE EXMOOR WHITE HORSE INN, EXFORD TA24 7PY (064 383229). Family run 17th century inn situated in charming Exmoor village. 19 bedrooms all en-suite, with colour TV and tea making. Fully licensed. Restaurant with varied menu.

Exmoor

One of the country's smaller National Parks, with many beautiful sights and places of interest. Much of the moor remains untouched by modern life.

SPRINGFIELD COTTAGE, EXMOOR. Unsurpassed views of open countryside. Sleeps 6, comfortable and well equipped. 3 bedrooms, central heating, colour TV, payphone, log fire, large enclosed garden. Well-behaved dogs welcome. From £180 per week. Write or phone Mrs Eeley, 26 St Margaret's Road, Oxford OX2 6RX (0865 54977). *[£7 weekly.]*

MRS M. R. G. SCOTT, RUGGS FARM, BROMPTON REGIS, DULVERTON (039-87 236). Comfortably furnished Farm Bungalow, sleeps 5 plus cot. Colour TV, washing machine, microwave. Linen inclusive. Large fenced garden, patio. Adjacent Wimbleball Lake. ETB 3 Keys. *[First pet free, others £7 weekly.]*

JANE & BARRY STYLES, WINTERSHEAD FARM, SIMONSBATH, EXMOOR TA24 7LF (064-383 222). Three tastefully furnished and well-equipped cottages plus small flat situated in the midst of beautiful Exmoor. Pets welcome, stables and grazing available. Colour brochure on request.

THE SHIP INN, HIGH STREET, PORLOCK TA24 8QT (0643 862507). Comfortable accommodation in famous old inn. Excellent English cooking, bar serving real ale and snacks. Car parking. *[🐕]*

CUTTHORNE FARM, LUCKWELL BRIDGE, WHEDDON CROSS TA24 7EW (064-383 255). Enjoy a touch of sheer luxury at our 14th century farmhouse in glorious Exmoor. En-suite facilities, log fires, candlelit dinners. Children's high teas. Stabling. 2 Crowns. *[🐕]*

Hillfarrance

4 miles west of Taunton with its 12th century castle. Situated in valley of Taunton Deane, famed for its apples and cider.

ANCHOR COTTAGES, THE ANCHOR INN, HILLFARRANCE, TAUNTON TA4 1AW (0823 461334). Three self-catering cottages, each sleeps up to 4. Full central heating, colour TV; tastefully furnished to high standard. Private gardens and ample parking. Anchor Inn renowned for good food. *[🐕]*

Huntworth

At base of Quantock Hills. Ideal for rambling. Bridgwater 3 miles.

Country Cottage at foot of Quantocks. Easy access M5 and sea. Sleeps 6. Children and pets welcome. SAE please. APPLY – MRS E. P. HART, HUNTWORTH HOUSE, BRIDGWATER, SOMERSET TA7 0AH (0278 662209). *[🐾 pw!]*

Ilminster

Market town founded in Saxon times, with charming Georgian houses and a 15th century Minster.

MRS GRACE BOND, GRADEN, PEASMARSH, NEAR DONYATT, ILMINSTER TA19 0SG (0460 52371). Friendly country house; log fire, central heating. Wash-basins and tea/coffee making in bedrooms. 12 miles Junction 25 M5. Two family rooms, double and twin. Bed and full English Breakfast from £12.

Minehead

Neat and stylish resort on Bristol Channel under the shelter of wooded North Hill. Small harbour, sandy bathing beach. Attractive gardens, golf course and good facilities for tennis, bowls and horse riding. Within easy reach of the beauties of Exmoor.

MERTON HOTEL, WESTERN LANE, THE PARKS, MINEHEAD TA24 8BZ (0643 702375). Pets and their families most welcome at this small, family hotel. 12 en suite rooms. Car park. Home cooking. *[🐾]*

HINDON FARM, NEAR MINEHEAD TA24 8SH (0643 705244). Lovely 18th century farmhouse on 500-acre working farm. B&B or Self Catering. Own horses and dogs welcome – kennel runs, stabling, grazing; qualified instruction available. SAE or phone for brochure. *[pw! £3 per night.]*

THE LANGBURY, BLUE ANCHOR BAY, MINEHEAD TA24 6LB (0643 821375). Small, family-owned Hotel known for high standards of comfort, service and cuisine. All rooms with TV and tea/coffee facilities; most en suite. Pets welcome by arrangement.

TRANMERE HOUSE, 24 TREGONWELL ROAD, MINEHEAD TA24 5DU (0643 702647). Friendly guest house situated only a few minutes from shops and sea. H&C, razor points, colour TV and tea making facilities in all rooms. Licensed. Excellent menus.

MERLIN HOUSE HOLIDAY APARTMENTS, BLUE ANCHOR BAY. Luxuriously appointed; central heating, hot water, bed linen, electricity all included. A relaxing base to explore Exmoor. Ample parking and pleasant gardens. APPLY: SHEILA AND ALAN COLE, APPLEDORE, HUNTSCOTT, MINEHEAD TA24 8RR (0643 841457). *[£1 per night.]*

16th Century Cottage for two and Cottage with inglenook and beamed ceilings for 7/9. Fully furnished. Pets welcome. APPLY – MR T. STONE, TROYTES FARM-STEAD, TIVINGTON, SOMERSET (0643 704531). *[🐾]*

Porlock

Most attractive village beneath the tree-clad slopes of Exmoor. Picturesque cottages, old Ship Inn and interesting Church (Perp.). Good bathing from pebble beach at delightful Porlock Weir (2 miles). Several picture-book villages nearby. Lynton 11 miles, Minehead 6.

MRS CHRISTINE FITZGERALD, 'SEAPOINT', UPWAY, PORLOCK TA24 8QE (0643 862289). Spacious Edwardian house overlooking Porlock Bay. Open log fires. Coastal/moorland walks. Excellent traditional or vegetarian food. All bedrooms en-suite with tea/coffee facilities. *[🐾]*

CASTLE HOTEL, PORLOCK TA24 8PY (0643 862504). Fully licensed, family-run hotel in centre of lovely Exmoor village. 11 en suite bedrooms, all with colour TV. Bar snacks and meals. Well-behaved children and pets welcome. 4 Crowns. *[↑]*

MR AND MRS A. D. HARDICK, PORLOCK CARAVAN PARK, HIGHBANKS, PORLOCK, NEAR MINEHEAD TA24 8NS (0643 862269). Well equipped Caravans for hire, with main drains and water, electric light, TV, launderette. Dogs welcome. Touring Caravans, Dormobiles and tents welcome. Write or phone for brochure. *[↑pw!]*

Shipham

Pleasant village on edge of Mendip Hills, Cheddar 3½ miles, Axbridge 3.

PENSCOT FARMHOUSE HOTEL, SHIPHAM, WINSCOMBE BS25 1PW (Winscombe [093 484] 2659). Take a break in Somerset with your Pet! Cosy, quiet Hotel near Cheddar. Good farmhouse food. Gardens and lovely walks.

Taunton

County town, rich in historical associations. Good touring centre. Many sporting attractions. Notable links with the past include the Castle part of which is believed to be 12th century. Bristol 43 miles, Exeter 32, Weston-super-Mare 29, Yeovil 26, Chard 16, Bridgwater 11.

THE BLORENGE GUEST HOUSE, 57 STAPLEGROVE ROAD, TAUNTON TA1 1DG (0823 283005). Large Victorian house, 4 original four-poster beds. Licensed bar, swimming pool. 5 minutes' walk to town centre and railway station. Warm and friendly atmosphere. ETB Registered. [pw!]

Watchet

Small port and resort with rocks and sands. Good centre for Exmoor and the Quantocks. Bathing, boating, fishing, rambling. Tiverton 24 miles, Bridgwater 19, Taunton 17, Minehead 9, Dunster 6.

WEST SOMERSET HOTEL, SWAIN STREET, WATCHET TA23 0AB (0984 34434). Small family-run former coaching inn. All bedrooms with colour TV, tea/coffee facilities; many en suite. Golf, fishing, pleasure cruises locally. Bed and Breakfast or Dinner, Bed and Breakfast.

SUNNY BANK HOLIDAY CARAVANS, DONIFORD, WATCHET TA23 0UD (0984 632237). Small picturesque family park on coast. All caravans with mains services. Colour TV. Showers. Heated swimming pool. Shop. Launderette. BHHPA 5 ticks. Also caravans for sale. Brochure. *[£12 per week.]*

LORNA DOONE CARAVAN PARK, WATCHET, SOMERSET TA23 0BJ (0984 631206). Small quiet park with beautiful views of the harbour and Quantock Hills. Fully equipped luxury caravans. Rose Award Park. *[£10 weekly.]*

Waterrow

Picturesque village on the Devon/Somerset border. Wiveliscombe 3 miles.

RICHARD & PAM GROOME, TONE VALLEY PINE LODGES, WATERROW, NEAR WIVELISCOMBE TA4 2AU (0984 623322). Six pine lodges in secluded woodland setting. Sleep up to 6. Colour TV, fitted kitchens and bathrooms. Laundry, fitness suite etc. Bed, Breakfast & Evening Meal also available. *[£15 weekly.]*

SYMBOLS

↑   Indicates no charge for pets.

£   Indicates a charge for pets: nightly or weekly.

pw! Indicates some special provision for pets: exercise, feeding etc.

Wheddon Cross

Beautifully situated between Brendon Hills and Dunkery Beacon. An ideal centre for exploring Exmoor. The seaside is within easy reach. Dulverton 10 miles, Minehead 9.

TRISCOMBE FARM, WHEDDON CROSS, MINEHEAD TA24 7HA (Winsford [064 385] 227). Modern self-catering Homes set in 50 acres of Exmoor National Park. An all-weather tennis court and games room available. Pets are welcome if kept under control *[£8.00 per week.]*

Withypool

Delightful Exmoor village on River Barle. Dulverton 8 miles.

WESTERCLOSE COUNTRY HOUSE HOTEL AND RESTAURANT, WITHYPOOL, EXMOOR TA24 7QR (064 383 302). Set in tranquillity of the National Park, ideal for a holiday with your horse and dog. Stabling and kennels available. 10 en suite bedrooms; excellent food and wines. 3 Crowns Commended, AA and RAC **.

STAFFORDSHIRE

STAFFORDSHIRE   *Burton-on-Trent*

Burton-upon-Trent

Historic brewing centre and Shire horse stables are included among 400 years of brewing heritage in Bass Museum.

LITTLE PARK HOLIDAY HOMES, TUTBURY, BURTON-ON-TRENT DE13 9JH (0283 812654). Barn conversion chalets overlooking Dove Valley and Peak District next to medieval castle of Tutbury. Few minutes' walk to numerous shops, pubs, restaurants.

SUFFOLK

SUFFOLK   *Kessingland*

Bury St Edmunds

Town on River Lark 23 miles north-west of Ipswich. Many old buildings, especially Georgian remains of abbey. 12th century flint and rubble building houses collections, including terrifying mantraps.

RAVENWOOD HALL COUNTRY HOUSE HOTEL AND RESTAURANT, ROUGHAM, BURY ST EDMUNDS IP30 9JA (0359 70345). 16th century heavily beamed Tudor Hall set in seven acres of perfect dog walks. Beautifully furnished en suite bedrooms; renowned restaurant; relaxing inglenook fires.

Hadleigh

Historic town on River Brett with several old buildings of interest, including unusual 14th century church. Bury St. Edmunds 20 miles, Harwich 20, Colchester 14, Sudbury 11, Ipswich 10.

EDGEHILL HOTEL, 2 HIGH STREET, HADLEIGH IP7 5AP (Ipswich [0473] 822458). 16th-century property offering a warm welcome. Comfortable accommodation and good home-cooked food. Licensed. Pets welcome. SAE or telephone for details. ETB 3 Crowns Commended. *[🐕]*

Kessingland

Little seaside place with expansive sandy beach, safe bathing, wildlife park, lake fishing. To the south is Benacre Broad, a beauty spot. Norwich 26 miles, Aldeburgh 23, Saxmundham 19, Lowestoft 5.

A three bedroomed cottage situated on beach. Fully furnished with colour TV. Self catering, kitchen with electric cooker, fridge. Children and disabled persons welcome. SAE TO MR S. MAHMOOD, 156 BROMLEY ROAD, BECKENHAM, KENT BR3 2PG (081-650 0539)

Quality seaside Bungalows, all with colour television, refrigerator, parking, linen service. Children and pets welcome. Direct access to beach. APPLY – KNIGHTS HOLIDAY HOMES, KESSINGLAND, LOWESTOFT, SUFFOLK NR33 7SF (0502 588533). *[£17.50 per week.]*

EAST SUSSEX

EAST SUSSEX *Brighton*

EAST SUSSEX *Chiddingly, Hastings, Herstmonceux, Polegate, Telscombe*

Chiddingly, East Sussex
Adorable small, well equipped cottage in grounds of Tudor Manor.
* Full central heating * Two bedrooms * Colour TV
* Fridge, freezer, microwave, laundry facilities, telephone
* Use of indoor heated swimming pool, sauna/ jacuzzi, tennis and badminton court. * Large safe garden.

FROM £230–£480 PER WEEK INCLUSIVE   PETS AND CHILDREN WELCOME
SEETB 4 Keys Commended

Apply: Eva Morris, "Pekes", 124 Elm Park Mansions, Park Walk, London SW10 0AR Tel: 071-352 8088 Fax: 071-352 8125

BEAUPORT PARK HOTEL
🦢🦢🦢🦢 AA/RAC***

A Georgian country house Hotel set amid 33 arcres of formal gardens and woodland. All rooms have private bath, satellite colour television, trouser press, hairdryer and auto dial telephone. Outdoor Swimming Pool, Tennis, Squash, Badminton, Outdoor Chess, French Boules, Croquet Lawn, Putting, Golf and Riding School. Own woodland walks. Special Country House Breaks available all year. Please telephone for Brochure and Tariff.
BEAUPORT PARK HOTEL
Battle Road, Hastings TN38 8EA
Tel: Hastings (0424) 851222

CLEAVERS LYNG
16TH CENTURY COUNTRY HOTEL
CHURCH ROAD, HERSTMONCEUX, E. SUSSEX. BN27 1QI
TEL: 0323 833131 FAX: 0323 833617

For excellent home cooking in traditional English style, comfort and informality, this small family-run hotel in the heart of rural East Sussex is well recommended. Peacefully set in beautiful landscaped gardens extending to 1.5 acres featuring a rockpool with waterfall. Adjacent to Herstmonceux Castle, the house dates from 1577 as its oak beams and inglenook fireplace bear witness. This is an ideal retreat for a quiet sojourn away from urban clamour. The castles at Pevensey, Scotney, Bodiam and Hever are all within easy reach as are Battle Abbey, Kipling's house, Batemans, Michelham Priory and the seaside resorts of Eastbourne, Bexhill and Hastings. Bedrooms all have central heating, wash-hand basins and tea-making facilities; some rooms en suite. On the ground floor there is an oak beamed restaurant with a fully licensed bar, cosy residents' lounge with television and an outer hall with telephone and cloakrooms. Peace, tranquillity and a warm welcome await you. Special attraction: Badger watch.

POLEGATE EAST SUSSEX
Lakeside Farm Holiday Bungalows

On the edge of Arlington Reservoir, with views of the South Downs. Eastbourne, Brighton and Lewes within 15 miles, Drusilla's Zoo two miles, shopping half a mile. Modern comfortable accommodation, two double rooms, lounge, diningroom, bathroom, toilet. Well equipped kitchen. Open April to October. Car essential, parking. Suitable for disabled guests. Children welcome, cot and high chair available. Well controlled pets accepted. Weekly terms from £140. Electricity included. **Mr. M. F. Boniface, Lakeside Farm, Arlington, Polegate BN26 6SB (0323 870111).**

DUCK BARN

ḯ ḯ ḯ ⁄ ḯ ḯ ḯ ḯ   Up to Highly Commended
DUCK BARN HOLIDAYS, TELSCOMBE VILLAGE
Beautifully converted Barn for 8/10 in large garden; Attractive Coach House for 4/5 and Cosy Cottage for 2/3. CH & woodburners. Exposed beams; pine furniture. Children and dogs welcome.
Brochure: **Duck Barn Holidays, 51 School Road, Firle, Near Lewes BN8 6LF (0273 858221)**

JEAKE'S HOUSE
Mermaid Street, Rye, East Sussex TN31 7ET
Telephone: 0797 222828 Fax: 0797 222623

Dating from 1689, this beautiful Listed Building stands in one of England's most famous streets. Oak-beamed and panelled bedrooms overlook the marsh to the sea. Brass, mahogany or four-poster beds with linen sheets and lace; honeymoon suite. En suite facilities, TV, radio, telephone. Residential licence. Traditional and vegetarian breakfast served. £19.50–£27.50 per person. Access, Visa & Mastercard accepted.

AA . QQQQQ PREMIER SELECTED   RAC Highly Acclaimed   César Award 1992
Good Hotel Guide   ETB ❦ ❦ Highly Commended

Brighton

Famous resort with shingle beach and sand at low tide. Varied entertainment and nightlife; excellent shops and restaurants. Portsmouth 48 miles, Hastings 37, Tunbridge Wells 32, Horsham 23, Worthing 11, Newhaven 9.

KEMPTON HOUSE HOTEL, 33/34 MARINE PARADE, BRIGHTON BN2 1TR (0273 570248). Private seafront Hotel, relaxed and friendly atmosphere, overlooking beach and Pier. En-suite rooms available, all modern facilities. Choice of Breakfasts, Dinner optional. Pets and children always welcome.

GEOFF AND MARION BURGESS, DIANA HOUSE, 25 ST GEORGE'S TERRACE, BRIGHTON BN2 1JJ (0273 605797). Two minutes to seafront, close town/ Conference Centre and Marina. All rooms have colour TV, tea/coffee facilities, central heating, showers; some en suite. Public phone. Own key. *[🐾]*

PASKINS HOTEL, 19 CHARLOTTE STREET, BRIGHTON BN2 1AG (0273 601203). Stylish Regency building in quiet location, walking distance to town centre. Imaginative organic cuisine always includes a vegetarian option. Prices from £21 per person, optional Evening Meal £9.95. 3 Crowns, AA QQQ. *[£1 per night.]*

Chiddingly

Charming village, 4 miles north-west of Hailsham off the A22 London–Eastbourne road.

Adorable small well equipped cottage in grounds of Tudor Manor. Two bedrooms. Full central heating. Colour TV. Fridge, freezer, laundry facilities. Large safe garden. Use indoor heated swimming pool, sauna/jacuzzi and tennis. From £230 to £480 per week inclusive. 4 Keys Commended. Contact: EVA MORRIS, "PEKES", 124 ELM PARK MANSIONS, PARK WALK, LONDON SW10 0AR (071-352 8088; Fax: 071-352 8125). *[🐾]*

Hastings

Seaside resort with a famous past – the ruins of William the Conqueror's castle lie above the Old Town. Many places of historic interest in the area, plus entertainments for all the family.

MISS M. COLEMAN, 38 TOWERSCROFT AVENUE, ST LEONARDS-ON-SEA TN37 7JB. Small cosy room in Georgian-style family house. Self catering facilities. Attractive bathroom. Pleasant outlook. Two miles seafront. £60 low-£80 high season for two persons. £10 reduction for one person. Access at all times. Privacy respected. SAE for details. *[🐾 pw!]*

MRS VICKI SAADE, "COPPERBEECHES", 41 CHAPEL PARK ROAD, ST LEONARDS-ON-SEA, HASTINGS TN37 6JB (0424 714026). Lovely Victorian Guest House with off-road parking. Friendly, relaxed atmosphere with pets most welcome. Rooms with colour TV, tea/coffee facilities and central heating. Close to BR Warrior Square. Good walks, ideal for touring 1066 country. £15–£17. Sorry, no smokers. SEETB 2 Crowns Approved. [🐕pw!]

BEAUPORT PARK HOTEL, BATTLE ROAD, HASTINGS TN38 8EA (0424 851222). Georgian country mansion in 33 acres. All rooms private bath, colour television, trouser press, hairdryer, telephone. Country house breaks available all year. [pw!]

MRS D. BEYNON, c/o HAVELOCK ACCOMMODATION SERVICE, CROSS WING, 72 ALL SAINTS STREET, HASTINGS (0424 436779; evenings and weekends 081-399 9605). 15th century Cottage. New fitted kitchen, colour TV. Sleeps 3. Just off sea front in Old Town and fishing quarter. Well behaved pets welcome. [🐕]

Herstmonceux

Small village four miles north-east of Hailsham. Royal Observatory at Herstmonceux Castle.

CLEAVERS LYNG 16TH CENTURY COUNTRY HOTEL, CHURCH ROAD, HERST-MONCEUX BN27 1QJ (0323 833131; Fax: 0323 833617). Small family-run Hotel in heart of rural East Sussex. Bedrooms have central heating, washbasins, tea making. Oak-beamed restaurant, bar, residents' lounge. Pets welcome.

Polegate

Quiet position 5 miles from the popular seaside resort of Eastbourne. LONDON 58 miles, Lewes 12.

MRS P. FIELD, 20 ST JOHNS ROAD, POLEGATE BN26 5BP (0323 482691). Homely private house 5 miles from Eastbourne. Quiet location; large enclosed garden. Parking space. Ideally situated for dog walking on South Downs and Forestry Commission land. All rooms tea/coffee facilities. Bed and Breakfast. Pets very welcome. [🐕pw!]

MR M. F. BONIFACE, LAKESIDE FARM, ARLINGTON, POLEGATE BN26 6SB (0323 870111). Situated on the edge of Arlington Reservoir; Eastbourne within 15 miles. Accommodation sleeps 4-6 with two double rooms, lounge, dining room, kitchen, bathroom. Open April to October. Weekly from £140.

Rye

Picturesque hill town with steep cobbled streets. Many fine buildings of historic interest. Hastings 12 miles. Tunbridge Wells 28.

JEAKE'S HOUSE, MERMAID STREET, RYE, EAST SUSSEX TN31 7ET (0797 222828; Fax: 0797 222623). Dating from 1689, this Listed Building has oak-beamed and panelled bedrooms overlooking the marsh. En suite facilities, TV, radio, telephone. Residential licence. £19.50–£27.50 per person. AA QQQQQ Premier Selected. [🐕]

MRS D. AVERY, "THACKER", OLD BRICKYARD, RYE TN31 7EE (0797 225870). Comfortable holiday home, quietly situated within easy walking distance of Rye's delightful "old town". Sleeps 2 to 3. Fully equipped including bed linen. Enclosed garden adjoining fields. Available all year – short breaks October to April. Dogs very welcome. [🐕]

Telscombe

Tranquil Downland hamlet, close to South Downs Way. 4 miles south of Lewes and 2 miles from coast.

DUCK BARN HOLIDAYS, 51 SCHOOL ROAD, FIRLE, NEAR LEWES BN8 6LF (0273 858221). Beautiful converted Barn, sleeps 8/10; Coach House for 4/5; Cosy Cottage for 2/3. Central heating, woodburners. Exposed beams; pine furniture. Children and dogs welcome. Brochure. *[pw! £10 weekly.]*

WEST SUSSEX

WEST SUSSEX   *Bognor Regis, Littlehampton, Pulborough*

CHEQUERS HOTEL

**Church Place, Pulborough,
West Sussex RH20 1AD
Tel: 0798 872486**

Delightful small Queen Anne Hotel on the edge of the Village, overlooking the Arun Valley towards the South Downs. All bedrooms with private bathrooms, plus colour TV, telephone, trouser press, hairdryer and tea/coffee making facilities. Restaurant serves fresh market produce from daily changing menu. New Garden Conservatory and Coffee Shop. Car Park. Superb centre for walking or touring, with safe walks for your dog available directly from the Hotel in our 9 acre meadow.

Walk for miles along the South Downs Way, or along the banks of the River Arun, or visit one of the many local places of interest, such as Parham House & Gardens, Petworth House & Park, Goodwood, Arundel, or the Weald & Downland Open Air Museum.

Children also very welcome. Major Credit Cards accepted, BARGAIN BREAKS all through the year, from £42 per person for Dinner, Bed and Breakfast. Reduced rates for longer stays. Winter bargain–any 3 nights, D, B&B for £99. AA**RAC. 2 RAC Merit Awards. Egon Ronay and Ashley Courtenay recommended.

No charge for dogs belonging to readers of Pets Welcome!

Bognor Regis

Renowned for its wide sands and safe bathing, Bognor is ideal for family holidays, with a pier, promenade, gardens and a variety of entertainments.

WANDLEYS CARAVAN PARK, EASTERGATE PO20 6SE (0903 745831) (0243 543235 9am-5pm weekdays). Comfortable holiday caravans in tranquil little country park. All with internal WC and shower. Only 15 minutes from Sussex Downs, Bognor and Chichester. *[🐾]*

JOAN AND ROGER TANN, ALANCOURT HOTEL, MARINE DRIVE WEST, BOGNOR REGIS (0243 864844). Fully licensed Hotel near Marine Park Gardens. All rooms colour TV, tea/coffee facilities, heating; many en-suite. Friendly atmosphere. Children and pets welcome. Goodwood and Fontwell racecourses nearby.

BLACK MILL HOUSE HOTEL, PRINCESS AVENUE, BOGNOR REGIS (0243 821945). Children and dogs most welcome. Situated in the quieter West End of town, near sea and Marine Gardens, West End shops and bus routes. Attractive cocktail bar. Games room, colour television, private bathrooms, central heating throughout. Lift. Enclosed garden. Open all year. Mini-Breaks – 2 days D, B&B from £60 (October to March). Own car park. No service charge. Short summer breaks. *[£1.50 per night.]*

Littlehampton

Neat resort backed by a wide green and with lovely sands. The River Arun enters the sea here. Motor-boat trips are run up-river. Chichester 14 miles, Bognor Regis 7, Arundel 4.

MRS A. T. BAIRD, HOME FARM, CLIMPING, LITTLEHAMPTON BN17 5RQ (0903 717981). Comfortably furnished cottages, sleep 4–6, fully equipped with colour TV etc. No linen. Pretty seaside village, convenient for Brighton, Portsmouth etc. Reduction for only 2 persons. SAE for details. *[£10 per week.]*

Pulborough

Popular fishing centre on the River Arun. Nearby South Downs Way makes it an ideal centre for walking. Arundel 8 miles.

THE BARN OWLS, LONDON ROAD, COLDWALTHAM, PULBOROUGH RH20 1LR (0798 872498). Small country Hotel specialising in gourmet breaks and holidays. 2 night breaks from £80. Bed and Breakfast (en suite) from £140 weekly. Gourmet Christmas and New Year breaks. Telephone for brochure.

CHEQUERS HOTEL, PULBOROUGH RH20 1AD (0798 872486). Lovely Queen Anne house in village overlooking Arun Valley. Excellent food. Children and dogs welcome. AA and RAC 2 Star. ETB 4 Crowns Highly Commended. No charge for dogs belonging to readers of *Pets Welcome!* *[pw!]*

WARWICKSHIRE

WARWICKSHIRE   *Stratford-upon-Avon*

RAYFORD CARAVAN PARK
RIVERSIDE, TIDDINGTON ROAD
STRATFORD-ON-AVON CV37 7BE
Tel: (0789) 293964

PETS WELCOME. A HAPPY AND INTERESTING HOLIDAY FOR ALL.

River
Launch
Service
to
Stratford

Situated within the town of Stratford-on-Avon, on the banks of the river, Rayford Park is ideally placed for visiting all Shakespearean attractions and the beautiful Cotswolds. In Stratford itself there is everything you could wish for: shops, pubs, restaurants, swimming pool, sports centre, the Royal Shakespeare Theatre and a generous helping of history and the Bard! The luxury 12ft wide Caravan Holiday Homes accommodate up to 6 persons in comfort. All have kitchen with full-size cooker, fridge; bathroom with shower/washbasin/WC; 2 bedrooms, one double-bedded, one with 2 single beds (cot sides available); double dinette/2 single settees in lounge; electric fire, colour TV, carpeted throughout. Also available, two Cottages, "Sleepy Hollow" and Kingfisher Cottage, all modern facilities, set on River bank. Private fishing. BROCHURE ON REQUEST.

Stratford-upon-Avon

Historic town famous as Shakespeare's birthplace and home. Many interesting old buildings; rebuilt Shakespeare Memorial Theatre. There is a steeplechase course here. Birmingham 24 miles, Banbury 20, Coventry 19, Broadway 15, Evesham 14, Warwick 8.

MRS J. M. EVERETT, NEWBOLD NURSERIES, NEWBOLD-ON-STOUR, STRATFORD-UPON-AVON CV37 8DP (0789 450285). Small farm and hydroponic tomato nursery close to Cotswolds, Stratford-upon-Avon, Warwick, and Blenheim. Comfortable rooms with colour TV, tea/coffee. Local pub serves evening meals at budget prices. En suite available. Bed and Breakfast from £14.50. Children half price. [🐾]

CROWN & CUSHION HOTEL AND LEISURE CENTRE, HIGH STREET, CHIPPING NORTON, NEAR STRATFORD-UPON-AVON OX7 5AD (0608 642533; Fax: 0608 642926; Colour Brochure Free Phone 0800 585251). 500-year-old coaching inn, tastefully modernised. "Old World" bar; indoor pool, solarium etc. Convenient Oxford, Stratford, London, Heathrow, Shakespeare Country. Price Busters from £19.50. [🐾]

MRS H. J. MELLOR, ARRANDALE, 208 EVESHAM ROAD, STRATFORD-UPON-AVON CV37 9AS (0789 267112). Guest House situated near River Avon, theatre, Shakespearean properties. Washbasins, tea making, TV, central heating, en-suite available. Children, pets welcome. Parking. Bed and Breakfast £13.50-£16.00. Weekly terms £90-£105. Evening Meal £5.50. [🐾]

RAYFORD CARAVAN PARK, TIDDINGTON ROAD, STRATFORD-UPON-AVON (0789 293964). Luxury Caravans, sleep 6. Fully equipped kitchens, bathroom/ shower/WC. Also two riverside Cottages, all modern facilities to first-class standards. Private fishing. On banks of River Avon. *[£10 weekly.]*

Warwick

Town on the River Avon, 9 miles south-west of Coventry, with medieval castle and many fine old buildings.

DOREEN E. BROMILOW, WOODSIDE, LANGLEY ROAD, CLAVERDON, WARWICK CV35 8PJ (0926 842446). Set in own grounds, one mile from Claverdon village. One double room, one family, one single; two bathrooms; TV lounge. All rooms have washbasins, tea/coffee making. Well-behaved dogs welcome.

MR & MRS D. CLAPP, THE CROFT, HASELEY KNOB, WARWICK CV35 7NL (0926 484447). This four acre smallholding has a friendly, family atmosphere and is situated in picturesque rural surroundings. Very comfortable accommodation. Bedrooms, most en suite, with colour TV, tea/coffee facilities. Ground floor en suite bedrooms available. Bed and Full English Breakfast from £19. Pets welcome.

THE OLD RECTORY, STRATFORD ROAD, SHERBOURNE, WARWICK CV35 8AB (0926 624562). Grade II Listed Georgian Country House offers Bed and Breakfast: en-suite bedrooms, brass beds; delicious home-cooked Breakfast. Beautiful surroundings. Half-mile M40 Junction 15. AA QQQQ Selected, ETB 2 Crowns Commended. *[🐕]*

WEST MIDLANDS

Birmingham

The second largest city in Britain, with Art Galleries to rival London. The Bull Ring has been modernised and includes an impressive shopping centre, but there is still plenty of the old town to see; the town hall, the concert hall and the Cathedral Church of St Phillip.

ANGELA AND IAN KERR, THE AWENTSBURY HOTEL, 21 SERPENTINE ROAD, SELLY PARK, BIRMINGHAM B29 7HU (021-472 1258). Victorian Country House. Large gardens. All rooms have colour TV, telephones and tea/coffee making facilities. Some rooms en-suite, some rooms with showers. All rooms central heating, wash-basins. Near BBC Pebble Mill, transport, University, City centre. Bed and Breakfast from £25. Dinner extra.

WILTSHIRE

WILTSHIRE *Amesbury*

Antrobus Arms Hotel
Church Street,
Amesbury, Wiltshire SP4 7EU
Tel: 0980 623163 Fax: 0980 622112

Attractive Town Hotel with magnificent walled garden at the rear featuring a three-tier Victorian Fountain. 6 miles from Salisbury and ½ mile off A303. All bedrooms have central heating, colour TV, tea/coffee making facilities, direct-dial telephone; mostly en suite. Excellent restaurant with Table D'Hôte and A la Carte menu. Meals also served in elegant bar. Full English Breakfast served in restaurant. Ideal base for touring many local places of interest, including Stonehenge and Salisbury Cathedral. Excellent fishing, golf courses. Tennis court available locally. Guests made welcome by owners John and Jill and their friendly staff.

Dairy/sheep farm on the Wiltshire/Gloucestershire borders. Ideal for touring, antique shops, market towns, stately homes and gardens. pretty villages. Horse riding, golf and water sports nearby. Malmesbury 3 miles and only 15 mins from M4 (Junctions 16 or 17). Children and pets will particularly enjoy the atmosphere.

3 rooms for B&B One en suite; central heating; tea/coffee.
2 bungalow-style barns, sleeps 2/3 plus cot, for s/c holiday.

**John & Edna Edwards, Stonehill Farm, Charlton, Malmesbury SN16 9DY
Tel: (0666) 823310**

Amesbury

Town on River Avon at S.E. corner of Salisbury Plain. Only two miles from Stonehenge.

ANTROBUS ARMS HOTEL, CHURCH STREET, AMESBURY SP4 7EU (0890 623163 Fax: 0980 622112). Attractive town hotel with magnificent walled garden at the rear. 6 miles from Salisbury. All bedrooms with CH, colour TV, tea/coffee facilities. Excellent restaurant.

Malmesbury

Country town on River Avon with a late medieval market cross. Remains of medieval abbey.

MRS A. HILLIER, LOWER FARM COTTAGE, SHERSTON, MALMESBURY SN16 0PS (0666 840391). Self-contained wing of Farmhouse, sleeps 3/5. Working farm. Large secluded lawn and fields, ideal for pets and children. Fishing. Half-a-mile from shops, pubs. Wiltshire/Gloucs. Border, ideal for Bath, Cotswolds etc. £85 to £140 per week; electricity by 50p meter. *[£5 per week.]*

JOHN AND EDNA EDWARDS, STONEHILL FARM, CHARLTON, MALMESBURY SN16 9DY (0666 823310). Family-run dairy/sheep farm, ideal for touring. 3 comfortable rooms, one en suite. Also 2 fully equipped bungalow style barns, each sleeps 2/3 plus cot, self catering.

WORCESTERSHIRE

WORCESTERSHIRE   *Great Malvern*

Whitewells Farm Cottages

Ridgway Cross, Malvern, Worcestershire WR13 5JS
Telephone Ridgway Cross (0886) 880607

ETB Highly Commended–4 Keys

Seven cottages including one for disabled, full of charm and character, converted from historic farm buildings. Fully furnished and equipped to the highest standards. Exceptionally clean and comfortable. Set in 9 acres in unspoilt Herefordshire countryside, this is an ideal base for touring Herefordshire, Worcestershire, Gloucestershire, Cotswolds, Welsh mountains, Shakespeare country. All electricity, linen, towels, cleaning materials, central heating in winter months included in price. Laundry room. Open all year. Short breaks in low season. Dogs welcome.

Mr and Mrs D. Berisford

Evesham

Quiet town with narrow streets of Georgian houses. Market place and churchyard. Abbey ruins with surviving bell tower. Stratford-upon-Avon 14 miles.

WATERSIDE HOTEL, 56 WATERSIDE, EVESHAM WR11 6JZ (0386 442420). Great accommodation at affordable prices overlooking river, parks. Highly recommended fun restaurant and bar. Bargain breaks. Central for touring Cotswold/Shakespeare country. 4 Crowns Commended.

Great Malvern

Situated 7 miles south west of Worcester on the slopes of the Malvern Hills. Developed as a spa town in the 19th century, and noted for its majestic priory church.

MR AND MRS D. BERISFORD, WHITEWELLS FARM COTTAGES, RIDGWAY CROSS, NEAR MALVERN WR13 5JS (0886 880607). Charming converted Cottages, sleep 2–6. Fully equipped with colour TV, fridge, iron, etc. Linen, towels also supplied. One cottage suitable for disabled guests. ETB 4 Keys Highly Commended. *[£10 per week.]*

NORTH YORKSHIRE

NORTH YORKSHIRE   *Bentham, Bolton Abbey, Brompton-by-Sawdon, Clapham*

Mrs L. J. STORY   **HOLMES FARM, LOW BENTHAM,**
Bentham (05242) 61198   **LANCASTER LA2 7DE**
Within easy reach of Dales, Lake District and Coast.
COTTAGE CONVERSION attached to farmhouse in peaceful countryside.
Central heating * Fridge * TV * Washer * Table Tennis
Tourist Board Approved   3 Keys Commended   **PETS WELCOME!**

Devonshire Arms Country House Hotel
Bolton Abbey, Near Skipton, North Yorkshire BD23 6AJ Tel: 0756 710441

A traditional country house set in the Yorkshire Dales National Park. Open log fires, gourmet restaurant, luxurious bedrooms and lounges bedecked with antiques from Chatsworth, the Derbyshire home of the Duke and Duchess of Devonshire.

AA★★★ 79% Rosette   👑👑👑👑👑 *HIGHLY COMMENDED*

HEADON FARM
WYDALE, BROMPTON-BY-SAWDON, SCARBOROUGH YO13 9DG Tel: 0723 859019
Five spacious character stone cottages situated in a quiet wooded setting on the edge of the North York Moors. Cottages are ideally situated within easy reach of the Heritage Coast, North York Moors, Herriot Country and Vale of York. Open all year from £130 per week with short breaks available from October to June. Brochure on request. Winner of YTB's White Rose Award 1991.
Mrs Denise Proctor   4 Keys Commended

New Inn Hotel
Clapham, Nr Settle, Via Lancaster,
North Yorkshire LA2 8HH
👑👑👑 Commended

Keith and Barbara Mannion invite you to their friendly eighteenth century residential coaching inn in the picturesque Dales village of Clapham. Ideal centre for walking the three peaks of Ingleborough, Pen-y-ghent and Whernside. All rooms have full en suite facilities, colour television and tea/coffee facilities. Enjoy good wholesome Yorkshire food in our restaurant, or bar meals in either of our two bars. Ring Barbara for details of special mid week breaks. **(05242) 51203**

NORTH YORKSHIRE *Harrogate, Hawes*

holiday **COTTAGES** and **LODGES**

Luxury Cottages and Lodges situated in an attractive setting near the picturesque village of Follifoot. All cottages have been restored retaining their traditional charm and are equipped to the highest standard. Facilities within the private country estate include heated swimming pool, mini golf course, children's playground and games room.

Please send for illustrated brochure.

RUDDING
holiday PARK

  Rudding Holiday Park, Follifoot, Harrogate, HG3 1JH. Tel: (0423) 870439

HELME PASTURE
FREEDOM HOLIDAYS
Ideal for Discriminating Dogs
Rosemary Helme, Helme Pasture,
Hartwith Bank, Summerbridge,
Harrogate, N. Yorks. HG3 4DR.
Tel: 0423 780279

* Great sniffing trails, highest paw category walks in the heart of unspoilt Nidderdale.
* Renowned snooze spots while owners explore. Central for Harrogate, York, Herriot and Bronte country. National Trust area.
* After your hard day, stretch out and watch woodland wildlife from the luxurious comfort of your Scandinavian lodge or converted Yorkshire Dales barn.

UP TO HIGHLY COMMENDED

Illustrated brochure

Hawes
Wensleydale
North Yorkshire
DL8 3LY

Tel: (0969) 667255
Fax: (0969) 667741

Simonstone Hall

Elegant 250 year old Country House Hotel enjoying unsurpassed views across James Herriot's Wensleydale. Comfortably furnished with antiques giving the aura and grace of a bygone age, but with all the essential luxuries of the twentieth century. Excellent cuisine including vegetarian and healthy choice menus, extensive and interesting wine list. All rooms en-suite with colour TV and tea-makers. Christmas and New Year house parties. Dogs always welcome. Winner of E.T.B. Warmest Hotelier and RAC Blue Ribbon Awards for last five years. Self-catering studio for 2 people also available. Personally managed by the resident owners, Mr & Mrs. C. Jeffryes.

Readers are requested to mention this guidebook when seeking accommodation (and please enclose a stamped addressed envelope).

HIGHLY ACCLAIMED

*Situated on
Scarborough's
famous Esplanade*

THE PREMIER
LICENSED PRIVATE HOTEL

This lovely Victorian licensed Hotel overlooking the sea and coastline has all the warmth and hospitality of a bygone era. It is conveniently situated for all Scarborough's attractions and is near the Italian, Rose and Holbeck Gardens; also convenient for the historic city of York, North York Moors, Whitby, and many stately homes in the area. The Premier has a high reputation for its standards of food and service, specialising in traditional English cuisine using the very best local produce. Peaceful relaxing atmosphere; lift to comfortable bedrooms, all with colour TV, tea tray, clock radio and hairdryer. Private car park.

PETS VERY WELCOME
Full details from:
MAUREEN and RON JACQUES
66/67 ESPLANADE, SCARBOROUGH,
NORTH YORKSHIRE YO11 2UZ
TEL: 0723 501038 or 0723 501062

NORTH YORKSHIRE *Scarborough, Settle, Skipton*

215

A wide choice of selected and personally inspected self-catering properties in most areas. APPLY – RECOMMENDED COTTAGES (0751 75555).

Bentham

Quiet village amidst the fells. Good centre for rambling and fishing. Ingleton 5 miles N.E.

MRS L. J. STORY, HOLMES FARM, LOW BENTHAM, LANCASTER LA2 7DE (Bentham [05242] 61198). Cottage conversion in easy reach of Dales, Lake District and coast. Central heating, fridge, TV, washer, table tennis. 3 Keys Commended. *[🐕]*

Bolton Abbey

In picturesque Wharfedale. Noted for ruins of 12th century abbey. Roads and footpaths run alongside a beautiful stretch of river.

DEVONSHIRE ARMS COUNTRY HOUSE HOTEL, BOLTON ABBEY, NEAR SKIPTON BD23 6AJ (0756 710441; Fax: 0756 710564). Fully licensed. Situated amidst beautiful scenery, hotel has 40 bedrooms all with private bathroom. Hotel interior features log fires, four-poster bedrooms, fine furnishings and paintings from Chatsworth. 5 Crowns Highly Commended. *[🐕]*

Brompton-by-Sawdon

Quiet village on edge of North Yorkshire Moors. Close to Northallerton.

MRS D. PROCTOR, HEADON FARM, WYDALE, BROMPTON-BY-SAWDON, SCARBOROUGH YO13 9DG (0723 859019). Five spacious character cottages situated in a quiet wooded setting on edge of North York Moors. Open all year from £130 per week. Brochure available.

Clapham

Attractive village with caves and pot-holes in vicinity, including Gaping Ghyll. Nearby lofty peaks include Ingleborough (2,373ft.) to the north. Kendal 24 miles, Settle 6.

NEW INN HOTEL, CLAPHAM, NEAR SETTLE LA2 8HH (05242 51203; Fax: 05242 51496). Friendly 18th century coaching inn. Ideal centre for walking. All rooms en suite, with colour TV and tea/coffee facilities. Restaurant and bar meals. Dogs welcome.

Coverdale

Small village set in Yorkshire Dales, in heart of Herriot country.

MRS JULIE CLARKE, MIDDLE FARM, WOODALE, COVERDALE, LEYBURN DL8 4TY (0969 40271). Peacefully situated traditional Farmhouse offering Bed and Breakfast, optional Evening Meal. Home cooking. Ideally positioned for walking and touring the Dales. [🐕pw!]

MRS C. HARRISON, HILL TOP FARM & RIDING SCHOOL, WEST SCRAFTON, LEYBURN DL8 4RU (0969 40663). Two luxurious cottages on peaceful Dales farm with panoramic views of open moorland and fields. Accommodation sleeps 4/6. Central heating, log fires, games room, private picnic area, fishing. Riding school offers professional tuition, all standards. Holiday courses and liveries with fully qualified instructor. [pw!]

Easingwold

Small market town with cobbled streets where weathered red brick dwellings are grouped around a large green. 12 miles north-west of York.

MRS R. RITCHIE, THE OLD RECTORY, THORMANBY, EASINGWOLD, YORK YO6 3WN (0845 501417). Ideal for touring Herriot Country, Moors, Dales. 3 spacious bedrooms, lounge with colour TV, dining room. Open all year. Ample parking. Bed and Breakfast from £15. Also two self-contained cottages sleeping 4/6. SAE or phone for brochure. [🐕]

Filey

Well-known resort with sandy beach. Off-shore is Filey Brig. Hull 40 miles, Bridlington 11, Scarborough 7.

MRS BUCKLEY, MAYFIELD GUEST HOUSE, 2 BROOKLANDS, FILEY YO14 9BA (0723 514557). Friendly, quiet, close to all amenities. Open all year. Ideal centre for touring Moors, Wolds, etc. From £21 nightly for Dinner, Bed and Breakfast. [🐕]

Goathland

Centre for moorland and woodland walks and waterfalls. Village of 19th century houses scattered over several heaths.

MRS MARION COCKREM, DALE END FARM, GREEN END, GOATHLAND, NEAR WHITBY YO22 5LJ (0947 85371). 500-year-old stone-built farmhouse on 140-acre working farm in North York Moors National Park. Rare breeds kept. Generous portions home cooked food. Guest lounge with colour TV and log fire. Homely olde-worlde interior. Many repeat bookings. SAE for brochure. *[🐾]*

Grassington

Wharfedale village in attractive moorland setting. Ripon 22 miles, Skipton 9.

YORKSHIRE DALES. "Rooftops", Grassington. Sleeps 2/7 plus cot. Splendid walks from "Rooftops", 3-bedroomed detached cottage with superb views. Well equipped for owners' use with colour TV, washer, microwave, telephone. Central heating and open fire. Open all year. From £125 per week incl. fuel. ETB 3 Keys Commended. *[£7 per week.]* Brochure (stamp appreciated) from MRS BRENDA BRITTON, 38 MEADLANDS, YORK (0904 416252).

FORESTERS ARMS, MAIN STREET, GRASSINGTON, SKIPTON (0756 752349). The Foresters Arms is situated in the heart of the Yorkshire Dales and provides an ideal centre for walking or tourism. Within easy reach of York and Harrogate.

GRASSINGTON HOUSE HOTEL, THE SQUARE, GRASSINGTON BD23 5AQ (0756 752406; Fax: 0756 752135). A small hotel with a big reputation. Les Routiers Newcomer of the Year! All rooms en suite, colour TV, telephone, tea making. Table d'Hôte Restaurant, Café Bar. Parking. 3 Crowns. *[🐾]*

Hackness

Village five miles west of Scarborough in National Park.

HACKNESS GRANGE HOTEL, HACKNESS, NEAR SCARBOROUGH YO13 0JW (0723 882345). Sensitively restored and idyllically tucked away in National Park. 26 superbly appointed rooms with en suite facilities. Kennels available. AA/RAC***. *[£6 per night.]*

Harrogate

Charming and elegant spa town set amid some of Britain's most scenic countryside. Ideal for exploring Herriot country and the moors and dales. York 22 miles, Bradford 19, Leeds 16.

Charming Cottages and Lodges sleeping 2–9 people. All equipped to a high standard. Pool, golf and children's playground on estate. Illustrated brochure available. 3/4 Keys. RUDDING HOLIDAY PARK, FOLLIFOOT, HARROGATE HG3 1JH (0423 870439). *[🐾]*

SCOTIA HOUSE HOTEL, 66 KINGS ROAD, HARROGATE HG1 5JR (0423 504361). Owner-managed licensed Hotel five minutes' walk town centre. En suite bedrooms with colour TV, hospitality tray, telephone. Central heating throughout. On site parking. Pets and owners welcome. 3 Crowns Commended, AA, RAC Acclaimed. *[🐾]*

ROSEMARY HELME, HELME PASTURE, HARTWITH BANK, SUMMERBRIDGE, HARROGATE HG3 4DR (0423 780279). Country accommodation for dogs and numerous walks in unspoilt Nidderdale. Central for Harrogate, York, Herriot and Brontë country. National Trust area. Illustrated brochure available. ETB 3/4 Keys up to Highly Commended. *[pw! £2 per day, £12 per week.]*

YOUNG'S HOTEL, 15 YORK ROAD (OFF SWAN ROAD), HARROGATE HG1 2QL (0423 567336). Licensed Hotel with large attractive garden. Colour television, tea/coffee making facilities in all rooms, all with en suite bathrooms. 4 Crowns Commended, AA 2 stars. *[🐕]*

Hawes

Small town in Wensleydale. Situated 14 miles south-east of Kirkby Stephen.

MR AND MRS C. JEFFRYES, SIMONSTONE HALL, HAWES, WENSLEYDALE DL8 3LY (0969 667255). Situated facing south across picturesque Wensleydale. All rooms en-suite with colour TV. Fine cuisine. Extensive wine list. Off season bargain breaks. Personal attention. Resident owners.

STONEHOUSE HOTEL, SEDBUSK, HAWES DL8 3PT (0969 667571; Fax: 0969 667720). This fine Edwardian country house has spectacular views and serves delicious Yorkshire cooking with fine wines. Comfortable en-suite bedrooms, some ground floor. Dogs welcome.

CLOCK TOWER STUDIO, SIMONSTONE HALL, HAWES DL8 3LY (0969 667255). First floor self-catering Studio for 2 persons, combining living and sleeping areas. Separate kitchen and bathroom. In East Wing of award-winning Country House Hotel. Open fire, central heating, well equipped kitchen. Large garden. Dogs welcome.

Hawes near (Mallerstang)

8 miles north-west on B6259 Hawes to Kirkby Stephen road.

COCKLAKE HOUSE, MALLERSTANG CA17 4JT (07683 72080). Charming, High Pennine country house in unique position above Pendragon Castle in Upper Mallerstang Dale. Offers good food and exceptional comfort to a small number of guests. Two double bedrooms with large bathrooms. 3 acres riverside rounds. Dogs welcome.

Helmsley

A delightful stone-built town on River Rye with a large cobbled square. Thirsk 12 miles.

Scandinavian Pine Lodges, each sleeping up to five persons. Fully centrally heated and double glazed. Set in 60 acres, surrounded by pine forests. Open all year. CRIEF LODGE HOLIDAY HOMES, WASS, YORK YO6 4AY (0347 868207 or 0850 598809). *[🐕]*

MRS ELIZABETH EASTON, LOCKTON HOUSE FARM, BILSDALE, HELMSLEY YO6 5N3 (043-96 303). 16th century Farmhouse; oak beams, central heating. All rooms washbasins, tea/coffee facilities. Good home cooking. Panoramic views. Bed and Breakfast from £13.50; BB & EM from £21. One dog per family.

CROWN HOTEL, MARKET SQUARE, HELMSLEY YO6 5BJ (0439 70297). Fully residential old coaching inn. Bedrooms are very well appointed, all have tea and coffee-making facilities, colour TV, radio and telephones. Traditional country cooking. Recommended AA and RAC 2 star. *[🐕]*

Horton-in-Ribblesdale

Moorland village in the Craven country in the shadow of Pen-y-Ghent (2273 ft.). Many caves and potholes in the vicinity. Settle 6 miles.

COLIN AND JOAN HORSFALL, STUDFOLD HOUSE, HORTON-IN-RIBBLESDALE, NEAR SETTLE BD24 0ER (07296 200) and (0729 860200). Georgian house standing in one acre of beautiful gardens. All rooms have central heating, washbasins, colour TVs and tea/coffee making facilities. Vegetarians, children and pets also welcome. Bed and Breakfast £14. Evening Meal £7.00. Also self-catering cottage. SAE please.

Huby

Small village 9 miles north of York. Ideal as base for exploring Dales, Moors and coast.

THE NEW INN MOTEL, MAIN STREET, HUBY, YORK YO6 1HQ (0347 810219). Ideal base for all Yorkshire attractions. Ground floor rooms, en-suite, colour TV etc. Bed and Breakfast from £18. Evening Meal optional. Vegetarians catered for. Suitable for disabled. Pets welcome. Special 3-day breaks. Telephone for brochure. AA Listed. [🐕]

Kilburn

Village to south of Hambleton Hills. Nearby is white horse carved into hillside. Helmsley 9 miles, Thirsk 6.

CLAIRE STRAFFORD, CHAPEL COTTAGE, KILBURN, YORK YO6 4AH (0347 868383). Converted farm buildings in excellent area for touring Moors, Dales and coast. Range of sports facilities and restaurants in area. ALL PETS VERY WELCOME.

Kirkbymoorside

Small town below North Yorkshire Moors, 7 miles west of Pickering. Traces of a medieval castle.

MRS F. WILES, SINNINGTON COMMON FARM, KIRKBYMOORSIDE, YORK YO6 6NX (0751 31719). Newly converted cottages, tastefully furnished and well equipped, on working family farm. Sleep 2/4 from £100 per week including linen and heating. Also spacious ground floor accommodation (teamakers, colour TV, radio alarms). Disabled facilities, separate entrances. B&B from £16. [🐕pw!]

Leeming Bar

Small pretty village two miles north-east of Bedale.

THE WHITE ROSE HOTEL, LEEMING BAR, NORTHALLERTON DL7 9AY (0677 422707; Fax: 0677 425123). Eighteen bedroom, two-star private Hotel situated in village on A684, half a mile from A1 motorway. Ideal base for touring North Yorks Moors, Dales and coastal resorts. [🐕]

Leyburn

Small market town, 8 miles south-west of Richmond, standing above the River Ure in Wensleydale.

PEN VIEW FARMHOUSE, THORALBY, LEYBURN DL8 3SU (0969 663319). Fully centrally heated with 1 single, 1 twin, 1 double, and 1 family room, 2 en-suite. Licensed. Ideal for walking or touring Dales. Children and pets welcome.

YORKSHIRE DALES NATIONAL PARK. Former 17th century Coaching Inn now run as a guest house. Oak beams, log fire, home cooking. En suite from £14. [🐕]

Litton

Village in Littondale, two miles north-west of Arncliffe.

LITTONDALE COUNTRY HOUSE HOTEL, LITTON, SKIPTON BD23 5QE (0756 770293). Charming hotel in beautiful dale. Glorious views. Fine food/service. All en-suite, colour TV, teamakers. Four-poster room with jacuzzi available. Two ground floor bedrooms. 3 Crowns Commended. Bed and breakfast from £20.50. *[pw!]*

Malham

In picturesque Craven District with spectacular Malham Cove (300ft.) and Gordale Scar with waterfalls. Malham Tarn (N.T.) is 4 miles N. Skipton 12 miles.

MRS V. SHARP, MIRESFIELD FARM, MALHAM, SKIPTON BD23 4DA (0729 830414). In beautiful gardens bordering village green and stream. Well known for excellent food. 14 bedrooms, 12 with private facilities. Full central heating. Two well furnished lounges and conservatory for guests' use.

Myton-on-Swale

Beautiful, rural surroundings. Very peaceful. Brafferton 2 miles.

MR R. W. HALL, THE HADDOCKS, MYTON-ON-SWALE, HELPERBY YO6 2RB (0423 360224). Three-bedroom farm cottages sleep 6 plus cot. Fridge/freezer, colour television, open fire. Ample parking. Quiet rural surroundings. Central for all Yorkshire. *[🛏pw!]*

Oldstead

Hamlet 7 miles east of Thirsk in beautiful North Yorkshire Moors.

THE BLACK SWAN INN, OLDSTEAD, COXWOLD, YORK YO6 4BL (0347 868387). 18th-century Country Freehouse offers Chalet-style accommodation, en-suite, colour TV, central heating, tea/coffee facilities. Real ale. A la Carte Restaurant. Fine wines. No charge for pets. Brochure available. *[🛏]*

Pateley Bridge

Picturesque and friendly small town in the heart of beautiful Nidderdale, bordering the Dales National Park. Excellent walking country and a good centre for touring the Dales, Moors, Herriot Country etc.

RIVULET COURT, PATELY BRIDGE. ETB rating 4 Keys Highly Commended. Spacious 18th century cottage, comfortable accommodation for six or more. Central heating, fully equipped for self catering with laundry, dishwasher, fridge freezer etc, and situated close to village amenities. Fully enclosed courtyard. Weekly rates £150–£340 incl. For colour brochure contact: ANNE RACK, BLAZEFIELD, BEWERLEY, HARROGATE HG3 5BS (0423 711001). *[🛏]*

Pickering

Pleasant market town on southern fringe of North Yorkshire Moors National Park with moated Castle (Norm.). Bridlington 31 miles, Whitby 20, Scarborough 16, Helmsley 13, Malton 8.

BEANSHEAF HOTEL, MALTON ROAD, KIRBY MISPERTON, MALTON YO17 0UE (065-386 614 or 488). RAC Merit Award for Comfort. Impressive menus. Gateway to North York Moors. Half an hour from coast resorts, York, Helmsley. Good value for money. AA and RAC 2 Stars. *[🛏]*

VIVERS MILL, MILL LANE, PICKERING YO18 8DJ (0751 473640). Bed and Breakfast in ancient Watermill in peaceful surroundings. Comfortable en-suite rooms with beamed ceilings. Tea making facilities. Ideal for Moors, coastline, and York. Bed and Breakfast from £22 per day, £135 weekly. [🐾]

Scarborough

Very popular family resort with fine coast scenery, good sands. Of interest is the ruined 12th century Castle. Wood End Museum and Oliver's Mount (viewpoint). York 41 miles, Whitby 20, Bridlington 17, Filey 7.

CHURCH FARMHOUSE HOTEL, 3 MAIN STREET, EAST AYTON, SCARBOROUGH YO13 9HL (0723 862102 and 863693). North York Moors National Park. Delightful village hotel. Home cooking. En-suite, colour TV, tea/coffee facilities. Games room. 3 Crowns Commended. Full disabled access. Les Routiers Recommended. RAC Highly Acclaimed. Also self-catering cottages, 5 Keys Commended. [🐾]

PARADE HOTEL, 29 ESPLANADE, SCARBOROUGH YO11 2AQ (0723 361285). Splendidly situated Victorian Hotel; superb views of sea and coastline; 17 comfortable bedrooms, all en-suite, with colour TV and tea/coffee trays. Emphasis on preparation of fresh food "home-style". Separate non-smoking lounge. Easy parking. ETB 2 Crowns Approved. RAC Acclaimed. [🐾]

THE PREMIER HOTEL, ESPLANADE, SCARBOROUGH, NORTH YORKSHIRE YO11 2UZ (0723) 501062/501038. The Premier Hotel is situated on the Esplanade. All rooms have private bath/shower and toilet en suite, colour TV, radio, tea/coffee facilities and full central heating.

SCARBOROUGH near. Two luxury detached Bungalows, each sleeps 7, on 170-acre park enjoying wonderful views. APPLY – MRS J. HOLLAND, 32 JOAN LANE, HOOTON LEVITT, ROTHERHAM, SOUTH YORKSHIRE S66 8PH (0709 815102) with SAE. [pw!]

Settle

Old world town high in the hills, characterised by gabled houses with oriel windows and turrets. Skipton 13 miles.

SETTLE, INGLETON AND HORTON, YORKSHIRE DALES. Idyllic stone self-catering cottages. Sleep 2–15, lovingly restored to the highest standards. Central heating, colour TV/video, fridge freezer, dishwasher etc. ALL PETS WELCOME. For brochure telephone YORKSHIRE PROPERTIES (0729 840499). [🐾]

Skipton

Airedale market town, centre for picturesque Craven district. Fine Castle (14th cent). York 43 miles, Manchester 42, Leeds 26, Harrogate 22, Settle 16.

PAT AMES, DALES HOLIDAY COTTAGES, CARLETON BUSINESS PARK, SKIPTON BD23 2DG (0756 799821 and 790919). Wide range of personally inspected, self-catering holiday properties. Many in the heart of 'Herriot' and 'Heartbeat' Country.

Over 200 super self-catering Cottages, Houses and Flats throughout Yorkshire Dales, York, Moors, Coast, Peak and Lake District. Telephone for free illustrated brochure. APPLY – HOLIDAY COTTAGES (YORKSHIRE) LTD., WATER STREET, SKIPTON (18) BD23 1PB (0756 700872).

Sleights

Village running down to River Esk, 3 miles south-west of Whitby.

MRS M. CANA, PARTRIDGE NEST FARM, ESKDALESIDE, SLEIGHTS, WHITBY YO22 5ES (0947 810450). Six caravans on secluded site, five miles from Whitby and sea. Ideal touring centre. All have mains electricity, colour TV, fridge, gas cooker. SAE or phone please.

Staithes

Fishing village surrounded by high cliffs on North Sea coast, 9 miles north-west of Whitby.

THE FOX INN, ROXBY, STAITHES, SALTBURN TS13 5EB (0947 840335). Family run village inn; all rooms colour TV, tea/coffee making. Open all year for B&B from £15; Bar Meals/Evening Meals on request. *[*↖*pw!]*

Thirsk

Market town with attractive square. Excellent touring area. Northallerton 8 miles.

EMMA SWIERS, FIR TREE FARM HOUSE, THORMANBY, EASINGWOLD, YORK YO6 3NN (0845 501201 and 501220). Attractive farmhouse with two double rooms and one family room, one en suite. Sittingroom with open fire and colour TV. Good home cooking and friendly welcome. Ideally located for visits to York, the North Yorks Moors and Dales. Pets and children welcome. B&B from £13.50; B, B & Dinner from £20.00. *[*↖*]*

BARLEY GARTH, BALK, THIRSK YO7 2AJ (0845 597524). 18th century Mill House twixt Dales and Moors. Bed and Breakfast from £14. Also self-catering apartment. Children welcome. ETB Listed 'Commended'/3 Keys Commended. *[£1 per night.]*

Wensleydale

Possibly the most picturesque of all the Dales, ideal for touring some of the most beautiful parts of Yorkshire and the nearby Herriot Country. Kendal 25 miles, Kirkby Stephen 15.

THE WENSLEYDALE HEIFER, WEST WITTON, WENSLEYDALE DL8 4LS (0969 22322). Sample the best of Yorkshire at this 17th century inn. 19 en-suite bedrooms, 3 four-poster suites. Real ales. Bistro. Restaurant serving finest cuisine. Traditional hospitality. *[£2 per night.]*

MRS P. M. KEEBLE, HAMMER FARM, MASHAM, RIPON HG4 4JF (0677 60306; Fax: 0677 60327). Three barn conversion cottages. All equipped to high standard. Central heating. Large gardens. Fabulous views, all the peace and quiet you could wish for.

MRS SUE COOPER, ST EDMUNDS, CRAKEHALL, BEDALE DL8 1HP (0677 423584). Set in Lower Wensleydale, these recently renovated cottages are fully equipped and are an ideal base for exploring the Dales and Moors. Sleep 2-5 plus cot. Up to 4 Keys Commended. *[*↖*]*

Whitby

Charming resort with harbour and sands. Cliffs and moors. Of note is the 13th century Abbey (ruins). Stockton-on-Tees 34 miles, Scarborough 20, Saltburn-by-the-Sea 19.

MRS K. E. NOBLE, SUMMERFIELD FARM, HAWSKER, WHITBY YO22 4LA (0947 601216). Between Whitby/Robin Hood's Bay. Six berth caravan. Private farm site. Beach one mile. 'Cleveland Way' footpath nearby. Set in secluded safe grassy area. SAE for details. *[pw! £5 per week.]*

MRS R. B. O'DONNELL, 'KINGSWOOD', THE AVENUE, SLEIGHTS, NEAR WHITBY YO22 5BS (0947 810280). Charming Edwardian House in own grounds on the edge of the Moors/sea. Centrally heated. One room en-suite. Guests' lounge and bedrooms with colour TV. Private parking. Good food and attentive service. Bed and Breakfast from £16.50. Brochure on request. *[pw!]*

MR W. BAKER, HAVEN CREST HOTEL, 137 UPGANG LANE, WHITBY YO21 3JW (0947 602726). Small, family-run, licensed Hotel. Close to beach. Pets welcome. Car parking. Telephone for brochure. 3 Crowns. *[ ]*

WHITE ROSE HOLIDAY COTTAGES, SLEIGHTS, NEAR WHITBY. Superior stone village cottages situated near Sleights Bridge. Available all year, including Christmas and New Year. 3 Keys Commended. APPLY – MRS J. ROBERTS (PW), 5 BROOK PARK, SLEIGHTS, NEAR WHITBY YO21 1RT. Telephone 0947 810763. *[pw! £5 per week.]*

York

Historic cathedral city and former Roman Station on River Ouse. Magnificent Minster (E.E. to Perp.) and 3 miles of ancient walls. Many interesting old churches and other notable buildings, including Palace Chapel, St. William's College (15th-17th cent.). Merchant Adventurers Hall, St. Anthony's Hall (15th cent.) and Treasurer's House (17th cent.); also old inns, museums. Facilities for a wide range of sports and entertainments. Horse-racing on Knavesmire. Bridlington 41 miles, Filey 41, Helmsley 24, Leeds 24, Harrogate 22, Malton 18, Selby 13.

ASTORIA HOTEL, 6 GROSVENOR TERRACE, BOOTHAM, YORK (0904 659558). Licensed Hotel, 15 bedrooms, many with private bathroom. Dogs welcome. Private parking. *[ ]*

3 attractive self-catering choices. 12 miles from York. WOODLEA detached house, sleeping 5–6, with kitchen, dining area, large lounge and colour TV, bathroom, cloakroom, 3 bedrooms. BUNGALOW adjacent to farmhouse sleeps 2–4. Kitchen, bathroom, lounge/dining room with colour TV and double bed settee. Twin room with cot. STUDIO adjacent to farmhouse, sleeping 2. Kitchen, lounge/dining room with colour TV, twin bedroom, bathroom/toilet. SAE for details: MRS M. S. A. WOODLIFFE, MILL FARM, YAPHAM, POCKLINGTON, YORK YO4 2PH (0759 302172).

ORILLIA HOUSE, 89 THE VILLAGE, STOCKTON-ON-FOREST, YORK YO3 9UP (0904 400600 or 0904 738595). Conveniently situated in centre of village 3 miles from York. All rooms with private facilities etc. Bed and Breakfast from £15. Telephone for brochure. *[£1 per night.]*

MRS JUNE WOOD, ASCOT HOUSE, 80 EAST PARADE, YORK YO3 7YH (0904 426826). Within 15 minutes' walk of City Centre. Attractive Victorian Villa with 12 en suite double bedrooms. Private car park. Own keys and access at all times. Well-behaved pets welcome. Two Crowns Approved.

MRS S. JACKSON, VICTORIA VILLA GUEST HOUSE, 72 HESLINGTON ROAD, YORK YO1 5AU (0904 631647). Ten minutes' walk from city centre. Comfortable double, twin, single and family bedrooms, all with TV. Children and pets welcome. Open all year. B&B from £13-£18. *[ ]*

ST GEORGE'S HOUSE HOTEL, 6 ST GEORGE'S PLACE, YORK YO2 2DR (0904 625056). Family-run licensed Hotel in quiet cul-de-sac near racecourse. All rooms with colour TV, radio. Tea/coffee facilities. Private parking. Pets welcome. 3 Crowns. RAC, AA. *[ ]*

YORK LAKESIDE LODGES, MOOR LANE, YORK YO2 2QU (0904 702346 or 0831 885824). Superbly equipped self-catering Scandinavian pine lodges. Parkland setting. Private fishing lake. Alongside Park and Ride – cheap coach to City centre. Open all year. Brochure. ETB 4 Keys Highly Commended. *[pw! £12 weekly.]*

WEST YORKSHIRE

WEST YORKSHIRE   *Huddersfield*

HUDDERSFIELD HOTEL
Kirkgate, Huddersfield, West Yorkshire HD1 1QT
Tel: 0484 512111
Friendly, 40-bedroomed, town centre hotel. All rooms en suite.
One first-class suite with roof garden and kennel. Open all year.
👑 👑 👑 👑 Commended   Yorkshire and Humberside in Bloom winners   RAC/AA★★

Haworth

Town situated above the River Worth Valley. Of interest is the parsonage, one-time home of the Brontë Family, now a museum; the revived Worth Valley Railway runs from Keighley to Oxenhope. Keighley 2 miles.

Superb small moorland Cottage, one mile Haworth. Sleeps 4–6. Luxuriously equipped, sunny lounge, patio garden, central heating. Breathtaking moorland views. Children welcome. Available all year round. Prices £85–£150 (Winter) and £130–£260 (Summer), includes sheets and heating. Tourist Board Category 3. APPLY – MRS P. M. SEABROOK, 30 NEWCOMBE STREET, MARKET HARBOROUGH, LEICESTERSHIRE LE16 9PB (0858 463723).

Holmfirth

Town on River Holme, five miles south of Huddersfield. Built on textiles and engineering industry.

FAIRVIEW GUEST HOUSE, 6 MEARHOUSE TERRACE, JACKSON BRIDGE, NEAR HOLMFIRTH HD7 7HD (0484 681643). Last of the Summer Wine country. Small friendly Guest House with hearty traditional or vegetarian breakfast. All rooms central heating, H&C, tea and coffee. En suite available. Pets welcome.

Huddersfield

Situated on River Colne, 11 miles south of Bradford. Museum with exhibits illustrating the development of the textile industry.

HUDDERSFIELD HOTEL, KIRKGATE, HUDDERSFIELD HD1 1QT (0484 512111). Friendly, 40-bedroom town centre hotel. All rooms en-suite. One first-class suite with roof garden and kennel. Open all year. *[pw!]*

Wales

SEASIDE COTTAGES

We have a selection of self catering seaside and country cottages, bungalows, farmhouses, caravans etc offering superb reasonably priced accommodation for owners and their pets. Our brochure contains details of all you need for a wonderful holiday–please telephone for your copy now.

0758 701 702 (24 hours)

MANN'S HOLIDAYS, GAOL STREET, PWLLHELI, GWYNEDD LL53 5DB (0758 701702 24 hours). Large selection of seaside and country cottages, bungalows, farmhouses, caravans etc offering reasonably priced accommodation for owners and their pets. Telephone for brochure.

ANGLESEY

ANGLESEY   *Trearddur Bay*

Cliff Cottages and Plas Darien Apartments

All year round holidays and short breaks in a choice of centrally heated apartments with wonderful sea views or stonebuilt cottages in village-like situation very near sea. Own private indoor leisure complex with adults' pool and children's pool, saunas, solarium, gym, snooker, bowls, table tennis. Outdoor heated pool, tennis courts, badminton, small golf, bowls, croquet. Adjacent 18 hole golf course, horse riding, windsurfing, canoeing, fishing.

Phone or write for brochure:
Plas Darien
The Cliff
Trearddur Bay
Anglesey LL65 2TZ
Tel: 0407 860789

Llanddaniel

Village just off the A5, Menai Bridge 5 miles E.

Secluded Farmhouse with views of Snowdonia, sleeps 7/8. Single 6-berth Caravan with shower, etc. on smallholding. B&B; en suite ground floor bedrooms. WTB 2 Crowns Highly Commended. APPLY – MRS M. WILLIAMS, TYDDYN GOBLET, BRYNSIENCYN, ANGLESEY (0248 430296).

Llanerchymedd

Pretty village on Anglesey. 6 miles south of Amlwch.

MRS J. THOMAS, GLEGIR FARM, BODAFON MOUNTAIN, LLANERCHYMEDD (0248 470244). Luxury Caravan (33' Pemberton) with all amenities, shower, colour TV, fridge. On secluded farm site with idyllic views. Lligwy beach three miles, Moelfre Bay four miles. Pets and children welcome.

Trearddur Bay

Attractive holiday spot set amongst low cliffs on Holy Island, near Holyhead. Golf, sailing, fishing, swimming.

CLIFF COTTAGES AND PLAS DARIEN APARTMENTS, TREARDDUR BAY LL63 3LD (0407 860789). Fully equipped holiday Cottages, sleeping 4/8 plus cot. Near sea. Children's playground. Indoor and outdoor heated pools. Colour television. Choice of centrally heated apartments or stone-built cottages. Own private leisure complex with bowls, sauna, snooker, table tennis etc. Also tennis, croquet. Adjacent golf course. [🐕]

CLWYD

CLWYD   *Colwyn Bay*

CLWYD

QUALITY COTTAGES

AROUND THE MAGNIFICENT WELSH COAST

Away from the madding crowd
Near safe sandy beaches

A small specialist agency with over 30 years' experience of providing quality self-catering, offer privacy, peace and unashamed luxury.
The first WTB self-catering award winners.
Highest residential standards.
Dishwashers, microwaves, washing machines
Central heating NO Slot Meters
Log Fires.
Linen Provided.

PETS WELCOME FREE

All in coastal areas famed for scenery, walks, wild flowers, birds, badgers and foxes.

Free colour brochure:

P.W. REES
"Quality Cottages"
Cerbid, Solva, Haverfordwest,
Pembrokeshire SA62 6YE

Tel: (0348) 837871

Colwyn Bay

Lively seaside resort with promenade amusements. Attractions include Mountain Zoo, Eirias Park; golf, tennis, riding and other sports. Good touring centre for Snowdonia. The quieter resort of Rhos-on-Sea lies at the western end of the bay.

EDELWEISS HOTEL, OFF LAWSON ROAD, COLWYN BAY LL29 8HD (0492 532314). Comfortable Country House Hotel set in own wooded grounds close to open parkland; ideal for dog owners. All rooms with en-suite facilities. Well-behaved dogs welcome. [🐾]

WESTWOOD HOTEL – COED GORLLEWIN, 51 PRINCES DRIVE, COLWYN BAY LL29 8PL (0492 532078). Friendly licensed Hotel, ideal for touring North Wales. All bedrooms colour TV, tea/coffee facilities, en-suite facilities. Bed and Breakfast from £13.00. WTB 3 Crowns. [🐾]

MR & MRS G. P. WALTERS, THE CONTINENTAL, WEST PROMENADE, COLWYN BAY LL28 4BT (0492 531516). Popular seafront holiday flats from £62. Dogs welcome if house trained and well behaved. Please send SAE for brochure and booking form. WTB Approved. [£10 per week.]

ALWYN HOUSE HOTEL, 4 UPPER PROMENADE, COLWYN BAY LL28 4BS (0492 532004). Small Family Hotel, one minute beach, 5 minutes shops/entertainments. Central heating. All rooms colour TV, washbasins, tea-making. Excellent meals. Children/pets welcome. Licensed. Open all year.

Llangollen

Famous for International Music Eisteddfod held in July. Plas Newydd, Valle Crucis Abbey nearby. Standard gauge steam railway; canal cruises; ideal for golf and walking.

Spacious country house in extensive grounds offering quality accommodation. Colour TV, tea/coffee in en suite rooms. Evening meals a short walk away. B&B £15. Brochure. THE OLD VICARAGE GUEST HOUSE, BRYN HOWEL LANE, LLANGOL-LEN LL20 7YR (0978 823018). *[🐕]*

PEN-Y-DYFFRYN COUNTRY HOUSE HOTEL, NEAR RHYDYCROESAU, OSWES-TRY SY10 7DT (0691 653700). Georgian Rectory set in Shropshire/Welsh Hills. Seven en-suite bedrooms, colour TV. Licensed restaurant. Very quiet and relaxed. Fishing. Dinner, Bed and Breakfast from £39.00 per person. 3 Crowns. *[🐕pw!]*

BRYN DERWEN HOTEL, ABBEY ROAD, LLANGOLLEN LL20 8EF (0978 860583). Imposing hotel in tranquil surroundings overlooking River Dee and mountains. Ideal touring base. Fine cuisine and wines. En suite, colour TV, tea-makers. Sauna/solarium.

DYFED

DYFED   *Broad Haven*

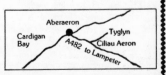

235

Aberaeron

Attractive little town on Cardigan Bay, good touring centre for coast and inland. The Aeron Express Aerial Ferry offers an exciting trip across the harbour. Marine aquarium; Aberarth Leisure Park nearby.

GILFACH-YR-HALEN HOLIDAY VILLAGE, LLWYNCELYN, NEAR ABERAERON SA46 0NN (0545 580288). Choice of modern Bungalows (6 persons) or luxury 2/3 person apartments. Fully equipped, linen, colour TV. Horse and pony riding. Write or phone for brochure pack to the Manager.

237

Aberporth

Popular seaside village offering safe swimming and good sea fishing. Good base for exploring Cardigan Bay coastline.

MR P. W. REES, 'QUALITY COTTAGES', CERBID, SOLVA, HAVERFORDWEST, PEMBROKESHIRE SA62 6YE (0348 837871). Cottages set in all coastal areas; unashamed luxury; all equipped to highest residential standards; dishwashers, microwave ovens, washing machines. Log fires. Linen supplied. Pets welcome. *[pw!]*

Beulah

Small hamlet four miles north-west of Newcastle Emlyn and seven miles east of Cardigan.

BRENDA SLADE, GLASFRYN, BEULAH, NEWCASTLE EMLYN SA38 9OP (0239 810745). Farm house offering Bed and Breakfast. Optional evening meal. Also caravan accommodation. Riding available. Adults, children, horses, dogs, etc. welcome. *[🐕 pw!]*

Bosherston

Village 4 miles south of Pembroke, bordered by 3 man-made lakes, a haven for wildlife and covered in waterlilies in early summer.

MR P. W. REES, 'QUALITY COTTAGES', CERBID, SOLVA, HAVERFORDWEST, PEMBROKESHIRE SA62 6YE (0348 837871). Cottages set in all coastal areas; unashamed luxury; dishwashers, microwaves, washing machines – highest residential standards. Log fires. Linen provided. Pets welcome. *[pw!]*

Broad Haven

Attractive little resort on St. Bride's Bay in the Pembrokeshire Coast National Park. Superb sandy beach; National Park Information Centre.

MILLMOOR FARM COTTAGES AND ROCKSDRIFT APARTMENTS. Enjoy a relaxing and peaceful holiday only yards from safe sandy beach and woodland walks. Personal supervision. Microwaves, fridge freezers, colour TV. Full central heating. Children's play areas; cots, high chairs. Brochure from E. & H. MOCK, MILLMOOR, BROAD HAVEN, HAVERFORDWEST SA62 3JB (0437 781507; Fax: 0437 781002).

JOHN BIRT-LLEWELLIN, THE BOWER FARM, LITTLE HAVEN, HAVERFORD-WEST SA62 3TY (0437 781554). Friendly, comfortable, working farmhouse over-looking Broad Haven sandy beach, offshore islands and coast path. Peaceful paradise. Convenient for all country and water sports and walking. Livery available. 2 Crowns Commended. *[🐕]*

BROAD HAVEN HOTEL, ENFIELD ROAD, BROAD HAVEN, NEAR HAVERFORD-WEST SA62 3JN (0437 781366). On sea-front. Heated swimming pool. Games room. Colour television in bedrooms. Quiet, well-behaved dogs welcome. Please send for colour brochure. *[£3.00 per day, £21 weekly.]*

Ciliau Aeron

Village in undulating country just inland from the charming Cardigan Bay resorts of New Quay and Aberaeron. New Quay 12 miles, Aberaeron 6.

TYGLYN HOLIDAY ESTATE, CILIAU AERON, NEAR LAMPETER SA48 8DD (0570 470684). In the heart of rural Wales and only four miles from the seaside town of Aberaeron. Twenty award-winning brick-built semi-detached two-bedroom Bunga-lows with all modern facilities and colour TV. Range of outdoor activities locally. £107–£220 per week.

Fishguard

Picturesque Lower Town clusters round the old quayside; Upper Town is spread out on a hill above the harbour. Many craft workshops in the area; ferry to Ireland from nearby Goodwick.

FISHGUARD HOLIDAY PARK, DEPT PW, GREENACRES, FISHGUARD SA65 9JH (0437 767172). Where good caravan holidays cost less. Superbly situated few minutes' walk from town; excellent leisure facilities incl. clubhouse, launderette, takeaway etc. Send for colour brochure. *[pw! £10 per week.]*

Haverfordwest

Administrative and shopping centre for the area; ideal base for exploring National Park. Historic town of narrow streets; museum in castle grounds; many fine buildings.

HAVEN COTTAGES, WHITEGATES, LITTLE HAVEN, HAVERFORDWEST, PEM-BROKESHIRE SA62 3LA (0437 781552). Cottages sleep two to twelve. On Coastal Path, 200 yards from beach. All facilities plus linen. WTB 4/5 Dragons Award. Also Bed and Breakfast available in fishing village. *[🛏🐕]*

CLARE HALLETT, KEESTON KITCHEN, KEESTON, HAVERFORDWEST SA62 6EJ (0437 710440). Two fully equipped comfortable Flats, sleeping 4/5, in beautifully converted Cottage with large garden. One suitable for wheelchair. Close to our first-class restaurant. Open all year; short breaks available. Central heating, electricity and linen included. WTB 4 Dragons. *[£5 per pet per week.]*

Llangrannog

Pretty little seaside village overlooking a sandy beach. Superb cliff walk to NT Ynys Lochtyn, a secluded promontory.

MR P. W. REES, 'QUALITY COTTAGES', CERBID, SOLVA, HAVERFORDWEST, PEMBROKESHIRE SA62 6YE (0348 837871). Cottages set in all coastal areas; unashamed luxury. All equipped to highest residential standards with washing machines, dishwashers, microwaves. Log fires. Linen supplied. Pets welcome. *[pw!]*

Manorbier

Unspoiled village on South Pembrokeshire coast near Tenby. Sandy bay and fine coastal walks. Impressive 12th century moated castle overlooks bay.

AQUARIUM COTTAGE, MANORBIER. Delightful detached country cottage. Two bedrooms. Sleeps 6. Also THE LOBSTER POT, MANORBIER. Pleasant modern ground floor flat. Two bedrooms. Sleeps 4. Both properties ½ mile sea. Pets welcome. Ample parking. Electricity and bed linen included in price. Brochure from: MRS J. HUGHES, ROSE COTTAGE, MANORBIER, PEMBROKESHIRE SA70 7ST (0834 871408). *[🐕]*

Newgale

On St Bride's Bay 3 miles east of Solva. Long beach where at exceptionally low tide the stumps of a submerged forest may be seen.

MR P. W. REES, 'QUALITY COTTAGES', CERBID, SOLVA, HAVERFORDWEST, PEMBROKESHIRE SA62 6YE (0348 837871). Cottages set in all coastal areas, unashamed luxury; equipped to highest residential standards with dishwashers, washing machines, microwave ovens. Log fires. Linen provided. Pets welcome. *[pw!]*

Nolton Haven

Hamlet at head of inlet on St Bride's Bay. Fine coastal views.

FOLKESTON HILL HOLIDAY BUNGALOWS. A small group of bungalows in a sheltered valley which winds down to the sea. WTB Graded. Pets welcome – no charge. Brochure from JOHN & CERI PRICE, CASHFIELD COTTAGE HOLIDAYS, NINE WELLS, SOLVA, HAVERFORDWEST SA62 6UH (0437 720027).

Quality beachfront Cottages 30 yards from Nolton Haven's sandy beach. Fully equipped, sleeping 4/6. Also nearby Farm Guest House offering Dinner, Bed and Breakfast. APPLY – J. CANTON, NOLTON HAVEN FARM, NOLTON HAVEN, HAVERFORDWEST SA62 6NH (0437 710263).

St. David's

Smallest cathedral city in Britain, shrine of Wales' patron saint. Magnificent ruins of Bishop's Palace. Craft shops, farm parks and museums; boat trips to Ramsey Island.

MR P. W. REES, 'QUALITY COTTAGES', CERBID, SOLVA, HAVERFORDWEST, PEMBROKESHIRE SA62 6YE (0348 837871). Cottages set in all coastal areas, unashamed luxury; highest residential standards. Dishwashers, microwaves, washing machines. Log fires. Linen supplied, pets welcome. *[pw!]*

RAMSEY HOUSE, LOWER MOOR, ST DAVID'S SA62 6RP (0437 720321). WTB 3 Crowns Highly Commended; RAC Acclaimed. Mac and Sandra Thompson offer a warm welcome in superior accommodation (most en suite). Cosy bar. Private parking. Open all year. Superb beaches and walks nearby – DOGS' PARADISE! *[pw!]*

TREVACCOON FARM, ST DAVID'S, HAVERFORDWEST SA62 6DP (0348 831438). Large comfortable farmhouse; four family rooms and one double, all en suite. TV lounge; dinner licence; play area. Children welcome; pets welcome by arrangement. Self catering cottages also available. *[£1 per night.]*

JILL AND ROBIN MOORE, IDYLLIC COTTAGES, TREVINE, NEAR ST DAVIDS SA62 5AG (0348 837865). Beautiful coast and country locations in Pembrokeshire. Our specialist agency can offer you a selection of warm, comfortable cottages sleeping from 2–8. Most welcome a pet.

Delightful farmhouse 6 miles from St. David's. 3 bedrooms sleeping 4 adults and 3 children. Fully equipped except linen. Electricity by coin meter. APPLY: MRS C. E. SKEEL JONES, AROSFYR FARM, DOLGELLAU LL40 2YP (0341 422 355).

Saundersfoot

Popular resort and sailing centre with picturesque harbour and sandy beach. Tenby 3 miles.

VINE FARM, THE RIDGEWAY, SAUNDERSFOOT SA69 9LA (0834 813543). Former Farmhouse close to village and beaches. Central heating, log fires. All rooms en-suite. Pets welcome – garden and paddock. AA Listed QQQ. *[pw! £1.00 per night.]* Also available, one-bedroomed Self Catering flat for 2.

Solva

Picturesque coastal village with sheltered harbour and excellent craft shops. Sailing and watersports; sea fishing; long sandy beach.

MRS M. J. PROBERT, YNYS DAWEL, SOLVA, HAVERFORDWEST SA62 6UF (0437 721491). Quality Cottages in Solva near safe, sandy beaches. Highest standards. Enclosed rear gardens. Modern central heating. Resident owners. Particularly warm welcome to Boxer dogs (and others) and their owners. *[£7/£10 per week.]*

MRS M. JONES, LOCHMEYLER FARM, PEN-Y-CWM, NR SOLVA, HAVERFORD-WEST SA62 6LL (0348 837724). Modernised farmhouse on 220 acre dairy farm retains all its old character. Smokers' lounge, video library. Choice of menus including traditional farmhouse and vegetarian. Children over 10 welcome. Open all year. *[pw! £3 per night in house. Free in outside kennels or in car.]*

MR P. W. REES, 'QUALITY COTTAGES', CERBID, SOLVA, HAVERFORDWEST, PEMBROKESHIRE SA62 6YE (0348 837871). Cottages set in all coastal areas; unashamed luxury; dishwashers, microwaves, washing machines – highest residential standards. Log fires. Linen provided. Pets welcome. *[pw!]*

UPPER VANLEY, PEN-Y-CWM, NEAR SOLVA, PEMBROKESHIRE SA62 6LJ (0348 831418). Old farmhouse, near coast and beaches, castles, Solva Harbour and St. David's. All rooms en-suite, colour TV, teamaking facilities. Traditional food. Diningroom. Lounge. Garden. Licensed. Bed and Breakfast from £16; Bed, Breakfast and Evening Meal £26. *[pw!]*

Tenby

Popular resort with two wide beaches. Fishing trips, craft shops, museum. Medieval castle ruins, 13th century church. Golf, fishing and watersports; boat trips to nearby Caldy Island with monastery and medieval church.

MRS J. N. FRAZER, HIGHLANDS FARM, MANORBIER-NEWTON, TENBY SA70 8PX (0834 871446). Spacious six-berth caravan situated in quiet three-acre meadow. Caravan has electric lighting and TV, gas cooker and heater. Two separate bedrooms, shower, kitchen/diner and lounge. Car essential. Peaceful setting, ideal for children or well-behaved pet. Please write or phone for details.

MR P. W. REES, 'QUALITY COTTAGES', CERBID, SOLVA, HAVERFORDWEST, PEMBROKESHIRE SA62 6YE (0348 837871). Cottages set in all coastal areas, unashamed luxury; highest residential standards. Dishwashers, microwaves, washing machines. Log fires. Linen provided, pets welcome. *[pw!]*

WEST GLAMORGAN

Gower

Britain's first designated Area of Outstanding Natural Beauty with numerous sandy beaches and countryside to explore.

POWELLS COTTAGE HOLIDAYS, 61 HIGH STREET, SAUNDERSFOOT, PEM-BROKESHIRE, DYFED SA69 9EJ (0834 813232). Cottages along the coasts of Pembrokeshire, The Gower, and West of England. Also inland riverside and the countryside. Well equipped; some with swimming pool. Jacuzzi baths. Pets welcome.

MRS D. A. STILL, CULVER HOUSE, PORT EYNON, GOWER SA3 1NN (0792 390755). Small, friendly hotel with fabulous food and quality service. Peacefully situated, with superb coast and countryside. En suite, sea views. DB&B from £29.50. WTB 3 Crowns Highly Commended. *[£2 per night.]*

GWENT

GWENT *Abergavenny, Raglan*

THE HALF MOON, LLANTHONY, NEAR ABERGAVENNY 🍺
NP7 7NN Tel: (0873 890611)
Friendly 17th-century inn. Serves good food and real ale. Enjoy wonderful
scenery of Black Mountains. Good base. Walking, pony trekking.
Dogs welcome.

THE GRANGE
PENRHOS, RAGLAN NP5 2LQ

Traditional 115-acre working farm off the beaten
track between Abergavenny and Monmouth. Walk,
picnic or join in work! Many interesting places to visit;
local golf, fishing, riding. Bring dogs and horses!
New large en-suite rooms. BED AND BREAKFAST
FROM £16.00, reductions for children and longer
holidays.
Come and share this beautiful place.

MRS J.E. THOM   WTB 🦢🦢   Tel: 0600 85202

Abergavenny

*Historic market town at south-eastern gateway to Brecon Beacons National Park. Pony trekking,
leisure centre; excellent touring base for Vale of Usk.*

CHRISTINE SMITH, THE HALF MOON, LLANTHONY, NEAR ABERGAVENNY NP7
7NN (0873 890611). Friendly 17th-century inn. Serves good food and real ale. Enjoy
wonderful scenery of Black Mountains. Good base. Walking, pony trekking. Dogs
welcome. 1 Crown. *[🐾]*

Newport

*Port and resort on the River Usk, 10 miles north-east of Cardiff. Noted for interesting transporter
bridge and ruins of 12th century castle.*

MR P. W. REES, 'QUALITY COTTAGES', CERBID, SOLVA, HAVERFORDWEST,
PEMBROKESHIRE SA62 6YE (0348 837871). Cottages set in all coastal areas,
unashamed luxury; highest residential standards. Dishwashers, washing machines,
microwaves. Log fires. Linen supplied. Pets welcome. *[pw!]*

Raglan

Village situated 7 miles south of Monmouth. Remains of 15th century castle nearby.

MRS J. E. THOM, THE GRANGE, PENRHOS, RAGLAN NP5 2LQ (0600 85202).
Traditional 115-acre farm, off beaten track between Abergavenny and Monmouth.
Local golf, fishing, riding and walks. Bring dogs, horses. Rooms en-suite. Bed and
Breakfast from £16; reductions children and longer stays. *[🐾]*

Wye Valley

Scenic area, ideal for relaxation.

MR & MRS J. LLEWELLYN, CWRT-Y-GAER, WOLVESNEWTON, CHEPSTOW
NP6 6PR (0291 650700). 1,4 or more dogs welcomed free. Owners self-cater in
attractively converted stone buildings of Welsh Long House. 20 acres, super views of
Usk Vale. Quiet. Brochure. Some units suitable for disabled. *[🐾]*

GWYNEDD *Llandudno, Tywyn*

☙ ☙ ☙ | Highly Commended

Hen Dŷ Hotel

10 North Parade, Llandudno, Gwynedd LL30 2LP
Tel: (0492) 876184

CHARLES & IRENE WATTS welcome you to the
Hen Dŷ Hotel, set on the promenade, opposite the Pier.
Wonderful panoramic views over the Bay. All bedrooms have radio, TV, teamakers, central heating; some
ensuite. Enjoy the Chef/Proprietor's menu and the cosy Residents' Bar. Tariff from £17.50
to £27.00 per night. Pets welcome by arrangement. We are close to shops, Happy Valley,
Dry Ski Slope, Great Orme Summit. Our priority is YOUR comfort and enjoyment.

COASTAL HOUSE TYWYN GWYNEDD
3 bedrooms
Sleeps five
£115–£185
per week

* 2 minutes' walk to sandy beach
* 2 minutes' walk to pub/bar meals
* Fully eqiupped as own home
* Garden front and rear. * Garage
* 8 doors from the home bakery
* Tal-y-llyn Steam Railway walking distance
* Pets welcome FREE OF CHARGE

Enquiries: **Mr and Mrs Ian Weston, 18 Elizabeth Road,**
Basingstoke, Hampshire RG22 6AX Tel: 0256 52364

Abergynolwyn

A pretty little village standing on the Dysynni and Gwernol Rivers. A few miles from the sea and ideal for Snowdonia National Park and nearby Cader Idris. Tywyn 5 miles.

RIVERSIDE GUEST HOUSE, SHOP AND CAFE, ABERGYNOLWYN, TYWYN LL36 9YR (0654 782235). Warm welcome, homely. Central heating, washbasins, tea/ coffee facilities. Access during day. TV lounge. Dogs welcome. Ideal for Talyllyn Railway, Cader Idris, birdwatching, seaside, fishing, sightseeing. Bed and Breakfast £11-£15. OAP/child reductions – up to 16 years. Weekly terms/Off Season Mini Breaks. SAE for details. *[🐾]*

Abersoch

Dinghy sailing and windsurfing centre with safe sandy beaches. Pony trekking, golf, fishing and sea trips.

MR P. W. REES, 'QUALITY COTTAGES', CERBID, SOLVA, HAVERFORDWEST, PEMBROKESHIRE SA62 6YE (0348 837871). Cottages set in all coastal areas, unashamed luxury; highest residential standards. Dishwashers, microwaves, washing machines. Log fires. Linen supplied. Pets welcome. *[pw!]*

Bala

Natural touring centre for Snowdonia. Narrow-gauge railway runs along side of Bala Lake, the largest natural lake in Wales. Golf, sailing, fishing, canoeing.

MRS ANN SKINNER, TALYBONT ISA, RHYDUCHAF, BALA LL23 7SD (0678 520234). Bed and Breakfast, optional Evening Meal, on the farm. Also two 6 to 8 berth Caravans with all modern conveniences. Just two miles from Bala Lake. Ideal for walking, sailing, fishing, golfing. *[🐕]*

Barmouth

Modern seaside resort with two miles of sandy beaches. Surrounding hills full of interesting archaeological remains.

LAWRENNY LODGE HOTEL, BARMOUTH LL42 1SU (0341 280466). Quiet, family-run hotel overlooking harbour and estuary but only 5 minutes from town. Most rooms en-suite, all with TV, tea/coffee making facilities and clock/radio alarms. Restaurant menu includes vegetarian dishes. Residential licence. Large car park. 3 Crowns.

Beddgelert

Delightfully picturesque village in scenic landscape 4 miles south of Snowdon.

COLWYN, BEDDGELERT, GWYNEDD (0766.86.276) ♛♛♛ Joan Williams. Small friendly 18th century cottage guesthouse, beams, original stone fireplace; most rooms en-suite, white linen, central heating. Overlooking river in picturesque village centre at the foot of Snowdon, surrounded by wooded mountains, lakes and streams. Small shops, inns, cafes in village. Discount on bookings of three or more days. B&B from £16–£19. Booking advisable. (Also cottage, sleeps two, £125–£185).

Betws-y-Coed

Popular mountain resort in picturesque setting where three rivers meet. Trout fishing, craft shops, golf, railway and motor museums, Snowdonia National Park Visitor Centre. Nearby Swallow Falls are famous beauty spot.

SUMMER HILL NON-SMOKERS' GUEST HOUSE, BETWS-Y-COED LL24 0BL (0690 710306). Quiet location, overlooking river. 150 yards from main road, shops. Washbasins, tea-making. Residents' lounge. TV. Singles, children, pets welcome. Car parking. EM available. B&B from £14.00. *[£1 per night.]*

Caernarvon

Historic walled town and resort, ideal for touring Snowdonia. Museums, Segontium Roman Fort, magnificent 13th century castle. Old harbour, sailing trips.

OUR WORLD BY THE SEA. Executive Beach Bungalows. Villa Chalets and Luxury Caravans with your own beach moments from your door. Fully equipped. Ideal base for touring. BEACH HOLIDAY, WEST POINT, THE BEACH, PONTLLYFNI, CAERNARVON LL54 5ET. *[£2/£5 nightly.]*

MRS B. CARTWRIGHT, TAN DINAS, LLANDDEINIOLEN, CAERNARVON LL55 3AR (0248 670098). Comfortable friendly farmhouse. Large grounds. Ideal touring, set between mountains and sea. TV lounge, separate dining room and tables. Open March to October. Evening Meal, Bed and Breakfast £16, Bed & Breakfast £13. WTB Listed. *[🐕pw!]*

Conwy

One of the best preserved medieval fortified towns in Britain on dramatic estuary setting. Telford Suspension Bridge, many historic buildings, lively quayside (site of smallest house in Britain). Golf, pony trekking, pleasure cruises.

GWERN BORTER COUNTRY MANOR, NEAR CONWY LL32 8YL (0492 650360). 3 miles from the coast. Total peace and quiet. 10 acres of beautiful grounds. Luxury accommodation (WTB Highly Commended) with fine food or choose one of our self catering cottages. *[🐕]*

THE LODGE, TAL-Y-BONT, CONWY LL32 8YX (0492 660766; Fax: 0492 660534). Family-run Hotel with lovely en suite bedrooms. Enjoy peace and quiet, superb food and attention from friendly and efficient staff. B&B from £20; 2 nights DB&B from £57.50. Pets welcome.

PINEWOOD TOWERS COUNTRY GUEST HOUSE, SYCHNANT PASS ROAD, CONWY LL32 8BZ (0492 592459). Dogs, cats. One of the few Guest Houses catering for animal lovers and their pets, being fully equipped in the right surroundings. 10 acres of gardens and paddocks, with own stream and woods. *[pw! 75p per night.]*

Criccieth

Popular family resort with safe beaches divided by ruins of 13th century castle. Salmon and sea trout fishing; Festival of Music & Arts in summer.

WERNOL CARAVAN PARK, CHWILOG FAWR, CHWILOG, PWLLHELI LL53 6SW (0766 810506). Family run park in elevated position offers accommodation in superior detached chalets with colour TV, microwave, etc. Luxury Farmhouse also available. Convenient for beach, touring, etc. *[£10 weekly.]*

M. JONES, YNYS GRAIANOG, YNYS, CRICCIETH LL52 0NT (076 675 234). Modernised cottages, sleep 2/12. Peaceful rural setting. Also 6-berth caravan. Convenient for Snowdonia, Lleyn Peninsula. Ample parking. Cot, colour TV. *[🐕]*

MR P. W. REES, 'QUALITY COTTAGES', CERBID, SOLVA, HAVERFORDWEST, PEMBROKESHIRE SA62 6YE (0348 837871). Cottages set in all coastal areas, unashamed luxury; equipped to highest residential standards with dishwashers, washing machines, microwaves. Log fires. Linen provided. Pets welcome. *[pw!]*

MRS A. M. JONES, BETWS-BACH, YNYS, CRICCIETH, GWYNEDD LL52 0PB (Tel and Fax: 0758 720 047/0766 810 295). Traditional stone-built Farm Cottages. Situated in peaceful secluded grounds amidst fine walking countryside. Sleep 2-6. All home comforts. Full heating – open all year. WTB Grade 5. *[🐕]*

Dolgellau

Picturesque market town with buildings made from dark local slate. Many interesting walks in the area giving fine views across Cambrian Mountains.

Delightful Cottage with panoramic views. Sleeps four adults plus one child. Cot available. Fully equipped except linen. Also available, new luxury Farm Bungalow for four, and a Flat for two in Dolgellau. APPLY: MRS C. E. SKEEL JONES, AROSFYR FARM, DOLGELLAU LL40 2YP (0341 422 355). *[One dog free, £15 each additional dog.]*

Fairbourne

Bright little resort facing Barmouth across the Mawddach estuary. Safe spacious sands. A short distance inland is Cader Idris. Dolgellau 9 miles.

THE FAIRBOURNE HOTEL, FAIRBOURNE LL38 2HQ (0341 250203). Views of Cardigan Bay from own grounds. Licensed. Private bathrooms. Bowls green. Games room. Car park. Open all year. Pets welcome. WTB 3 Crowns Highly Commended. [🛏]

Harlech

Small stone-built town dominated by remains of 13th century castle. Golf, theatre, swimming pool, fine stretch of sands.

FRON DEG GUEST HOUSE, LLANFAIR, HARLECH LL46 2RE (0766 780448). Small Georgian cottage overlooking beach at Harlech. Pretty bedrooms. Central for unspoiled beaches and countryside; within easy reach of Porthmadog. Reasonable terms for Bed and Breakfast, also Dinner.

Llandudno

Premier holiday resort of North Wales coast flanked by Great Orme and Little Orme headlands. Wide promenade, pier, two beaches; water ski-ing, sailing, fishing trips from jetty. Excellent sports facilities: golf, indoor pool, tennis, pony trekking, Leisure Centre. Summer variety shows, Alice in Wonderland Visitor Centre.

MR AND MRS C. WATTS, HEN DŶ HOTEL, 10 NORTH PARADE, LLANDUDNO LL30 2LP (0492 876184). Experience the warm welcome extended by the proprietors of this charming Hotel, set opposite the Pier, with panoramic views. All rooms with central heating, TV, radio, teamakers; some en suite. Good food. Cosy bar. From £17.50 per night. 3 Crowns Highly Commended. [🛏]

MR AND MRS J. WILLIAMS, 'DEVA', 34 TRINITY AVENUE, LLANDUDNO LL30 2TQ (0492 877059). Holiday Flats for 2/4 adults. House-trained pets welcome. Car parking. Colour Television. Bed linen provided. Park opposite to walk your dog. Stamp please for brochure. [🛏]

HEADLANDS HOTEL, HILL TERRACE, LLANDUDNO LL30 2LS (0492 877485). Personal service and comfort at this AA, RAC, Ashley Courtenay recommended Hotel. Adjoining Snowdonia. All rooms with TV, Teasmaid; most with private facilities. Telephone for brochure.

THE WILSON FAMILY, EDCLIFFE HOTEL, PROMENADE, LLANDUDNO LL30 1BG (0492 878494). Friendly family Hotel. Colour TV, tea/coffee facilities and central heating all 25 bedrooms. Bed and Breakfast, optional Evening Dinner. Bar snacks. 13 bedrooms en-suite, 22 have sea views. [🛏]

Porthmadog

Harbour town with mile-long Cob embankment, along which runs Ffestiniog Narrow Gauge Steam Railway to Blaenau Ffestiniog. Pottery, maritime museum, car museum. Good beaches nearby.

BLACK ROCK SANDS, PORTHMADOG. Private site, beach 150 yards. 14 Caravans only. Fully equipped 6 berths. Own flush toilets. Showers and televisions. Shop and tavern near. APPLY – E. H. HUMPHRIES, 251 HEDNESFORD ROAD, NORTON CANES, CANNOCK, STAFFORDSHIRE WS11 3RZ (Heath Hayes [0543] 279583 evenings).

Pwllheli

Popular sailing centre with harbour and long sandy beach. Golf, leisure centre, river and sea fishing.

MRS M. PARRY ROBERTS, 'TY FRY', ABERDARON, PWLLHELI LL53 8BY (075 886 274). Modernised, fully furnished Cottage with views over Aberdaron Bay. Two bedrooms sleeping 5, cot; bathroom; large lounge, TV; kitchen/diner, cooker, fridge; metered electricity. Ample parking. Sandy beaches and coves, mountain walks nearby. Pets welcome. Booking March-October; SAE please.

Snowdonia

Craggy mountains, steep valleys and jewel-like lakes make up the Snowdonia National Park, whose chief attraction is Snowdon itself. Also tranquil villages and castles built by Welsh princes.

UPPER LLANDWROG. WTB 3 Dragon Award. Cherished crafted, comfortable, family mountain cottages, sleep 4/6. Posture beds, patchworked. Cots. Fitted kitchens, washing machines. Showers, bath. Stone-walled peaceful gardens. Magnificent views. £100–£275. The REVD & MRS E. J. S. PLAXTON, THE VICARAGE, VICARAGE ROAD, LINGFIELD, SURREY RH7 6HA (0342 832021).

Tywyn

Pleasant seaside resort, start of Talyllyn Narrow Gauge Railway. Sea and river fishing, golf.

Fully equipped coastal house, close to sandy beach. Sleeps five. Gardens; garage. Pets welcome free of charge. APPLY – MR AND MRS WESTON, 18 ELIZABETH ROAD, BASINGSTOKE, HAMPSHIRE RG22 6AX (0256 52364). [🐕]

POWYS

POWYS   *Brecon, Crickhowell, Llandrindod Wells*

MAES-Y-COED FARM, LLANDEFALLE, BRECON LD3 0WD

Three Crowns. Comfortable, friendly, 17th century farmhouse with oak beams offers you a warm welcome. Ideal centre for walking and touring. One family and one double bedded room en suite; one twin-bedded room with washbasin. All rooms have tea-making facilities. Bed and Breakfast; Evening Dinner by arrangement.
Mrs Sue Morgan
Tel: 0874 754211

Mrs P. Llewelyn WHITE HALL, Glangrwyney, Crickhowell, Powys NP8 1 EW

Comfortably furnished and well placed for exploring Black Mountains, Brecon Beacons, Big Pit Mine, Abergavenny and Hay-on-Wye. Double and twin-bedded rooms with TV and tea-making. Terms: from £15 (en suite available). Small single £13.00. **Phone (0873) 811155 or 840267.**

WTB 2 Crowns

The Park Motel
Crossgates
Llandrindod Wells,
Powys LD1 6RF
Tel: (0597) 851201
W.T.B. 2 Crowns

Set in 3 acres, amidst beautiful Mid-Wales countryside, near the famous Elan Valley reservoirs and centrally situated for touring. Accommodation in modern luxury self-contained centrally heated Chalets, each with twin-bedded room and shower room with WC, tea/coffee-making facilities. Colour TV, kitchenette for self-catering option. Licensed restaurant open all day for meals and bar snacks. Lounge bar. Swimming-pool. Children's play area. Ample parking. Pets welcome. Resident proprietors. Games room. Brochure available.

Brecon

Main touring centre for National Park. Busy market, Jazz Festival in summer. Brecknock Museum, ruined castle, cathedral of interest. Golf, walking, fishing, canal cruising, pony trekking.

BEACONS GUEST HOUSE, 16 BRIDGE STREET, BRECON LD3 8AH (0874 623339). All friendly doggies (and owners) welcome to our guest house, close to town centre. Comfortable rooms, most en-suite, all with colour TV and beverage trays. Private parking. Cosy bar, residents' lounge and coffee shop. Excellent home cooking. "Taste of Wales" Recommended. AA Listed. WTB 3 Crowns Commended. Bargain Breaks from £49. Brochure available.

MRS ANN PHILLIPS, TYLEBRYTHOS FARM, CANTREF, BRECON LD3 8LR (0874 86329). WTB Grade 4. Self catering cottages situated amongst spectacular scenery in Brecon Beacons. Well equipped. Personally supervised. Open all year. Short Breaks. Ideal location for touring and lovers of "Great Outdoors". ⋔⋋pw!⏌

MRS SUE MORGAN, MAES-Y-COED FARM, LLANDEFALLE, BRECON LD3 0WD (0874 754211). Comfortable, friendly 17th century farmhouse offers you a warm welcome. One family and one double room en suite; one twin-bedded room with washbasin. Bed and Breakfast; Evening Dinner by arrangement. Three Crowns.

Builth Wells

Old country town in lovely setting on River Wye amid beautiful hills. Lively sheep and cattle markets; host to Royal Welsh Agricultural Show.

R. I. AND M. C. WILTSHIRE, BRON WYE GUEST HOUSE, 5 CHURCH STREET, BUILTH WELLS LD2 3BS (0982 553587). Bed and Breakfast. Evening Meals by prior arrangement. Snacks, home cooking. Licensed. TV Lounge. Tea/coffee making all rooms, en suites available. Car park. Children and pets welcome. Bed & Breakfast from £12, en suite £15 per person. Evening Meal £6.50 per person. WTB Three Crowns. *[🛪]*

Crickhowell

Pleasant village in the Usk Valley at foot of Black Mountains. 16th cent. bridge, fine Georgian houses, fragments of a castle, gateway of a long-vanished manor house, and 14th cent. church with elaborate tombs and memorials.

PRISCILLA LLEWELYN WHITE HALL, GLANGRWYNEY, CRICKHOWELL NP8 1EW (0873 811155 or 840267). Comfortably furnished and well placed for exploring Black Mountains, Brecon Beacons etc. En suite double and twin rooms with TV and tea-making. Terms on request. Pets welcome. WTB 2 Crowns. *[🛪]*

Garthmyl

Situated on A483 between Welshpool and Newtown in unspoiled countryside.

Self-catering luxury in beautiful log cabins set in 30 acres of unspoilt woodland. Central heating, colour TV, microwave, etc. Pets welcome. From £175 to £535 per week. APPLY – PENLLWYN LODGES, GARTHMYL SY15 6SB (0686 640 269).

Gladestry

Rural village on the Powys/Hereford & Worcester border, ideal for touring. Hay-on-Wye 10 miles, Kington 3.

MRS E. M. PINCHES, GWAITHLA BUNGALOW, GLADESTRY, KINGTON, HERE-FORD HR5 3NT (postal) (054 422 256). Hereford/Wales border. Remote farm Cottage. 3 bedrooms. All modern conveniences. Sleeps 7/8 plus cot. Ideal for walking and bird watching.

Llandrindod Wells

Popular inland resort, Victorian spa town, excellent touring centre. Golf, fishing, bowling, boating and tennis. Visitors can still take the waters at Rock Park Gardens.

THE PARK MOTEL, CROSSGATES, LLANDRINDOD WELLS LD1 6RF (0597 851201). In three acres, amidst beautiful countryside near Elan Valley. Luxury, self-contained, centrally heated Chalets. Licensed restaurant open all day. Swimming pool. Children's play area. Pets welcome. *[£1 per night, £5 per week.]*

Llangurig

Village on River Wye 4 miles south-west of Llanidloes. Craft centre and monastic 14th century church. Ideal walking countryside.

THE OLD VICARAGE COUNTRY GUEST HOUSE, LLANGURIG, MONTGOMERY-SHIRE SY18 6RN (05515 280). Charming Victorian house, ideal base for exploring the mountains and valleys of this unspoiled area. All bedrooms en suite. Two guest lounges; licensed dining room. WTB 3 Crowns Highly Commended. [🐾]

BLACK LION HOTEL, LLANGURIG, MONTGOMERYSHIRE SY18 6SG (05515 223). Small friendly hotel with licensed bar. Some rooms en suite, some with colour TV. Residents' lounge. Home cooked food lunchtime and evening. Large car park. Excellent centre for touring or walking. Pets free if "Pets Welcome" mentioned. [🐾]

Presteigne

An attractive old town with half-timbered houses. Ideal for hillside rambles and pony trekking.

MRS R. L. JONES, UPPER HOUSE, KINNERTON, NEAR PRESTEIGNE LD8 2PE (WHITTON [054 76] 207). Charming Tudor cottage in lovely Border countryside. 2 miles from Offa's Dyke. Children and pets welcome. Storage heaters, colour TV, log fire. Linen hire optional. Sleeps 5 plus 2 cots. Ample parking. Sun trap garden. On working farm in peaceful hamlet. WTB Grade 3. [🐾]

Welshpool

Lively market town with medieval streets. Narrow gauge Welshpool and Llanfair Light Railway runs along restored 8-mile track. Shrewsbury 17 miles.

LORDS BUILDINGS FARM, LEIGHTON, NEAR WELSHPOOL. Set in 73 acres with panoramic views. Sleeps 7 plus cot. Everything provided except linen. Ideal touring base. Children and pets welcome. MR G. R. EDWARDS, WINDMILL FARM, HALFWAY HOUSE, NEAR SHREWSBURY, SHROPSHIRE SY5 9EJ (0743 884 356). [🐾]

SCOTLAND

SCOTLAND   *Ballindalloch, Beattock, Biggar, Blairgowrie, Brechin, Burnhouse*

♛♛♛♛! Commended **BEECHGROVE COTTAGES, TOMNAVOULIN & GLENLIVET**
Traditional Highland Cottages near the Rivers Livet and Avon, in very scenic area. Each sleeps 2 to 6 persons; 2 double bedrooms, bathroom/shower; fully equipped dining/kitchen, livingroom with colour TV. All electric. Linen supplied. Central for Coast, Spey Valley, Aviemore, Dee Valley, Balmoral. Skiing at Lecht Ski Centre 20 minutes, Glen Shee 45 minutes. Open all year. Car essential. Children and pets welcome. Terms £150 to £250.
Apply: **MRS J. WHITE, BEECHGROVE, TOMNAVOULIN, BALLINDALLOCH AB3 9JA (0807 590220)**

♛♛♛ **BEATTOCK HOUSE HOTEL & CARAVAN PARK**   AA/▶▶
This 2 Star hotel is an ideal place to rest from the busy A74 from Glasgow to the South. Restaurant and bar (full day licence) 11am to 11pm. Unrivalled as a touring base for Galloway, Burns Country and the Lake District. Free fishing on River Evan in grounds, permits available for parts of the Annan, stalking and rough shooting can be arranged. Golf, tennis and riding nearby. Caravan Park has toilets and showers with H&C, and electric hook-ups for touring vans. Patrons welcome in Hotel restaurant and bars.
Beattock, Dumfriesshire DG10 9QB-Tel: Beattock (06833) 403

CARMICHAEL COUNTRY COTTAGES
CARMICHAEL ESTATE, BY BIGGAR, CLYDESDALE ML12 6 PG
Tel: 08993 336 Fax: 08993 481 *3 Crowns Commended–5 Crowns Highly Commended*
Our stone cottages nestle in the woods and fields of our historic family-run estate. Ideal homes for families, pets and particularly dogs. Walking trails, private tennis, fishing, restaurant/farm shop. 12 cottages, 25 bedrooms. Open all year. Central location. £160 to £425 per week.

PERTHSHIRE AND CENTRAL HIGHLANDS

* A choice of 1–3 bedroom self-catering Scandinavian-style chalets in 2 acres parkland, only 5 minutes walk from shops and town centre.
* OPEN ALL YEAR. Spring/Autumn short breaks welcome in warm, fully-equipped, comfortable accommodation. Colour TV. Tennis. Children's amenities on site.

* Ideal centre for touring in all directions. Golf (40 courses within an hour's drive), walking and fishing holidays.

For detailed brochure and bookings, please write or telephone:
ALTAMOUNT CHALETS, BLAIRGOWRIE, PERTHSHIRE PH10 6JN
Tel: (0250) 873324 Fax: (0250) 875733

NORTHERN HOTEL   STB AA**   ♛♛♛ Approved
2 CLERK STREET, BRECHIN DD9 6AE Tel: (0356) 625505

Family run hotel; 90% rooms en suite. All with TV, direct-dial phones, tea/coffee making facilities. Halfway between Dundee and Aberdeen. Plenty of parks and walks for pets and owners. Fishing, golf. Lots of wildlife in glens, nearest 7 miles; coast 9 miles.

Manor Farm Hotel
Burnhouse, By Beith, Ayrshire KA15 1LJ
Tel: 0560 484006

En suite accommodation within a farmhouse setting provides an ideal "home" for a tranquil holiday with a few added luxuries–without the added price!
We are situated 50 yards from the A736 Glasgow to Irvine road, making us the perfect base for touring Burns Country, the South West coastline, the Trossachs and Glasgow, with plenty of things to see and do for the whole family e.g. Magnum Leisure Centre, Kelburn Country Park, Culzean Castle.
9 rooms (some family), most en suite, all with washbasin, colour TV, tea making facilities and central heating.
Personally run by the Robertson family.   **Brochure on request.**

256

Roslin Cottage Guest House

Lagrannoch, Callander, Perthshire FK17 8LE
Telephone: 0877 330638 Lynne & Alistair Ferguson
"Good Walkies Area"

Situated on the outskirts of Callander, the Gateway to the Trossachs. Roslin Cottage has recently been restored yet still retains many original features including stone walls, beams and an open fireplace in the lounge. We offer a varied Scottish breakfast with Evening Meals on request. We use our own produce when available which includes eggs from our hens, ducks or geese, and honey from our apiary. We have 1 double, 1 twin and 2 single rooms, all with central heating, washbasins and tea/coffee makers. Bed and Breakfast from £12.50 per peson per night; four course evening meal from £11 per person. Brochure on request. Ideal touring base, with sailing, fishing, walking, climbing, mountain biking etc. all on the doorstep. Your dogs sleep in your room and are welcome in the lounge and in our large enclosed garden.

REDUCED WEEKLY RATES   **DOGS ESPECIALLY WELCOME (and stay free)**

BARNCROSH FARM
CASTLE DOUGLAS

Write or 'phone for brochure to:
P. W. Ball, Barncrosh, Castle Douglas
Kirkcudbrightshire DG7 1TX. Tel: Bridge of Dee (055-668) 216.

Enjoy a peaceful relaxing holiday in beautiful rural surroundings on a working farm near coast and hills. Comfortable Cottages for 2-6. Heated and fully equipped including linen. Colour TV. Children and dogs welcome. Scottish Tourist Board Commended 🌸 🌸 🌸 🌸

Our views are breath-taking – both from the hotel and the numerous miles of wonderful walks around us. "Skye" and "Raasay", our lovable labradors (together with owners, Ann and Martyn) look forward to welcoming you and your dog(s) to their lovely home. You'll enjoy good "Taste of Scotland" food, log fires and a well-equipped bedroom, in which you are as welcome as your dog!

Coul House Hotel

Contin, By Strathpeffer,
Ross-shire IV14 9EY
Tel: 0997 421487 Fax: 0997 421945

TORGUISH HOUSE, DAVIOT, INVERNESS

Once the local Manse, TORGUISH HOUSE is now a homely Guest House offering comfortable bedrooms, some with en suite facilities. Comfortable lounge with TV and welcoming log fire. B&B from £11, £15 en suite; D, B&B from £20, £24 en suite. Adventure play area for children, and reduced rates. Ideal base for touring; golf and fishing nearby. Self-catering also available.

DIRECTIONS: From the North on the A9, four miles south of Inverness, Torguish is 150 yards on the **LEFT** past the sign for Croy and Culloden. **From the South** on the A9, move into the right hand lane after passing the Daviot East junction (B9154). Access to Torguish approx. 200 yards on the **RIGHT** across central reservation.

For detailed brochure
phone **0463 772208**

Redheugh Hotel

Bayswell Park, Dunbar EH42 1AE
(0368) 62793

Cliff top location. Small comfortable licensed hotel with emphasis on personal attention. All rooms en suite, with colour TV, tea/coffee facilities, telephone etc. Only 28 miles from Edinburgh yet ideal for touring Borders. Country Park and scenic walks nearby. Pets welcome. Good home cooking. B&B from £55 per night for two people. AA/RAC**. Les Routiers.

🌸🌸🌸
Commended

FREE and REDUCED RATE Holiday Visits!
Don't miss our Readers' Offer Vouchers on
pages 5 to 20.

CHARACTER COTTAGES. Hundreds of unique cottages to spend the perfect holiday in. Pets welcome in most cottages, for just £10 per week. Let us help you discover your ideal holiday home. CHARACTER COTTAGES, ADMAIL 334, SIDMOUTH, DEVON EX10 8AD (0282 445142).

Aberdour (Fife)

Small resort on north shore of Firth of Forth 3 miles west of Burntisland. Remains of 17th century castle.

THE WOODSIDE HOTEL, HIGH STREET, ABERDOUR KY3 0SW (0383 860328). You will be made welcome in 3 star comfort. Enjoy the good restaurant, or the tasty food in the bar. You will find the hotel ideally situated for walking your dog. Easy reach to Edinburgh. B&B from £26.50 each. [🐶]

Aultbea (Highland)

Village on east shore of Loch Ewe, five miles north of Poolewe on west coast of Ross and Cromarty.

MRS P. MACRAE, 'COVEVIEW', 36 MELLON CHARLES, AULTBEA IV22 2JL (0445 731351). Wester Ross is ideal for hill walking or a quiet, restful holiday. Two detached cottages in own garden, each with two double bedrooms, sitting room, bathroom and mini kitchen. From £140 per week. B&B also available. [🐶]

Ballachulish (Highland)

Impressively placed village at entrance to Glencoe and on Loch Leven. Magnificent mountain scenery including Sgorr Dhearg (3362ft.). Good centre for boating, climbing and sailing. Glasgow 89 miles, Oban 38, Fort William 14, Kinlochleven 9.

BALLACHULISH HOTEL, BALLACHULISH, NEAR FORT WILLIAM PA39 4JY (08552 606; Fax: 08552 629). Escape to the magnificent West Highlands and enjoy a stylish, high value break. Luxurious accommodation and warm, friendly service. Set above Loch Linnhe, ideal base for touring.

Cottages and Chalets in natural woodland sleeping 4 to 15 people. The Glencoe area is lovely for walking and perfect for nature lovers too. All pets welcome. No VAT. Brochure available. APPLY – HOUSE IN THE WOOD HOLIDAYS, GLENACHULISH, BALLACHULISH, ARGYLL PA39 4JZ (085 52 379). [🐶]

THE ISLES OF GLENCOE HOTEL AND LEISURE CENTRE, BALLACHULISH, ARGYLL PA39 4HL (08552 602; Fax: 08552 629). Almost afloat! Scotland's wonderful new Hotel, tiered down a hillside. Stylish bedrooms, breathtaking views. Superb Restaurant. 40 acres surrounding parkland. Swimming pool. Pets welcome. SPECIAL OFFER FOR 1994 – Any 2 nights for just £39.95 per room per night! [pw! £2 per night.]

Ballindalloch (Grampian)

Baronial Castle with modern additions and alterations is the most noteworthy building in this area; set on right bank of River Avon near its confluence with River Spey 7 miles south-west of Charleston of Aberlour.

MRS J. WHITE, BEECHGROVE COTTAGES, TOMNAVOULIN, BALLINDALLOCH AB3 9JA (0807 590220). Traditional Highland Cottages in scenic area. Each sleeps 6 maximum; two double bedrooms, fully equipped dining/kitchen, living room, colour TV. All electric. Linen supplied. Central for coast and ski slopes. Open all year. Car essential. Childen and pets welcome.

Beattock (Dumfries & Galloway)

Picturesque Dumfriesshire village, ideally placed for touring Borders region and Upper Clyde Valley.

BEATTOCK HOUSE HOTEL AND CARAVAN PARK, BEATTOCK DG10 9QB (068 33 403). Ideally situated Hotel and Caravan Park for travellers wishing to rest awhile from the busy A74 or to tour the lovely Borders country, Burns Country and the Lake District. Fishing, stalking and rough shooting available. Restaurant; all-day bar licence. AA, RAC.

Biggar (Strathclyde)

Small town set round broad main street. Gasworks museum, puppet theatre seating 100, street museum displaying old shopfronts and interiors. Peebles 13 miles.

CARMICHAEL COUNTRY COTTAGES, CARMICHAEL ESTATE, BY BIGGAR ML12 6PG (08993 336 Fax: 08993 481). Our stone cottages nestle in the woods and fields of our historic family-run estate. Ideal homes for families, pets and dogs. 12 Cottages, 25 bedrooms. Open all year. £160 to £425 per week. *[᛭᛭]*

MRS MARGARET KIRBY, WALSTON MANSIONS FARMHOUSE, WALSTON, CARNWATH, LANARK ML11 8NF (089-981 338). Friendly and relaxed atmosphere. Good home cooking with home-produced meat, eggs and organic vegetables. Guest lounge with log fire, TV and video. Bedrooms with colour TV. Cot and high chair available. Biggar 5 miles. Edinburgh 24 miles. B&B £11.50, en suite £13.50; Evening Meal £7.00. FHB member. 3 Crowns Commended. *[᛭]*

Blairgowrie (Tayside)

Town in picturesque situation near Ericht Gorge. Fine touring centre. Several castles in vicinity. Pitlochry 23 miles, Dundee 20, Forfar 20, Perth 15.

ALTAMOUNT CHALETS, CUPAR ANGUS ROAD, BLAIRGOWRIE, PERTHSHIRE PH10 6JN (0250 873324). Modern, fully equipped 1, 2 and 3 bedroom Scandinavian-style Chalets. Colour television. Centrally situated for touring Highlands. Children's amenities on site. Pets welcome. *[£1.50 per night.]*

Brechin (Tayside)

Town rising steeply from River South Esk. Of note are 13th century cathedral and 11th century watchtower.

NORTHERN HOTEL, 2 CLERK STREET, BRECHIN DD9 6AE (0356 625505). Family-run Hotel; 90% rooms en suite. All with TV, direct-dial phones, tea/coffee making facilities. Halfway Dundee/Aberdeen. Good walking, fishing, golf. Lots of wildlife in glens, nearest 7 miles, coast 9 miles. STB 3 Crowns Approved, AA 2 Star. *[᛭]*

Burnhouse (Strathclyde)

In the heart of Ayrshire. Ideal for touring Burns country. Many wonderful golf courses nearby.

MANOR FARM HOTEL, BURNHOUSE, BY BEITH KA15 1LJ (0560 484006). Situated 50 yards from A736 Glasgow to Irvine, a perfect base for touring Burns' country, Trossachs and Glasgow. Nine rooms, most en suite, all with washbasin, colour TV and central heating.

Callander (Central)

Holiday resort and base for walks and drives around the Trossachs and Loch Katrine. Stirling 14 miles.

LYNNE AND ALISTAIR FERGUSON, ROSLIN COTTAGE GUEST HOUSE, LAG-RANNOCH, CALLANDER, PERTHSHIRE FK17 8LE (0877 330638). Bed and good Scottish Breakfast from £12.50 to £14.00 per person. Evening Meal optional. Comfortable accommodation in 18th century Cottage, historic features. Good "walkies" area – dogs are especially welcome. [🐾pw!]

E. L. MACLEOD, CRAIGROYSTON, 4 BRIDGE STREET, CALLANDER FK17 8AA (0877 31395). Family run Guest House. Warm welcome, home cooking. Comfortable rooms, all en suite with tea/coffee facilities, colour TV, central heating. Pets welcome. Prices from £16.50. [🐾]

Castle Douglas (Dumfries & Galloway)

Old market town northern end of Carlingwalk Loch, good touring centre for Galloway. Nearby Threave House surrounded by woodland walks and wildfowl refuge.

MR P.W. BALL, BARNCROSH FARM, CASTLE DOUGLAS, KIRKCUDBRIGHT-SHIRE DG7 1TX (Bridge of Dee [055 668] 216). Comfortable Cottages for 2-6. Fully equipped, including linen. Colour TV. Children and dogs welcome. Beautiful rural surroundings. Brochure on request. [£10 weekly.]

Contin (Highland)

Village in Ross and Cromarty district two miles south-west of Strathpeffer.

COUL HOUSE HOTEL, CONTIN, BY STRATHPEFFER IV14 9EY (0997 421487; Fax: 0997 421945). Skye and Raasay, our lovable labradors look forward to welcoming you. "Taste of Scotland" food, log fires, well-equipped bedrooms. Miles of wonderful walks. 4 Crowns Highly Commended. [🐾pw!]

Daviot (Highland)

Village 5 miles south-east of Inverness, the Highland "capital".

TORGUISH HOLIDAY HOMES, DAVIOT, INVERNESS IV1 2XQ (0463 772208; Fax: 0463 772308). Situated in the grounds of Torguish House. Local activities include fishing, golf, horse riding, hill walking; many beauty spots and places of historic interest. From £120–£280 weekly; exclusive electricity (lighting and linen supplied).

TORGUISH HOUSE, DAVIOT, INVERNESS (0463 772208). Homely Guest House, comfortable bedrooms, some with en-suite facilities. TV Lounge with log fire, armchairs. Children's adventure play area. Pets welcome. Ideal for golf, fishing, touring. Brochure on request.

Dunbar (Lothian)

Coastal resort with small harbour. Good bathing at White Sands to the south.

REDHEUGH HOTEL, BAYSWELL PARK, DUNBAR EH42 1AE (0368 62793). Small, comfortable licensed hotel, all rooms en-suite. Edinburgh 28 miles, ideal for touring Borders. Pets welcome. B&B from £55 per night for two people. STB 4 Crowns Commended.

Dunkeld (Tayside)

Charming, tiny cathedral town set in the wooded valley of the Tay. Excellent for touring Perthshire. Perth 10 miles.

BIRNAM HOTEL, DUNKELD, PERTHSHIRE PH8 0BQ (0350 727462; Fax: 0350 728979). Nestling in the Perthshire Highlands, just off the A9. 30 bedrooms with en-suite facilities. Brochure and tariff available on request. AA, RAC Three Star. [🐕]

Dunoon (Strathclyde)

Lively resort reached by car ferry from Gourock. Cowal Highland Gathering held at end of August.

ENMORE HOTEL, MARINE PARADE, DUNOON PA23 8HH (0369 2230). Small luxury Hotel with well-tended garden, situated overlooking the beautiful Firth of Clyde. Own shingle beach. Promenade and superb walking in the hills and forests within five minutes' drive. Owners have retriever and standard poodle. STB 4 Crowns Highly Commended. [pw! £2.50 per night.]

Duns (Borders)

Picturesque Borders town with nearby ancient fort, castle, and Covenanters stone to commemorate the army's encampment here in 1639. Excellent touring centre. Berwick-upon-Tweed 13 miles.

BARNIKEN HOUSE HOTEL, MURRAY STREET, DUNS, BERWICKSHIRE TD11 3DE (0361 82466). Dogs most welcome, colour TV and tea/coffee facilities in all rooms. Luxurious bar, sun lounge, large garden and car park. Central heating. Near spectacular scenery and ideal for walks for dogs. 2 Crowns Commended. [🐕]

Elie (Fife)

Popular golf centre; golden sandy beaches set in sheltered bay. Ideal base for exploring East Neuk, including St Andrews.

THE ELMS, PARK PLACE, ELIE KY9 1DH (0333 330404). Small family run hotel offering private facilities and home cooking. For details please refer to our Display Ad under Elie or send for a brochure. STB 3 Crowns Commended, AA QQQ Recommended. [£1 per night.]

Fort William (Highland)

Small town at foot of Ben Nevis, ideal base for climbers and hillwalkers. West Highland Museum, Scottish crafts.

MRS J. MacLEAN, FORESTERS BUNGALOW, INCHREE, ONICH, FORT WILLIAM PH33 6SE (Onich [08553] 285). Quarter-mile from A82, quiet, peaceful; perfect for touring North-West Highlands; 9 miles Fort William. Good home cooking. One family, two twin rooms. Parking. Children, dogs welcome. D, B & B from £18; B & B from £12. Weekly reductions.

LINNHE CARAVAN PARK, DEPT PW, CORPACH, FORT WILLIAM PH33 7NL (0397 772376). One of the best and most beautiful lochside parks in Scotland. Thistle Award caravans for hire. Graded "Excellent". Private beach, free fishing. Prices from £150. [£5 weekly; pw!]

Glasgow (Strathclyde)

Scotland's largest city is famed for its Victorian architecture and Art Nouveau. Against this backdrop, the art galleries and museums have ensured its outstanding cultural heritage. 13th century cathedral, three universities and airport.

WESTERWOOD HOTEL, GOLF AND COUNTRY CLUB, ST ANDREW'S DRIVE, CUMBERNAULD, GLASGOW G68 0EW (0236 457171; Fax: 0236 738478). Our rural setting provides a peaceful away-from-it-all break, with a selection of country walks to exercise man's best friend. From £40 per person Bed and Breakfast. 5 Crowns Highly Commended, AA/RAC 4 Stars. *[🐕]*

Glenelg (Highland)

Village in Lochaber district on mainland at head of Sound of Sleat. Iron Age Pictish forts lie to the south.

MR & MRS LAMONT, CREAGMHOR, GLENELG IV40 8LA (059982 231). Bungalow, centrally heated plus open fire. Superb area for the peaceful outdoor life and many sites of historic interest. Write or phone for terms.

Grantown-on-Spey (Highland)

Popular ski resort and market town. Excellent trout and salmon fishing in Spey and Dulnain rivers.

MR AND MRS J. R. TAYLOR, MILTON OF CROMDALE, GRANTOWN-ON-SPEY, MORAYSHIRE PH26 3PH (0479 2415). Fully modernised Cottage with large garden and views of River Spey and Cromdale Hills. Golf, tennis and trekking within easy reach. Fully equipped except linen. Two double bedrooms. Shower, refrigerator, electric cooker, colour television. Car desirable. Children and pets welcome. Available Easter to October. *[🐕]*

Haddington (Edinburgh & Lothians)

Historic town on River Tyne, 16 miles east of Edinburgh. Birthplace of John Knox, 1505. Renovated Church of St Mary, 14c–15c; St Martin's Church, AM.

THE MONK'S MUIR, HADDINGTON EH41 3SB (Tel and Fax: 0620 860340). Secluded and tranquil amidst beautiful countryside, only 25 minutes from Edinburgh. Tourers, tents and luxury hire caravans. Off season midweek and weekend breaks, discount golf tickets. Open all year.

Hawick (Borders)

Town on River Teviot. Noted for rugby, knitwear and tweed. Midway between Edinburgh and Carlisle.

MRS PHILIPPA McCARTER, DYKES FARM, DENHOLM, HAWICK TD9 8TB (045-087 323). Delightful semi-detached farm Cottage. Sleeps 4. Linen, electricity and logs supplied. Wonderful walks. Maximum two large dogs welcome. Weekly terms £150–£225. Brochure available.

Innerleithen (Borders)

An old woollen manufacturing town set in beautiful Borders countryside. Peebles 6 miles.

MRS JENNIFER CAIRD, TRAQUAIR BANK, INNERLEITHEN, PEEBLESSHIRE EH44 6PS (0896 830425). Stone House with rambling garden, overlooks Tweed. Walking, fishing, riding. Help on farm. Edinburgh ¾ hour. Animals welcome. Bed and Breakfast; Evening Meals by arrangement. *[🐕]*

Isle of Mull (Strathclyde)

Quiet, attractive and very varied Inner Hebridean island with 300-mile coastline carved by sea lochs and with white sandy bays and shingle coves. Inland are mountains, notably Ben More (3169 ft). Tobermory is a picturesque fishing village set in a wooded bay. Ferry from Craignure to Oban on the mainland.

DERRYGUAIG FARMHOUSE, GRIBUN. In an elevated position at foot of Ben More. Modernised farmhouse with four twin bedrooms, kitchen with dishwasher, washing machine etc. Other lodges, farmhouses and cottages available on Mull and mainland Argyll. WEST HIGHLAND ESTATES OFFICE, 21 ARGYLL SQUARE, OBAN PA34 4AT (0631 63617; Fax: 0631 62218).

GLENAROS FARM COTTAGES, AROS. Five traditional farm cottages on working farm on east side of Mull. Sleep four to six. Fishing available by arrangement. Full details from MRS C. SCOTT, KILMORE HOUSE, KILMORE, BY OBAN PA34 4XT (063 177 369). SAE please.

Kilmelford (Argyll)

Village at head of Loch Melfort. Ideal base for walking and touring. Many watersports nearby.

MELFORT VILLAGE, KILMELFORD, BY OBAN PA34 4XD (08522 257; Fax: 08522 321). Luxury cottages overlooking beautiful Loch Melfort. Excellent walking and touring area. Indoor pool and leisure facilities. Riding, fishing and watersports nearby. Pets welcome. 3-4 Crowns Commended/Highly Commended. [🛏🐕]

Kinloch Rannoch (Tayside)

Village at eastern end of Loch Rannoch. Views of 3554 ft. Schiehallion from car parks around the loch. Stone cottages, baronial-style hotel, forge and shops.

WEST TEMPAR HOUSE, KINLOCH RANNOCH, BY PITLOCHRY PH16 5QE (0882 632338 sometimes Ansaphone). Millions of trees plus miles of open country tracks – sounds great for new walks, doesn't it? Country house, three rooms, private baths. Bed and Breakfast £17.50 per person. Dinner/children's tea if pre-booked. House-trained healthy dogs welcome. [🐕]

Kinross

Town and resort on west side of Loch Leven, nine miles north of Dunfermline. Angling on Loch Leven. Formal gardens at Kinross House.

THE GREEN HOTEL, 2 THE MUIRS, KINROSS KY13 7AS (0577 863467; Fax: 0577 863180). Independently owned Hotel with well-appointed bedrooms and family suites. Restaurant, bar meals. Leisure facilities include indoor pool, golf courses, tennis and fishing. M90 five minutes.

Langholm (Dumfries & Galloway)

Small mill town at the junction of three rivers. Common Riding held in July.

THE ESKDALE HOTEL, LANGHOLM DG13 0JH (03873 80357). Former Coaching Inn. All rooms with central heating, colour TV, radio. En-suite available. Licensed. Two bars. Restaurant. Games room. Golf, shooting, fishing. AA 2 STAR. 3 Crowns Commended. [🐕]

Lochearnhead (Central)

Popular little touring centre on wooded Loch Earn, dominated by Ben Vorlich (3,224ft). Edinburgh 65 miles, Glasgow 50, Aberfeldy 30, Crieff 19, Crianlarich 16, Callander 14.

CLACHAN COTTAGE HOTEL, LOCHSIDE, LOCHEARNHEAD FK19 8PU (0567 830247; Fax: 0567 830300). Ideal holiday venue for pets and their owners. Spectacular Highland scenery, walking, fishing, watersports. Open fires, wonderful food. Three Day, Golf and Off-Season Breaks. *[pw!]*

MR ANGUS CAMERON, LOCHEARNHEAD HOTEL, LOCHEARNHEAD FK19 8PU (0567 830229). Small family-run hotel (2 Crowns Approved), restaurant and self-catering chalets (4 Crowns Highly Commended) at the west end of Loch Earn with lovely views across the loch. Excellent golf and touring centre with water ski-ing, sailing and windsurfing on our doorstep. Ample hill walking. AA 1 Star. *[pw! £1 per night.]*

Lochgoilhead (Strathclyde)

Village at head of Loch Goil in Argyll.

MRS ROSEMARY DOLAN, THE SHOREHOUSE INN, LOCHGOILHEAD PA24 8AJ (03013 340). The Shorehouse Inn has seven letting rooms, central heating and double glazing. There is a bar, lounge and licensed restaurant. Local amenities include water sports, fishing, tennis, bowls, golf, swimming pool and good area for walking. Rates from £13.50 B&B. Well trained dogs welcome.

Lockerbie (Dumfries & Galloway)

Annandale town noted as the scene of a battle in 1593 which ended one of the last great Border feuds. This and the surrounding area comprised the lands of Robert Bruce. Ecclefechan six miles south was the birthplace of Thomas Carlyle. Gretna 15 miles.

LOCKERBIE MANOR COUNTRY HOTEL, LOCKERBIE DG11 2RG (0576 202610). Splendid Georgian mansion house set in 78 acres of beautiful grounds. Ideal base for exploring countryside. Single, twin, double and family rooms, all en suite, and equipped with colour TV, tea-making etc.

Longformacus (Borders)

Village on Dye Water 6 miles west of Duns.

MRS SHEILA M. PATE, HORSEUPCLEUGH, LONGFORMACUS, DUNS TD11 3PF (03617 225). Pretty stonebuilt Cottage peacefully situated in the lovely Lammermuir Hills. Comfortably furnished. Sleeps 3. Bed linen included. Fishing, hill-walking, wildlife. Duns – shopping, swimming, golf. Max. £195 per week. 3 Crowns Commended.

Mey (Highland)

Village near north coast, 6 miles West of John O'Groats.

THE CASTLE ARMS HOTEL, MEY, CAITHNESS KW14 8XH (Tel and Fax: 0847 85244). Former 19th Century coaching inn near Castle of Mey. Fully modernised, with eight centrally heated en suite bedrooms. Lounge bar and dining room. Dinner, B&B from £39. *[🛌pw!]*

Moffat (Dumfries and Galloway)

At head of lovely Annandale, grand mountain scenery. Good centre for rambling, climbing, angling and golf. The 'Devil's Beef Tub' is 5 miles N. EDINBURGH 52 miles, Peebles 33, Dumfries 21, Beattock 2.

BUCCLEUCH ARMS HOTEL, MOFFAT DG10 9ET (0683 20003). Renowned for its excellent food and wine cellar, this elegant Georgian hotel has welcomed man and beast for over 230 years. All rooms en-suite with central heating etc. B&B £28 per person. Taste of Scotland. 3 Crowns Commended. Les Routiers. Good Food Guide. [🐶]

Oban (Strathclyde)

Popular Highland resort and port, yachting centre; ferry services to Inner and Outer Hebrides. Sandy bathing beach at Ganavan Bay. McCaig's Tower above town is Colosseum replica built in 1890s.

MR HENRY P. WOODMAN, COLOGIN HOMES LTD, LERAGS, BY OBAN PA34 4SE (Oban [0631] 64501 Fax: 0631 66925). Modern centrally heated timber bungalows, sleep 2-6, all conveniences. Situated on farm, wildlife abundant. Games room, licensed bar with all-day bar meals. Cycle hire, fishing. Scottish entertainment. [🐶 pw!]

MRS DONALD CHISHOLM, "MOORCROFT", NORTH CONNEL, NEAR OBAN PA37 1QZ (063 171 403). Bed and Breakfast from £15.00 in a Croft Cottage overlooking sea loch. Seven miles from Oban. Wonderful scenery. Well-controlled pets welcome. SAE or telephone for details. [pw!]

MR & MRS H. DAVIDSON, 'DUNMOR', BONAWE ROAD, NORTH CONNEL PA37 1RA (0631 71386). Situated on Loch Etive, 5 miles from Oban, we offer accommodation with the emphasis on good food. Ideally placed to explore Argyll and the islands; famed for fishing, walking and scenery. Bed and Breakfast £13, Dinner £9. Open all year. [🐶]

MRS G. CADZOW, DUACHY, KILNINVER, BY OBAN PA34 4QU (085 26 244). Three self-catering Cottages overlooking Loch Seil. Properties sleep three/five. Fully equipped, linen and electricity included in price. From £170. [🐶]

Fully equipped Scandinavian chalets in breathtaking scenery near Oban. Chalets sleep 4-7, are widely spaced and close to Loch Tralaig. Car parking. From £180 per week per chalet. APPLY – GILL AND ANDREW STEVENS, INNIE, KILNINVER, BY OBAN PA34 4UX (085 22 225).

D. R. KILPATRICK, KILNINVER, BY OBAN PA34 4UT (08526 272). Five self-catering houses on coastal estate near Oban. Sleep 4–8. All fully equipped; electricity, newspapers, trout fishing included in rental. From £220 including VAT. 4 Crowns. [🐶 pw!]

J. AND F. TURNBULL, LAG-NA-KEIL CHALETS, LERAGS, BY OBAN, ARGYLL PA34 4SE (0631 62746). One, two or three bedroomed Bungalows or Chalets; fully equipped (except linen); colour TV. Free fishing; boat hire. Launderette. Telephone. Pets welcome. Up to 4 Crowns Commended.

Onich (Highland)

On shores of Loch Linnhe, near entrance to Loch Leven. Good boating, fishing. Fort William 10 miles N.E.

MRS K. A. McCALLUM, TIGH-A-RIGH GUEST HOUSE, ONICH, FORT WILLIAM PH33 6SE (085 53 255). Well-equipped, comfortable accommodation in licensed Guest House. Ideal touring centre. Pets and children welcome. Open all year. Bed, Breakfast and Dinner from £23.50. En suite rooms £26. [🐶]

Peebles (Borders)

Town on River Tweed (noted for salmon). Renowned for knitwear and tweeds. Cross Kirk ruin dates from 13th c.

GLENRATH HOLIDAY HOMES. Country cottages and farmhouses offering the highest standards of comfort. Three peaceful locations, all within 10 miles of Peebles. Ideal for children; pets welcome under control. Brochure with full details from MRS J. CAMPBELL, GLENRATH FARM, KIRKTON MANOR, PEEBLES EH45 9JW (0721 740265; Fax: 0968 676957).

Perth (Tayside)

Historic Royal Burgh and one-time Scottish capital on the River Tay. Lovely countryside. Ideal touring centre. Fine views of the city from Kinnoull Hill. Buildings of interest include St John's Church (15th cent.), associated with John Knox, Fair Maid of Perth's House, art gallery and museum. Excellent sporting facilities, especially salmon fishing and golf, good entertainments. EDINBURGH 44 miles, Callander 40, Stirling 35, St Andrews 31, Dundee 22, Crieff 18, Blairgowrie 15.

MURRAYSHALL COUNTRY HOUSE HOTEL AND GOLF COURSE, SCONE, PERTH PH2 7PH (0738 51171; Fax: 0738 52595). Located four miles from the city of Perth amidst 300 acres of scenic countryside. Country walks, golf, tennis, croquet, bowls. DB&B from £55 per person sharing. *[⛾]*

Pitlochry (Tayside)

Popular resort on River Tummel in beautiful Perthshire Highlands. Excellent golf, loch and river fishing. Famous for summer Festival Theatre; distillery, Highland Games.

JACKY AND MALCOLM CATTERALL, "TULLOCH", ENOCHDHU, BY KIRK-MICHAEL, STRATHARDLE PH10 7DY (Tel and Fax: 0250 881404). Former farmhouse. Two family, one twin, all with washbasins, colour TV, tea/coffee facilities. All rooms facing open country to mountains beyond, peace and quiet guaranteed. We make a fuss of dogs and owners. B&B £14, optional dinner £7. *[⛾]*

ROSEMOUNT HOTEL, 12 HIGHER OAKFIELD, PITLOCHRY PH16 5HT (0796 472302/472262; Fax: 0796 474216). Fully licensed Hotel with 20 fully en suite bedrooms. Central location for touring. Delightful restaurant; fitness centre with sauna, gym, sunbed. Ample parking.

FOUR SEASONS, HIGHER OAKFIELD, PITLOCHRY (0796 472080)/BOBBIN BUT-TERY, FERRY ROAD, PITLOCHRY (0796 473945). Enjoy a holiday with your pet. Ideal touring, walking, fishing, golfing, theatre base. Bedrooms with washbasins, tea/coffee, central heating, TV, also en suite. B&B from £13.50. Self catering available. Write for full details. *[⛾]*

KILLIECRANKIE HOTEL, KILLIECRANKIE, BY PITLOCHRY PH16 5LG (0796 473220; Fax: 0796 472451). Charming small Hotel set in 4 acres. Wonderful views. Superb food, high standard of comfort. Open Christmas and New Year. 4 Crowns Commended. AA 2 Star Rosette. *[⛾]*

Port William (Dumfries & Galloway)

Small resort with quay, on east shore of Luce Bay, seven miles south-west of Wigtown.

Two self catering cottages, each sleeping 6 adults plus cot. On fringe of beautiful fishing village. Opposite beach and sea. Local activities include fishing, golf, bowls and tennis. Brochure from: MRS F. SHAW, BLEW HOUSE FARM, FINGHALL, NEAR LEYBURN, NORTH YORKSHIRE DL8 5ND (0677 50374).

Rockcliffe (Dumfries and Galloway)

Quiet resort on wooded Rough Firth; sandy and rocky bays. Bird sanctuary on Rough Island (N.T. Scot). Dumfries 20 miles.

KIRKLAND FARMHOUSE AND COTTAGES. 3/4 Crowns Commended. One mile safe sandy beach; surrounded by owner's fields. Superbly equipped and comfortable; private gardens. Sleep 6/8, 5/6, 2/3 persons plus cots. Forestry and seaside walks. Bicycle hire; golf, sailing, fishing. Terms from £95; special rates for couples only. MRS K. SINCLAIR, ROCKCLIFFE, DALBEATTIE, KIRKCUDBRIGHTSHIRE DG5 4QC (055663 205).

TORBAY GUEST HOUSE, TORBAY FARMHOUSE, ROCKCLIFFE, BY DALBEATTIE DG5 4QE (0556 630403). Our Galloway farmhouse stands in beautiful gardens overlooking the sea. Imaginative cooking and baking using our garden produce and tastefully appointed en suite rooms. Well-behaved dogs welcome. STB 3 Crowns Highly Commended. B&B & EM from £25; weekly terms. *[£1 per night.]*

Roy Bridge (Highland)

Located in Glen Spean at foot of Glen Roy in Lochaber. 3 miles east of Spean Bridge.

BUNROY HOLIDAY PARK, ROY BRIDGE PH31 4AG (0397 712332). In a quiet woodland setting with enough space for pets to exercise without traffic worries. Modern chalets, fully equipped for self catering for up to four persons. From £160 per week.

MR P. W. MATHESON, THE LITTLE HOUSES, EAST PARK, ROY BRIDGE PH31 4AG (0397 712 370/436). Holiday bungalows and chalets on peaceful site with splendid mountain views. Central for shops and hotels. Sleep 2/8, all modern facilities, site laundry, payphone. ASSC, BH&HPA. Weekly terms £125–£425 (inc. VAT).

St. Andrews (Fife)

Home of golf – new British Golf Museum has memorabilia dating back to the origins of the game. Remains of castle and cathedral. Sealife Centre and beach Leisure Centre. Excellent sands. Ideal base for exploring the picturesque East Neuk of Fife.

EDENSIDE HOUSE, EDENSIDE, ST ANDREWS KY16 9SQ (0334 838108; Fax: 0334 838493). Converted 19th century Listed farmhouse on nature reserve convenient A91, St Andrews 2 miles. En suite double/twin rooms, colour TV, beverage trays, some ground floor rooms. Totally non-smoking. Private parking. Golf packages. Quality accommodation, reasonable prices. STB 3 Crowns Commended. *[🐕]*

MRS A. WEDDERBURN, MOUNTQUHANIE HOLIDAY HOMES, MOUNTQUHANIE, CUPAR KY15 4QJ (082 624 252). Good quality self-catering houses, flats or cottages in tranquil, rural countryside. Central heating, modern kitchens, fitted carpets, colour TV, telephone. STB 4 Crowns Commended to 5 Crowns De Luxe. *[🐕]*

Spean Bridge (Highland)

At western end of Glen Spean amidst grand mountain scenery. Bridge built by Telford. Commando memorial nearby. Fort William 10 miles S.W.

DRUIMANDARROCH, SPEAN BRIDGE PH34 4EU (0397 712335). "HELLO MR/MS DOG". On your best behaviour you are welcome at Druimandarroch Guest House, Spean Bridge, Fort William and/or Brimar Self Catering Cottages, Laggan, Newtonmore. Open all year at cottages. Full details of both 0397 712335 or write to Druimandarroch. *[🐕pw!]*

Stanley (Tayside)

Pretty village on River Tay 8 miles south-east of Dunkeld and 6 miles north of Perth.

MRS A. GUTHRIE, NEWMILL FARM, STANLEY PH1 4QD (0738 828281). On A9, six miles north of Perth. Twin, double, family rooms. Bed and Breakfast from £13. Evening meal on request. Reductions for children. Ideal for touring, fishing, golf.

Strathyre (Central)

Village set in middle of Strathyre Forest, just off A84 north of Callander. Information centre and picnic area to south of village.

ARDOCH LODGE, STRATHYRE (08774 666). Log cabins and cottage in wonderful mountain scenery. Comfortably furnished and fully equipped. Country house accommodation also available. Phone for brochure. Open all year. Pets most welcome. 3 Crowns Highly Commended. [🐕]

West Linton (Borders)

Village on east side of Pentland Hills, 7 miles south west of Penicuik. Edinburgh 18 miles.

MRS C. M. KILPATRICK, SLIPPERFIELD HOUSE, WEST LINTON EH46 7AA (0968 660401). Two excellently equipped converted cottages set in 100 acres of lochs and woodlands. America Cottage sleeps 6, Loch Cottage sleeps 4. Car essential. [🐕]

KENNELS AND CATTERIES

Are you having difficulty locating a boarding kennel/cattery in an area other than your own? Have you words of praise (or criticism) for a kennel/cattery you have used? Perhaps you're even thinking of opening an Animal Boarding Establishment? The Boarding Kennels Advisory Bureau is a free service for the general public and monitors progress within the industry. Please write with your enquiry (enclosing SAE) or comments: The Boarding Kennels Advisory Bureau, c/o Blue Grass Animal Hotel, Little Leigh, near Northwich, Cheshire CW8 4RJ. Tel: 0606 891303.

ROSETOWN LUXURY BOARDING KENNELS & CATTERY
The Bungalow, Pitsmingle, Roche, St Austell, Cornwall PL26 8LZ
Tel: 0726 890531
All breeds of dogs and cats boarded in block-built heated kennels with fully enclosed runs. 40' outdoor runs + two walks daily. All pets receive their normal home diet, and a grooming service is available for dogs.
All animals must have current vaccination certificates
Rosetown is family-run – lots of love and cuddles for pets.

Bedfordshire
APPLEDOWN BOARDING KENNELS & CATTERY, HARLING ROAD, EATON BRAY, DUNSTABLE LU6 1QY
(Tel: 0525 220383)

Dogs, cats, small animals; individual or family kennels with runs; exercise compound; cats in individual or family pens; heating available; current vaccination certificate must be produced; all animals groomed regularly; also: food sales, dog training.

Devon
STOCKLAND BOARDING KENNELS & CATTERY, QUANTOCK FARM, STOCKLAND, HONITON EX14 9DX
(Tel: 0404 86301)

Dogs and cats; individual kennels and runs; dogs walked twice daily in paddocks; full vaccination required, certificates to be produced on arrival; all kennels and catteries individually heated; extensive range of diets catered for. Collection and delivery service. Lots of TLC for those of nervous disposition. Member of BARK.

Gloucestershire
AVONLEY KENNELS AND CATTERY, MOOREND ROAD, ELDERSFIELD GL19 4NS
(Tel: 0452 840247)

Dogs and Cats; large individual kennels with attached concrete runs for dogs and large pens for cats, both heated in winter; all animals must have up-to-date inoculations and boosters; delivery and collection service available; inspection welcome; problem and temperamental dogs a speciality; full grooming service available.

Hampshire

NOARCK BOARDING KENNELS & CATTERY, 217 RINGWOOD ROAD, ST LEONARDS, RINGWOOD BH24 2QB
(Tel: 0202 873664)

Dogs (50), cats (50); very large individual chalets with large patios attached for dogs. For cats – large sleeping and dining areas with own heaters; attached is large individual play area with patio chairs for each cat. All animals must show up-to-date inoculation certificates. Family-run kennels; brochure on request.

Hertfordshire

THE ANIMAL WELFARE TRUST (AWT TRADING LTD), TYLER'S WAY, WATFORD BY-PASS, WATFORD WD2 8HQ
(Tel: 081-950 1320)

Dogs, Cats and small domestic pets; concrete kennels with runs for dogs and cats, heated in winter; all dogs must be inoculated against hard pad, distemper, leptospirosis, hepatitis, parvovirus; inoculation against kennel cough desirable; cats must be inoculated against feline enteritis and cat flu; inspection welcomed.

Kent

THE ANIMAL INN, DOVER ROAD, RINGWOULD, NEAR DEAL CT14 8HH
(Tel: 0304 373597; Fax: 0304 380305)

Dogs, cats and other small animals and birds – in their own cages. All individual kennels; individual switched infra-red heat lamps over beds; large outdoor covered runs. Daily visit from vet (also quarantine). All inoculations must be up to date. Dogs walked in grounds and woods nearby. Individual diets catered for. Collection and delivery. Inspection welcome. Open 8am–6pm daily and 8am–1pm Sundays. Only 5 minutes from Dover Docks.

London

CHINGFORD BOARDING KENNELS AND CATTERY, 160 CHINGFORD MOUNT ROAD, CHINGFORD E4 9BS
(Tel: 081-529 0112/0979)

Dogs, cats, birds, rabbits and other children's pets. Individual kennels; dogs walked in runs individually; cats have own runs. Dogs and cats must be fully vaccinated. Collection and delivery arranged; exports world-wide; quarantine for cats and dogs. Vets' surgery on site.

LOGGERHEADS PUSSERY, 48 MARLBOROUGH ROAD, UPPER HOLLOWAY, LONDON N19 4NB
(Tel: 071-272 9146)

Cats (20); large indoor pens twice the legal requirement, fully licensed, fully heated. All cats are allowed out to exercise, individually or in families. No strange cats are allowed to mix. Feline enteritis and cat flu vaccinations are essential. Inspection welcome.

LOGGERHEADS PET SHOP AND BOARDING CATTERY, 33 WINCHESTER ROAD, HIGHAMS PARK, CHINGFORD, LONDON E4 9LH
(Tel: 081-531 2134)

Cats (80); extra large indoor pens, 6 feet long. Cats allowed out while pens are cleaned. Cat flu and enteritis inoculations essential. Birds, rabbits, gerbils and hamsters etc. will be looked after for a nominal fee. Inspection welcome.

Surrey

KINGSWOOD KENNELS, PIGEONHOUSE LANE, MUGSWELL CHIPSTEAD CR3 3SP
(Tel: 0737 832966)

Dogs (70); Cats (12); heated brick kennels, spacious runs and compounds; full inoculations required; collections and deliveries available; special diets catered for, close to Gatwick; clipping and grooming service. All visits welcome.

OAA RIDE FARM KENNEL & CATTERY, TITHE BARN LANE, SEND, WOKING GU23 7LE
(Tel: 0483 223312)

Dogs (45), cats (100); individual rooms for cats or one family of cats, heated; dogs in centrally heated kennels; current vaccination certificates must be shown; pick-ups can be arranged; high standards of care and hygiene; vet's assistance available 24 hours; open daily; inspection invited.

East Sussex
SALTDEAN KENNELS, WESTFIELD AVENUE NORTH, SALTDEAN BN2 8HP
(Tel: 0273 301331)

Dogs and cats; very clean; large kennels; own runs; also small quiet room for small dogs; individual pens and large exercise areas; current inoculations required for both cats and dogs.

West Sussex
SENLAC BOARDING KENNELS, SHOREHAM ROAD, HENFIELD BN5 9SE
(Tel: 0273 492925)

Dogs (35); Cats (12); concrete blocks, large airy kennels each with individual runs for both dogs and cats; regular exercise in our 4 acre field (for dogs), cats have individual runs; dogs, compulsory vaccination against distemper, hard pad, hepatitis, leptospirosis and parvovirus, also kennel cough; cats, compulsory vaccination against feline influenza and enteritis; animal nursing homes with veterinary surgeons in attendance.

WARNHAM KENNELS & ANIMAL SANCTUARY, MAYES LANE, WARNHAM, NEAR HORSHAM RH12 3SG
(Tel: 0403 268095)

Dogs (30), cats (30); all-brick heated kennel and cattery; all dogs in very large runs, plus walked daily; choice of any food; cats very comfortable; full inoculations required. Collection 25 miles; grooming, bathing; registered charity; viewing very welcome.

West Midlands
KAMA KENNELS, SPRINGFIELD ROAD, WALMLEY, SUTTON COLDFIELD B76 2SL
(Tel: 021-378 0911)

Dogs (50), cats (50); dogs in individual or family kennels, large exercise areas; cats in individual pens with heating when necessary; must have current inoculations – dogs against hard pad, distemper, hepatitis, leptospirosis, parvovirus, kennel cough; cats against flu and enteritis. Rabbits and guinea pigs also boarded. Open all year. Tattooist for National Dog Tattoo Register. Inspection welcome.

West Yorkshire
CARLTON BOARDING KENNELS, CHURCH HOUSE, CARLTON, YEADON, Nr LEEDS LS19 7BG
(Tel: 0532 505113)

Dogs (40); cats (10); concrete individual accommodation with outside runs; dogs walked on lead twice daily in farm land; full vaccination required; trimming by qualified staff.

SPARTH KENNELS & CATTERY, SPARTH COTTAGES, MARSDEN LANE, HUDDERSFIELD HD7 5XB
(Tel: 0484 844844)

Dogs (22), cats (30); purpose built accommodation; dogs walked twice daily; wide choice of menu; special diets catered for; open all year. All animals must have current vaccination certificate.

FLEET BOARDING KENNELS AND CATTERY, FLEET LANE, QUEENSBURY, NEAR BRADFORD BD13 2JR
(Tel: 0274 880408)

Fully licensed breeding, boarding kennels and cattery situated in a pleasant country setting above the highest village in England; local authority and veterinary approved. Open all year round; heated accommodation; all breeds of dogs welcome; special diets catered for; fully qualified staff; N.S.A.C. certificates; collection and delivery service; current vaccination certificate essential; professional grooming service available.

The Golden Bowl Supplement for Pet-Friendly Pubs

BETA *petfoods*

THIS YEAR *Recommended Wayside Inns* and Beta Petfoods have joined forces to provide the first guide to the nation's top 100 pet-friendly pubs.

Beta Petfoods launched its search for Britain's warmest pet welcome, in the form of the Beta Petfoods Golden Bowl Awards Scheme in late 1993. The response was staggering. Hundreds wrote in to nominate their pubs for a 'Golden Bowl Approved' sticker and a chance to become the outright winner of the 1994 award. Judging of regional winners and for the national award was still underway as we went to press. The results will be announced as soon as possible during 1994.

Beta Petfoods, petshops' leading name in complete food for dogs and cats, launched the award scheme to reward kind-hearted publicans for their traditional willingness to provide a bowl of water for their smallest customer. The pick of pet pubs (and hotels) have gone into this Supplement to enable owners travelling, holidaying or just walking their dogs to find a warm welcome for *everyone* in the party when they stop for refreshment. We only wish we had room to include more!

BETA PETFOODS has been the leading brand of complete pet food (you don't need to add anything to it to feed it) in pet shops for many years. Its range of food ensures that owners can feed their dogs the right food for every stage of their lives, from puppyhood and the active adolescent and young adult years through to later life when the pace slows down a little.

More than that, Beta Petfoods provides the right food for individual dogs' lifestyles. Sporting, working and very active dogs demand more from their food for energy and stamina to keep them happy and busy all day while some pet dogs are happy with just a short walk. To keep everyone happy and healthy, Beta Petfoods has just the right food for individual needs.

The familiar names in the Beta Petfoods range are *Beta Puppy, Pet, Field* and *Recipe. Beta Brutus* and *Bravo* are superior flaked foods, *Brutus* with a little added crunch and *Bravo* with its own rich gravy when mixed with water. Cats have their own crisp and appetising food in *Beta Purr* with a choice of two flavours. All are easy and pleasant to store and can be served straight from the bag. Ask your pet shop for details or contact: **Beta Petfoods, Beta Petcare Advice Service, Paragon Petcare UK Ltd, Wincham, Northwich, Cheshire CW9 6DF. Telephone (0606) 42822.**

The Golden Bowl Supplement
for Pet-Friendly Pubs

AVON

PRINCE'S MOTTO
Barrow Gurney, near Bristol, Avon.

Dogs allowed in non-food areas and beer garden.

Pet Regulars: Martha (Golden Retriever), serious eating and sleeping.

BERKSHIRE

THE GREYHOUND (known locally as 'The Dog')
The Walk, Eton Wick, Berkshire.

Dogs allowed throughout the pub.

Pet Regulars: Include Lady (GSD), at one o'clock sharp she howls for her hot dog; Trevor (Labrador/Retriever), who does nothing; Skipper (Jack Russell), the local postman's dog and Natasha (GSD) who simply enjoys the ambience.

NOTE
A few abbreviations and 'pet' descriptions have been used in this section which deserve mention and, where necessary, explanation as follows: ***GSD:*** German Shepherd Dog. *. . . -cross:* a cross-breed where one breed appears identifiable. *57:* richly varied origin. You will also enounter *'mongrel'*, *'Bitsa'* and *'???!'* which are self-evident and generally affectionate.

THE QUEEN

Harts Lane, Burghclere, near Newbury, Berkshire.

Dogs allowed throughout the pub.

Pet Regulars: Sam (Border Terrier), makes solo visits to the pub to play with resident long-haired Dachshund Gypsy.

THE SWAN

9 Mill Lane, Clewer, Windsor, Berkshire.

Dogs allowed throughout the pub.

Pet Regulars: Include Luke (Samoyed), enjoys a glass of Tiger beer.

THE TWO BREWERS

Park Street, Windsor, Berkshire.

Dogs allowed, public and saloon bars.

Pet Regulars: Missy and Worthey (Huskies), prefer to remain outside; Sam (Golden Retriever), will retrieve any food and eat it while owner is not looking; Bumble (Highland Terrier), better known as the Highland Hooverer.

BUCKINGHAMSHIRE

WHITE HORSE

Village Lane, Hedgerley, Buckinghamshire SL2 3UY.

Dogs allowed at tables on pub frontage, beer garden (on leads), public bar.

Pet Regulars: Digby (Labrador), the entertainer; Cooper (Boxer), tries hard to better himself – also drinks!

CAMBRIDGESHIRE

THE OLD WHITE HART

Main Street, Ufford, Peterborough.

Dogs allowed in non-food areas.

Pet Regulars: Henry and Robotham (Springer Spaniels), 'pub dog' duties include inspection of all customers and their dogs and, on occasion, seeing them home after last orders.

CHESHIRE

JACKSONS BOAT
Rifle Road, Sale, Cheshire.

Dogs allowed throughout with the exception of the dining area.

Pet Regulars: Bix (Labrador), will share pork scratchings with pub cat, chases beer garden squirrels on solo missions; hamburger scrounging a speciality.

CLEVELAND

TAP AND SPILE
27 Front Street, Framwellgate Moor, Durham DH1 5EE

Dogs allowed throughout the pub except between 12 and 1.30 lunchtimes.

Pet Regulars: These include Smutty (Labrador) who brings her own beer bowl and is definitely *not* a lager Lab – traditional brews only.

CORNWALL

THE WHITE HART
Chilsworthy, near Gunnislake, Cornwall.

Dogs allowed in non-food bar, car park tables, beer garden.

Pet Regulars: Joe (Terrier-cross), sleeps on back under bar stools; Max (Staffordshire-cross) lager drinker; Tatler (Cocker Spaniel), pork cracklings fan; Sheba (GSD), welcoming committee.

CUMBRIA

BRITANNIA INN
Elterwater, Ambleside, Cumbria.

Dogs allowed throughout.

Pet Regulars: Bonnie (sheepdog/Retriever), beer-mat catching, scrounging, has own chair.

THE MORTAL MAN HOTEL
Troutbeck, Windermere, Cumbria LA23 1PL

Dogs allowed throughout and in guest rooms.

Pet Regulars: Include James (Labrador) who will take dogs for walks if they are on a lead and Snip (Border Collie), makes solo visits.

STAG INN

Dufton, Appleby, Cumbria.

Dogs allowed in non-food bar, beer garden, village green.

Pet Regulars: Bachus (Newfoundland), enjoys a good sprawl; Kirk (Dachshund), carries out tour of inspection unaccompanied – but wearing lead; Kim (Weimarawer), best bitter drinker; Buster (Jack Russell), enjoys a quiet evening.

WATERMILL INN

School Lane, Ings, near Staveley, Kendal, Cumbria.

Dogs allowed in beer garden, Wrynose bottom bar.

Pet Regulars: Smudge (sheepdog); Gowan (Westie) and Scruffy (mongrel). All enjoy a range of crisps and snacks. Scruffy regularly drinks Theakstons XB. Pub dogs Misty (Beardie) and Thatcher (Lakeland Terrier).

DERBYSHIRE

DOG AND PARTRIDGE COUNTRY INN & MOTEL

Swinscoe, Ashbourne, Derbyshire.

Dogs allowed throughout, except restaurant.

Pet Regulars: Include Mitsy (57); Rusty (Cairn); Spider (Collie/GSD) and Rex (GSD).

RIFLE VOLUNTEER

Birchwood Lane, Somercotes, Derbyshire DE55 4ND.

Dogs allowed in non-food bar, car park tables, beer garden.

Pet Regulars: Flossy (Border Collie), bar stool inhabitant; Pepper (Border Collie), has made a study of beer mat aerodynamics; Tara (GSD), pub piggyback specialist.

WHITE HART

Station Road, West Hallam, Derbyshire DE7 6GW.

Dogs allowed in all non-food areas.

Pet Regulars: Ben and Oliver (Golden Retrievers), drinking halves of mixed; Sid (Greyhound), plays with cats.

DEVON

BRENDON HOUSE HOTEL

Brendon, Lynton, North Devon EX35 6PS.

Dogs allowed in garden, guest bedrooms.

Pet Regulars: Mutley (mongrel), cat chasing; Pie (Border Terrier), unusual 'yellow stripe', was once chased – by a sheep! Farthing (cat), 20 years old, self appointed cream tea receptionist. Years of practice have perfected dirty looks at visiting dogs.

THE BULLERS ARMS

Chagford, Newton Abbot, Devon.

Dogs allowed throughout pub, except dining room/kitchen.

Pet Regulars: Miffin & Sally (Cavalier King Charles Spaniels), celebrated Miffin's 14th birthday with a party at The Bullers.

CROWN AND SCEPTRE

2 Petitor Road, Torquay, Devon TQ1 4QA.

Dogs allowed in non-food bar, family room, lounge.

Pet Regulars: Samantha (Labrador), opens, consumes and returns empties when offered crisp packets; Toby & Rory (Irish Setters), general daftness; Buddy & Jessie (Collies), beer-mat frisbee experts; Cassie (Collie), scrounging.

THE DEVONSHIRE INN

Sticklepath, near Okehampton, Devon EX20 2NW.

Dogs allowed in non-food bar, car park, beer garden, family room, guest rooms.

Pet Regulars: Bess (Labrador), 'minds' owner; Annie (Shihtzu), snoring a speciality; Daisy (Collie), accompanies folk singers; Duke (GSD) and Ben (Collie-cross), general attention seeking.

THE JOURNEY'S END

Ringmore, near Kingsbridge, South Devon TQ7 4HL.

Dogs allowed throughout the pub.

Pet Regulars: Lager, Cider, Scrumpy and Whiskey (all Terriers) – a pint of real ale at lunchtime between them.

THE ROYAL OAK INN

Dunsford, near Exeter, Devon EX6 7DA.

Dogs allowed in non-food bars, beer garden, accommodation for guests with dogs.

Pet Regulars: Tom Thumb (Jack Russell), pub bouncer – doesn't throw people out, just bounces.

THE SEA TROUT INN

Staverton, near Totnes, Devon TQ9 6PA.

Dogs allowed in non-food bar, car park tables, beer garden, owners' rooms (but not on beds).

Pet Regulars: Billy (labrador-cross), partial to drip trays; Curnow (Poodle), brings a blanket.

THE WHITE HART HOTEL

Moretonhampstead, Newton Abbott, Devon TQ13 8NF.

Dogs allowed throughout, except restaurant.

Pet Regulars: Poppie, Rosie (Standard Poodles) and Bobby (Collie).

ESSEX

THE OLD SHIP

Heybridge Basin, Heybridge, Maldon, Essex.

Dogs allowed throughout pub.

Pet Regulars: Toby (57), monopolising bar stools; Tag (Spaniel), nipping behind the bar for biscuits; Toto (57), nipping behind the bar to 'beat up' owners' Great Dane; Happy (terrier), drinking beer and looking miserable.

THE WINGED HORSE

Luncies Road, Vange, Basildon, Essex SS14 1SB.

Dogs allowed throughout pub.

Pet Regulars: Gina (Newfoundland), visits solo daily for a pub lunch – biscuits and a beer; Roxy (Bull Terrier), fond of making a complete mess with crisps and loves a glass of beer. There are 14 canine regulars in all, not including the pub dog Tinka.

THE WOODEN FENDER

Harwich Road, Ardleigh, Essex CO7 7PA.

Dogs allowed in non-food bar, car park tables, beer garden.

Pet Regulars: Holly (Labrador), part-time door stop and vacuum cleaner (paid in marrow-bones); Busty (Labrador), when not eating crisps, thinks/dreams of eating crisps.

GLOUCESTERSHIRE

THE OLD LODGE INN

Minchinhampton Common, Stroud, Gloucestershire GL6 9AQ.

Dogs allowed throughout the pub with the exception of the restaurant.

Pet Regulars: Bess (Labrador) waits nibbling on a carrot while her owners dine in the restaurant; Dotty (Labrador) was a bridesmaid and came to her owner's wedding reception at the pub last year; Katar (Boxer), a fixation with 'chews', distinguished for having won Crufts 'Best Veteran' last year.

GREATER LONDON

THE PHOENIX

28 Thames Street, Sunbury on Thames, Middlesex.

Dogs allowed in non-food bar, beer garden, family room.

Pet Regulars: Pepe (57), fire hog; Cromwell (King Charles), often accompanied by small, balled-up sock. Drinks Websters, once seen with a hangover; Fred (Labrador), would be a fire hog if Pepe wasn't always there first; Oliver (Standard Poodle), still a pup, pub visits are character-building!

THE TIDE END COTTAGE

Ferry Road, Teddington, Middlesex.

Dogs allowed throughout the pub.

Pet Regulars: Angus (Setter), "mine's a half of Guinness"; Dina (GSD), guide dog, beautiful, loyal and clever; Harry (Beagle), partial to sausages, a greeter and meeter; Lady (cross), likes a game of tug o' war with Angus.

HAMPSHIRE

THE CHEQUERS

Ridgeway Lane, Lower Pennington, Lymington.

Dogs allowed in non-food bar, outdoor barbecue area (away from food).

Pet Regulars: Otto (Hungarian Vizsla), eats beer-mats and paper napkins. Likes beer but not often indulged.

FLYING BULL

London Road Rake, near Petersfield, Hampshire GU33 7JB.

Dogs allowed throughout the pub.

Pet Regulars: Flippy (Labrador/Old English Sheepdog), partial to the biscuits served with coffee. Status as 'pub dog' questionable as will visit The Sun over the road for a packet of cheese snips.

THE VICTORY

High Street, Hamble-le-Rice, Southampton.

Dogs allowed throughout the pub.

Pet Regulars: Sefton (Labrador), his 'usual' chew bars are kept especially.

HERTFORDSHIRE

THE BLACK HORSE

Chorly Wood Common, Dog Kennel Lane, Rickmansworth, Hertfordshire.

Dogs allowed throughout the pub.

Pet Regulars: Spritzy (mongrel), pub hooligan, former Battersea Dogs' Home resident.

THE FOX

496 Luton Road, Kinsbourne Green, near Harpenden, Hertfordshire.

Dogs allowed in non-food bar, car park tables, beer garden.

Pet Regulars: A tightly knit core of regulars which includes assorted Collies, German Shepherd Dogs and Retrievers. Much competition for dropped bar snacks.

THE ROBIN HOOD AND LITTLE JOHN

Rabley Heath, near Codicote, Hertfordshire.

Dogs allowed in non-food bar, car park tables, beer garden, pitch and putt.

Pet Regulars: Willow (Labrador), beer-mat catcher. The locals of the pub have close to 50 dogs between them, most of which visit from time to time. The team includes a two Labrador search squad dispatched by one regular's wife to indicate time's up. When they arrive he has five minutes' drinking up time before all three leave together.

HUMBERSIDE

BARNES WALLIS INN

North Howden, Howden, North Humberside.

Dogs allowed throughout the pub.

Pet Regulars: A healthy cross-section of mongrels, Collies and Labradors. One of the most popular pastimes is giving the pub cat a bit of a run for his money.

BLACK SWAN

Asselby, Goole, North Humberside.

Dogs allowed in non-food bar.

Pet Regulars: A variety of canine customers.

KINGS HEAD INN

Barmby on the Marsh, North Humberside DN14 7HL.

Dogs allowed in non-food bar.

Pet Regulars: Many and varied!

ISLE OF WIGHT

THE CLARENDON HOTEL AND WIGHT MOUSE INN

Chale, Isle of Wight.

Dogs allowed throughout.

Pet Regulars: Guy (mongrel), calls in for daily sausages. Known to escape from house to visit solo. Hotel dog is Gizmo (Spoodle – Toy Poodle-cross King Charles Spaniel), child entertainer.

KENT

KENTISH HORSE
Cow Lane, Mark Beech, Edenbridge, Kent.

Dogs allowed throughout.

Pet Regulars: Include Boozer (Greyhound), who enjoys a beer and Kylin (Shihtzu), socialising. Pub grounds also permanent residence to goats, sheep, lambs, a horse and geese.

THE OLD NEPTUNE
Marine Terrace, Whitstable, Kent CT5 1EJ.

Dogs allowed in non-food bar and beach frontage.

Pet Regulars: Josh (mongrel), solo visits, serves himself from pub water-bowl; Bear (GSD), insists on people throwing stones on beach to chase, will drop stones on feet as quick reminder; Trigger (mongrel), accompanied by toys; Poppy & Fred (mongrel and GSD), soft touch and dedicated vocalist – barks at anything that runs away!

PRINCE ALBERT
38 High Street, Broadstairs, Kent CT10 1LH.

Dogs allowed in non-food bar.

Pet Regulars: Buster (King Charles), a health freak who likes to nibble on raw carrots and any fresh veg; Suki (Jack Russell), Saturday-night roast beef sampler; Sally (Airdale). official rug; Bruno (Boxer), particularly fond of pepperami sausage.

THE SWANN INN
Little Chart, Kent TN27 0QB.

Dogs allowed – everywhere except restaurant.

Pet Regulars: Rambo (Leonbergers), knocks on the door and orders pork scratchings; Duster (Retriever), places his order – for crisps – with one soft bark for the landlady; Ben (GSD), big licks; Josh (Papillon), hind-legged dancer.

UNCLE TOM'S CABIN
Lavender Hill, Tonbridge, Kent.

Dogs allowed in non-food bar, beer garden.

Pet Regulars: Bob Minor (Lurcher); Tug (mongrel); Bitsy (mongrel); Tilly (Spaniel): 10pm is dog biscuit time!

LANCASHIRE

ABBEYLEE
Abbeyhills Road, Oldham, Lancashire.

Dogs allowed throughout.

Pet Regulars: Include Susie (Boxer), so fond of pork scratchings they are now used by her owners as a reward in the show ring.

MALT'N HOPS
50 Friday Street, Chorley, Lancashire PR6 0AH.

Dogs allowed throughout pub.

Pet Regulars: Freya (German Shepherd Dog), greets everyone by rolling over to allow tummy tickle; Abbie (GSD), under-seat sleeper; Brandy (Rhodesian Ridgeback), at the sound of a bag of crisps opening will lean on eater until guest's legs go numb or offered a share; Toby (Labrador), valued customer in his own right, due to amount of crisps he eats, also retrieves empty bags.

LEICESTERSHIRE

CHEQUERS INN
1 Gilmorton Road, Ashby Magna, near Lutterworth, Leicestershire.

Dogs allowed throughout the pub.

Pet Regulars: Bracken (Labrador), barmaid; Jessie (Labrador), socialite; Blue (English Setter), 'fuss' seeker.

LINCOLNSHIRE

THE BLUE DOG INN
Main Street, Sewstern, Grantham NG33 5QR.

Dogs allowed in non-food bar, beer garden. Dog-hitching rail outside.

Pet Regulars: The Guv'nor (Great Dane), best draught-excluder in history; Jenny (Westie) shares biscuits with pub cats; Jemma (98% Collie), atmosphere lapper-upper, JoJo (Cavalier King Charles), enjoys a drop of Murphys.

MERSEYSIDE

AMBASSADOR PRIVATE HOTEL

13 Bath Street, Southport PR9 0DP.

Dogs allowed in non-food bar, lounge, guest bedrooms.

THE SCOTCH PIPER

Southport Road, Lydiate, Merseyside.

Dogs allowed throughout the pub.

Pet Regulars: Pippa (Rescued Russell), one dog welcoming committee, hearth rug, scrounger. Landlord's dogs very much second fiddle.

MIDLANDS

AWENTSBURY HOTEL

21 Serpentine Road, Selly Park, Birmingham B29 7HU.

Dogs allowed in non-food bar, car park tables, beer garden.

Pet Regulars: Well-behaved dogs welcome.

THE MITRE

Lower Green, off Lower Street, Tettenhall, Wolverhampton.

Dogs allowed throughout the pub.

Pet Regulars: Sultan (Dobermann); Annie (mongrel); Bengie (Boxer); Blackie (mongrel): all adore pork scratchings.

TALBOT HOTEL

Colley Gate, Halesowen, West Midlands.

Dogs are allowed throughout the pub.

Pet Regulars: Include Inga, Gil, Jack and Red, all Border Collies. Every Christmas canine customers are treated to gift-wrapped dog chews.

NORFOLK

MARINE BAR

10 St Edmunds Terrace, Hunstanton, Norfolk PE36 5EH.

Dogs allowed throughout, except dining room.

Pet Regulars: Many dogs have returned with their owners year after year to stay at The Marine Bar.

THE OLD RAILWAY TAVERN
Eccles Road, Quidenham, Norwich, Norfolk NR16 2JG.

Dogs allowed in non-food bar, beer garden.

Pet Regulars: Maggie (Clumber Spaniel); Indi (GSD), Soshie (GSD) and pub dogs Elsa (GSD) & Vell (Springer). Elsa is so fond of sitting, motionless, on her own window ledge; new customers often think she's stuffed!

THE ROSE AND CROWN
Nethergate Street, Harpley, King's Lynn, Norfolk.

Dogs allowed in non-food bar, car park tables, beer garden.

Pet Regulars: A merry bunch with shared interests – Duffy (mongrel); Tammy (Airdale); Bertie & Pru (Standard Poodles) all enjoy pub garden romps during summer and fireside seats in winter.

OXFORDSHIRE

THE BELL
High Street, Adderbury, Oxon.

Dogs allowed throughout the pub.

Pet Regulars: Include Wilf (mongrel), supplies full cabaret including talking to people and singing.

SHROPSHIRE

LONGMYND HOTEL
Cunnery Road, Church Stretton, Shropshire SY6 6AG.

Dogs allowed in owners' hotel bedrooms.

Pet Regulars: Sox (Collie/Labrador), occasional drinker and regular customer greeter; Kurt (German Shepherd Dog), entertainments manager; Sadie (Retriever), self appointed fire-guard.

REDFERN HOTEL
Cleobury Mortimer, Shropshire CY14 8AA.

Dogs allowed throughout and guests' bedrooms.

SOMERSET

THE BUTCHERS ARMS

Carhampton, Somerset TA 24

Dogs allowed throughout the pub.

Pet Regulars: Lobo and Chera (Samoyeds), eating ice cubes and drinking; Emma (Spaniel), a whisky drinker; Benji (Spaniel-cross), self-appointed rug. Jimmy, a pony, also occasionally drops in for a drink.

HALFWAY HOUSE

Pitney, Langport, Somerset TA10 9AB.

Dogs allowed throughout (except kitchen!).

Pet Regulars: Pip (Lurcher), enjoys bitter, cider and G&T; Bulawayo (Ridgeback-cross), the advance party, sometimes three hours in advance of owner; Potter (57), sits at the bar.

THE SHIP INN

High Street, Porlock, Somerset.

Dogs allowed throughout and in guests' rooms.

Pet Regulars: Include Buster, Hardy and Crackers (Jack Russells), terrorists from London; Bijoux (Peke), while on holiday at The Ship enjoys Chicken Supreme cooked to order every evening.

STAFFORDSHIRE

WATERLOO

Ashby Road, Burton on Trent, Staffordshire.

Dogs allowed throughout pub.

Pet Regulars: They include Tuesday (Collie/German Shepherd), has first claim on a particular corner and won't budge.

SURREY

THE CRICKETERS

12 Oxenden Road, Tongham, Farnham, Surrey.

Dogs allowed in non-food bar, beer garden.

Pet Regulars: Include Lucy (a 'Bitsa'), surreptitious beer drinker and Chocolate Labradors Marston – after the beer – and Tullamore Dew – after the whisky.

WATTENDEN ARMS
Old Lodge Lane, Kenley, Surrey CR2 5RU.

Dogs allowed in non-food bar, beer garden.

Pet Regulars: Freya (GSD), partial to seafood; Karrie (Spaniel), children's entertainer; Ollie (Collie), shakes 'hands' with anyone with a drink; Sam (Springer), likes to fight and run up walls.

SUSSEX

CHARCOAL BURNER
Weald Drive, Furnace Green, Crawley, West Sussex RH10 6NY.

Dogs allowed in non-food bar areas and beer garden.

Pet Regulars: Lucy (Irish Setter), dedicated to cheese snips.

THE FORESTERS ARMS
High Street, Fairwarp, near Uckfield, Sussex TN22 3BP.

Dogs allowed in the beer garden and at car park tables, also inside.

Pet Regulars: Include Scampi (Jack Russell) who enjoys a social interlude with fellow canine guests.

THE INN IN THE PARK (CHEF & BREWER)
Tilgate Park, Tilgate, Crawley, West Sussex RH10 5PQ.

Dogs allowed in non-food bar, beer garden, family room, upstairs lounge and balcony.

Pet Regulars: Tuffy (Staffordshire Bull Terrier) leans, on hind legs, on bar awaiting beer and nibbles; Ted (Weimaraner), a 'watcher'; Jacko (Dalmatian), a crisp howler who, once given a pack, opens them himself; Meg (Border Collie), hoovers fallen bar snacks.

THE PLOUGH
Crowhurst, near Battle, Sussex TN33 9AY.

Dogs allowed in non-food bar, car park tables, beer garden.

Pet Regulars: Kai (Belgian Shepherd), drinks halves of Websters; Poppy and Cassie (Springer Spaniels), divided between the lure of crisps and fireside.

THE PRESTONVILLE ARMS

64 Hamilton Road, Brighton, East Sussex.

Dogs allowed in beer garden, throughout the pub (no food served).

Pet Regulars: These include Katie and Susie, a Yorkie and a ???!, who have been known to jump onto the pool table and help out by picking up the balls.

QUEENS HEAD

Village Green, Sedlescombe, East Sussex.

Dogs allowed throughout the pub.

Pet Regulars: Misty (Whippet) partial to Guinness and Bacardi and Coke. Hogs the dog biscuits kept especially for guests' dogs – proceeds to Guide Dogs for the Blind.

THE SLOOP INN

Freshfield Lock, Haywards Heath, Sussex RH17 7NP.

Dogs allowed in non-food bar, at car park tables, beer garden, family room, public bar.

Pet Regulars: Pub dogs are Staffordshire Bull Terriers Rosie and Chutney. Customers include Solo (Labrador), crisp burglar, beer drinker; Tania (Rottweiller), sleeping giant. All bedraggled gun-dogs are especially welcome to dry out by the fire.

THE SMUGGLERS' ROOST

125 Sea Lane, Rustington, West Sussex BN16 25G.

Dogs allowed in non-food bar, at car park tables, beer garden, family room.

Pet Regulars: Moffat (Border Terrier), beer makes him sneeze; Leo (Border Terrier), forms instant affections with anyone who notices him; Max (Cocker Spaniel), eats crisps only if they are 'plain'; Tim (King Charles Spaniel), quite prepared to guard his corner when food appears. The landlord owns a Great Dane.

THE SPORTSMAN'S ARMS

Rackham Road, Amberley, near Arundel BN18 9NR.

Dogs allowed throughout the pub.

Pet Regulars: Ramsden (Labrador), likes pickled onions. Landlord's dogs will not venture into the cellar which is haunted by the ghost of a young girl.

WELLDIGGERS ARMS

Lowheath, Petworth, West Sussex GU28 0HG.

Dogs allowed throughout the pub.

Pet Regulars: Angus (Labrador), crisp snaffler; Benji (Cavalier King Charles), hearth rug.

THE WYNDHAM ARMS

Rogate, West Sussex GU31 5HG.

Dogs allowed in non-food bar, at outside tables and in B&B guest rooms.

Pet Regulars: Henry (wire-haired Dachshund), hooked on Bristol Cream Sherry; Blot (Labrador), welcoming-committee and food fancier; Scruffy (Beardie), completely mad; Oscar (Labrador), floor hog.

WILTSHIRE

ARTICHOKE

The Nursery, Devizes, Wiltshire SN10 2AA.

Dogs allowed throughout pub.

Pet Regulars: Heidi (mongrel), pub tart; Monty (Dalmatian), trifle fixated; Rosie (Boxer), customer 'kissing'; Triffle (Airdale) and Shandy (mongrel) pub welcoming-committee.

THE PETERBOROUGH ARMS

Dauntsey Lock, near Chippenham, Wiltshire SN15 4HD.

Dogs allowed in non-food bar, at car park tables, beer garden, family room (when non-food).

Pet Regulars: Include Winston (Jack Russell), will wait for command before eating a biscuit placed on his nose; Waddi (GSD), can grab a bowling ball before it hits the skittle pins; Harry 4 Legs (GSD), always wins the Christmas prize draw.

THE THREE HORSESHOES

High Street, Chapmanslade, near Westbury, Wiltshire.

Dogs allowed in non-food bar and beer garden.

Pet Regulars: Include Clieo (Golden Retriever), possibly the youngest 'regular' in the land – his first trip to the pub was at eight weeks. Westbury and District Canine Society repair to the Three Horseshoes after training nights (Monday/Wednesday). The pub boasts six cats and two dogs in residence.

WAGGON AND HORSES

High Street, Wootton Bassett, Swindon, Wiltshire.

Dogs allowed in non-food bar.

Pet Regulars: Include Gemma, a very irregular Whippet/Border collie-cross. She likes to balance beer-mats on her nose, then flip them over and catch them, opens and shuts doors on command, walks on her hind legs and returns empty crisp bags. She is limited to one glass of Guinness a night.

YORKSHIRE

THE FORESTERS ARMS

Kilburn, North Yorkshire YO6 4AH.

Dogs allowed throughout, except restaurant.

Pet Regulars: Ebony (Labrador) and Jess (Labrador), eating ice cubes off the bar and protecting customers from getting any heat from the fire.

FOX INN

Roxby Staithes, Whitby, North Yorkshire.

Dogs allowed throughout including guests' bedrooms.

Pet Regulars: B&B guests include Lucy and Mouse (Jack Russell & Dachshund); Mattie & Sally (Spaniels) and Meg and George (Bassetts); Lady (57) and another Lady, also a Heinz 57.

THE GOLDEN FLEECE

Lindley Road, Blackley, near Huddersfield.

Dogs allowed in non-food bar, at outside tables.

Pet Regulars: Ellie & Meara (Rhodesian Ridgebacks), starving dog impressions, animated hearthrugs.

THE GREENE DRAGON INN

Hardraw, Hawes, North Yorkshire DL8 3LZ.

Dogs allowed in non-food bar, at car park tables, beer garden, family room.

THE HALL

High Street, Thornton Le Dale, Pickering, North Yorkshire YO18 7RR.

Dogs allowed usually throughout the pub.

Pet Regulars: Include Lucy (Jack Russell), she has her own beer glass at the bar, drinks only Newcastle Brown and Floss (mongrel), partial to Carlsberg.

NEW INN HOTEL

Clapham, near Settle, Yorkshire LA2 8HH.

Dogs allowed in non-food bar, beer garden, family room.

Pet Regulars: Ben (Collie-cross), a model customer.

PREMIER HOTEL

66 Esplanade, South Cliff, Scarborough, Yorkshire YO11 2UZ.

Dogs allowed throughout in non-food areas of hotel.

Pet Regulars: enjoy sharing their owners' rooms at no extra cost. There is a walking service available for pets with disabled owners.

THE SHIP

6 Main Street, Greasbrough, Rotherham S61 4PX.

Dogs allowed throughout the pub.

Pet Regulars: Include Hans (Guide Dog), reverts to puppy behaviour when 'off duty' and Ben (Border Terrier), 'frisks' customers for tit-bits.

SIMONSTONE HALL

Hawes, North Yorkshire DL8 3LY.

Dogs allowed throughout hotel except dining area.

Pet Regulars: account for 2,000 nights per annum. More than 50% of guests are accompanied by their dogs, from Pekes to an Anatolian Shepherd (the size of a small Shetland pony!). Two dogs have stayed, with their owners, on 23 separate occasions.

THE SPINNEY

Forest Rise, Balby, Doncaster, South Yorkshire DN4 9HQ.

Dogs allowed throughout the pub.

Pet Regulars: Shamus (Irish Setter), pub thief. Fair game includes pool balls, beer mats, crisps, beer, coats, hats. Recently jumped 15 feet off pub roof with no ill effect. Yan (Labrador), a dedicated guide dog; Sam (Boxer), black pudding devotee.

THE ROCKINGHAM ARMS

8 Main Street, Wentworth, Roherham, South Yorkshire S62 7LO.

Dogs allowed throughout pub.

Pet Regulars: Tilly (Beardie), does nothing but has adopted the quote of actor Kenneth Williams – "Sometimes I feel so unutterably superior to those around me that I marvel at my ability to live among them"; Sasha & Penny (Terriers), enjoy a social coffee; Kate & Rags (Airdale and cross-breed), prefer lager to coffee; Holly (terrier and pub dog), dubbed 'the flying squirrel', likes everyone, whether they like it or not!

ROTHERHAM COMPANIONS CLUB

The Fairways, Wickersley, Rotherham, South Yorkshire.

Dogs allowed throughout the pub (some restrictions if wedding party booked).

Pet Regulars: All chocolate fanatics who receive their favourite treat on arrival include Viking (Springer), Duke (Chow), Max (Border Collie) and Willie (Yorkshire Terrier). Viking keeps a box of toys and a ball behind the bar.

WALES

ANGLESEY

THE BUCKLEY HOTEL

Castle Street, Beaumaris, Isle of Anglesey LL58 8AW.

Dogs allowed throughout the pub, except in the dining room.

Pet Regulars: Cassie (Springer Spaniel) and Rex (mongrel), dedicated 'companion' dogs.

DYFED

THE ANGEL HOTEL
Rhosmaen Street, Lalndeilo, Dyfed.

Dogs allowed throughout the pub.

Pet Regulars: Skip (Spaniel/Collie), a Baileys devotee; Crumble (GSD) a devotee of anything edible.

SCOTLAND

ABERDEENSHIRE

BULL AND TERRIER BAR
Huntly Hotel, 18 The Square, Huntly, Aberdeenshire AB54 5BR.

Dogs allowed in non-food bar, beer garden, family room, guests' rooms.

Pet Regulars: Manni (English Bull Terrier), likes to have his tummy tickled by lady customers; Samantha (Rottweiller), eyes never leave the biscuit barrel; Megan (57), chasing Manni. Manni is also the local football team mascot.

ARGYLL

THE BALLACHULISH HOTEL
Ballachulish, Argyll PA39 4JY.

Dogs allowed in the lounge, beer garden and guests' bedrooms.

Pet Regulars: Thumper (Border Collie/GSD-cross), devoted to his owner and follows him everywhere.

DUMFRIES & GALLOWAY

CULGRUFF HOUSE HOTEL
Crossmichael, Castle Douglas, Dumfries & Galloway DG7 3BB.

Dogs allowed at car park tables, family room, guest bedrooms.

Pet Regulars: A cross section of canine visitors.

MORAYSHIRE

THE CLIFTON BAR

Clifton Road, Lossiemouth, Morayshire.

Dogs allowed throughout pub.

Pet Regulars: Include Zoe (Westie), has her own seat and is served coffee with two lumps and Rhona (Labrador) who makes solo visits.

ROYAL OAK

Station Road, Urquhart, Elgin, Moray.

Dogs allowed throughout pub.

Pet Regulars: Murphy (Staffordshire Bull Terrier) – food bin. Biscuits (from the landlady), Maltesers (from the landlord), sausages and burgers (from the barbecue).

PERTHSHIRE

CLACHAN COTTAGE HOTEL

Lochside, Lochearnhead, Perthshire, Scotland.

Dogs allowed in all non-food areas.

Pet Regulars: Regulars are few but passing trade frequent and welcome. Previous owner's dog was a renowned water-skier.

CHANNEL ISLANDS   *JERSEY*

LA PULENTE INN

La Pulente, St Brelade, Jersey.

Dogs allowed throughout the pub.

Pet Regulars: Include Bridie (Border Collie), darts, pool, watching TV, beer-mat skiing, stone shoving. Also responsible for fly catching. Drinks Bass and Guinness.

The

Countryman
comes from the country

THE COUNTRYMAN COMES FROM THE HEART OF THE BRITISH COUNTRYSIDE

The Countryman is unique - every other month this magazine will bring you all the peoples and places, crafts, characters and customs, wildlife and waysides of the British countryside.

Whatever your interests and wherever you live **The Countryman** is the ideal way to learn about the heritage that belongs to all of us. It will show you places to visit, reveal the history and traditions of everyday life and discuss the changes that are affecting our countryside.

Whether for yourself, a relative or friend **The Countryman** is the ideal gift. An attractive greetings card will be sent with a gift subscription to say that it is from you.

Subscribe now and wherever you are **The Countryman** will bring the heart of the countryside a lot closer.

ONE FOR YOUR FRIEND 1994

FHG Publications have a large range of attractive holiday accommodation guides for all kinds of holiday opportunities throughout Britain. They also make useful gifts at any time of year. Our guides are available in most bookshops and larger newsagents but we will be happy to post you a copy direct if you have any difficulty. We will also post abroad but have to charge separately for post or freight.

The inclusive cost of posting and packing the guides to you or your friends in the UK is as follows:

**Farm Holiday Guide
ENGLAND, WALES and IRELAND**
Board, Self-catering, Caravans/Camping,
Activity Holidays. Over 400 pages.   **£4.50**

Farm Holiday Guide SCOTLAND
All kinds of holiday accommodation.   **£3.00**

**SELF-CATERING & FURNISHED
HOLIDAYS**
Over 1000 addresses throughout for
Self-catering and caravans in Britain.   **£3.80**

BRITAIN'S BEST HOLIDAYS
A quick-reference general guide
for all kinds of holidays.   **£3.00**

**The FHG Guide to CARAVAN &
CAMPING HOLIDAYS**
Caravans for hire, sites and
holiday parks and centres.   **£3.00**

BED AND BREAKFAST STOPS
Over 1000 friendly and comfortable
overnight stops. Non-smoking, The
Disabled and Special Diets
Supplements.   **£3.80**

**CHILDREN WELCOME! FAMILY
HOLIDAY GUIDE**
Family holidays with details of
amenities for children and babies.   **£4.00**

**Recommended SHORT BREAK
HOLIDAYS IN BRITAIN**
'Approved' accommodation for
quality bargain breaks. Introduced by
John Carter.   **£4.00**

**Recommended COUNTRY HOTELS
OF BRITAIN**
Including Country Houses, for
the discriminating.   **£4.00**

**Recommended WAYSIDE INNS
OF BRITAIN**
Pubs, Inns and small hotels.   **£4.00**

**PGA GOLF GUIDE
Where to play and where to stay**
Over 2000 golf courses in Britain with
convenient accommodation. Endorsed
by the PGA. Holiday Golf in France,
Portugal and Majorca.   **£8.50**

PETS WELCOME!
The unique guide for holidays for
pet owners and their pets.   **£4.00**

BED AND BREAKFAST IN BRITAIN
Over 1000 choices for touring and
holidays throughout Britain.
Airports and Ferries Supplement.   **£3.00**

**THE FRENCH FARM AND VILLAGE
HOLIDAY GUIDE**
The official guide to self-catering
holidays in the 'Gîtes de France'.   **£8.50**

Tick your choice and send your order and payment to FHG PUBLICATIONS, ABBEY MILL BUSINESS CENTRE, SEEDHILL, PAISLEY PA1 1TJ (TEL: 041-887 0428. FAX: 041-889 7204). **Deduct** 10% for 2/3 titles or copies; 20% for 4 or more.

Send to: NAME ....

ADDRESS ....

....

.... POST CODE ....

I enclose Cheque/Postal Order for £ ....

SIGNATURE .... DATE ....

MAP

SECTION

The following seven pages of maps indicate the main
cities, towns and holiday centres of Britain. Space
obviously does not permit every location featured in
this book to be included but the approximate position
may be ascertained by using the distance indications
quoted and the scale bars on the maps.

Map 1

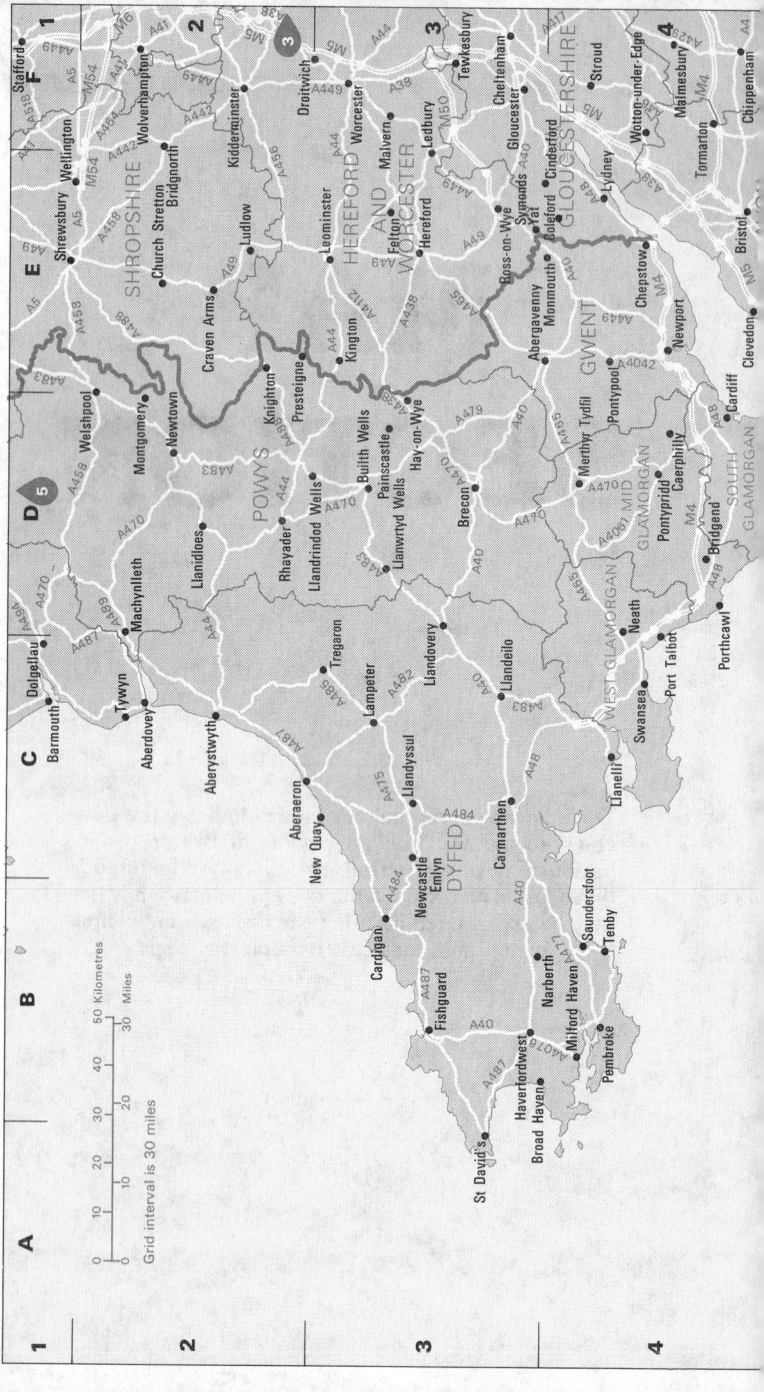
A
B
C
D
E
F
1
2
3
4
Stafford
Wolverhampton
Wellington
Shrewsbury
Bridgnorth
Church Stretton
SHROPSHIRE
Kidderminster
Ludlow
Craven Arms
Droitwich
Worcester
Malvern
Leominster
HEREFORD AND WORCESTER
Felton
Hereford
Ledbury
Tewkesbury
Cheltenham
Gloucester
Ross-on-Wye
Symonds Yat
Coleford
Cinderford
GLOUCESTERSHIRE
Stroud
Lydney
Wotton-under-Edge
Malmesbury
Tormarton
Chippenham
Bristol
Clevedon
Chepstow
Monmouth
Abergavenny
GWENT
Newport
Pontypool
Cardiff
Caerphilly
Pontypridd
Merthyr Tydfil
MID GLAMORGAN
SOUTH GLAMORGAN
Bridgend
Porthcawl
Port Talbot
Neath
WEST GLAMORGAN
Swansea
Llanelli
Welshpool
Montgomery
Newtown
Knighton
Presteigne
Kington
Hay-on-Wye
Painscastle
Builth Wells
Llandrindod Wells
Rhayader
POWYS
Llanwrtyd Wells
Brecon
Llanidloes
Machynlleth
Dolgellau
Barmouth
Tywyn
Aberdovey
Aberystwyth
Tregaron
Lampeter
Llandovery
Llandeilo
Aberaeron
New Quay
Llandyssul
Carmarthen
DYFED
Newcastle Emlyn
Cardigan
Fishguard
Narberth
Saundersfoot
Tenby
Haverfordwest
Milford Haven
Pembroke
Broad Haven
St David's
A5
A41
A449
M6
M54
A518
A442
A464
A458
A49
A488
A483
A38
M5
A44
A456
A4112
A438
A465
A40
M50
A417
A48
A429
A46
M4
A4
A4042
A479
A470
A4061
A489
A487
A494
A485
A482
A475
A484
A477
A4076
0
10
20
30
40
50 Kilometres
Miles
Grid interval is 30 miles

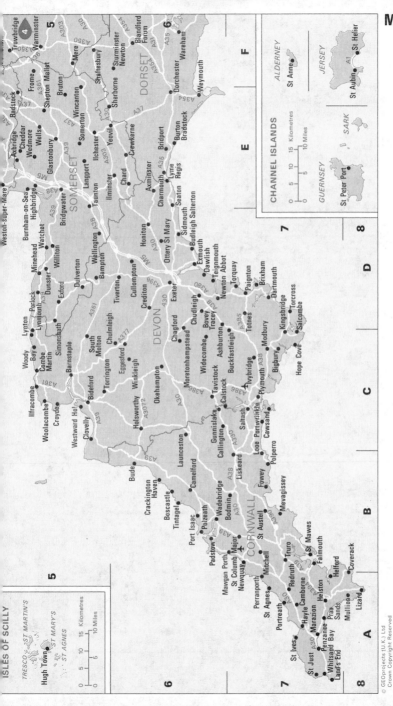

Map 2

ISLES OF SCILLY

TRESCO · ST MARTIN'S
ST MARY'S
ST AGNES

Hugh Town

0 5 10 15 Kilometres
0   5   10 Miles

CHANNEL ISLANDS

ALDERNEY
St Anne

GUERNSEY
St Peter Port

SARK

JERSEY
St Aubin St Helier

0 5 10 15 Kilometres
0   5   10 Miles

CORNWALL

DEVON

SOMERSET

DORSET

© GEOprojects (U.K.) Ltd
Crown Copyright Reserved

Map 3

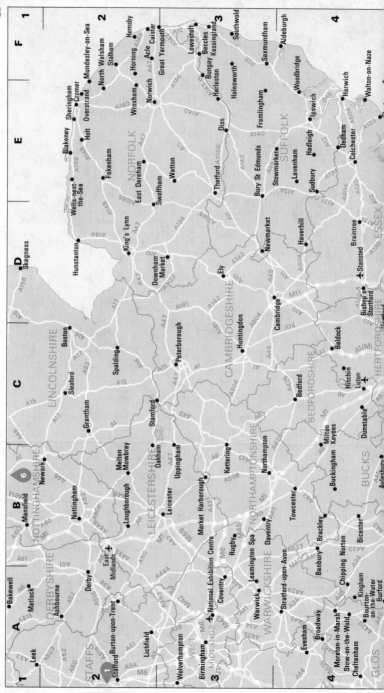

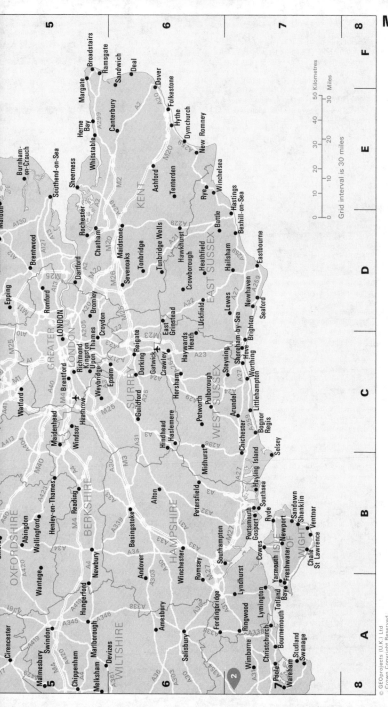

Map 4

Grid interval is 30 miles

0 10 20 30 40 50 Kilometres
0   10   20   30 Miles

© GEOprojects (U.K.) Ltd
Crown Copyright Reserved

Map 5

Girvan

A   B   C   7   D

DUMFRIES AND GALLOWAY   NORTH

Langholm   Bellingha

New Galloway   Dumfries   Gretna   Longtown   Greenhead

Newton Stewart   Annan   Brampton   A69

Wigtown   Castle Douglas   Carlisle   Alston

Gatehouse of Fleet   Silloth   Wigton

Port William   Kirkcudbright   Maryport   Bassenthwaite   Penrith

Cockermouth   Brampton

Workington   Keswick   Appleby

Whitehaven   Ennerdale Bridge   Ullswater   Shap   Kirkby Stephen

CUMBRIA

Ramsey   Gosforth   Little Langdale   Ambleside   Sedbergh

Peel   Seascale   Hawkshead   Windermere

Coniston   Kendal   Kirkby Lonsdale

ISLE OF MAN   Newby Bridge   Ingleton

Port Erin   Douglas   Broughton-in-Furness   Settle

Castletown   Millom   Ulverston   Grange-over-Sands

Port St Mary   Barrow-in-Furness   Morecambe

Lancaster

Fleetwood   Clitheroe

Blackpool   LANCASHIRE

Lytham St Annes   Preston   Blackburn

Southport   Chorley

Formby   Wigan   Bolton

GREATER MANCHESTER

Amlwch   MERSEYSIDE   Manchester

ANGLESEY   Hoylake   Liverpool

Holyhead   Llanerchymedd   Llandudno   Colwyn Bay   Prestatyn   Birkenhead

Menai Bridge   Beaumaris   Rhyl   Knutsford   Northwich

Llangefni   Conwy   Abergele

Bangor   CHESHIRE

Caernarvon   Llanrwst   Denbigh   Chester

Llanberis   Betws-y-Coed   Ruthin   Nantwich

CLWYD   Newcastle-under-Lyme

GWYNEDD   Corwen   Wrexham

Nefyn   Portmadoc   Ffestiniog   Bala   Llangollen   Wem   Market Drayton

Criccieth   Penrhyndeudraeth

Pwllheli   Oswestry   Wellington

Llanbedrog   Harlech   SHROPSHIRE

Aberdaron   Abersoch   Dolgellau   Shrewsbury

Barmouth   Welshpool   1

POWYS   C   D

Tywyn   Machynlleth

© GEOprojects (U.K.) Ltd
Crown Copyright Reserved

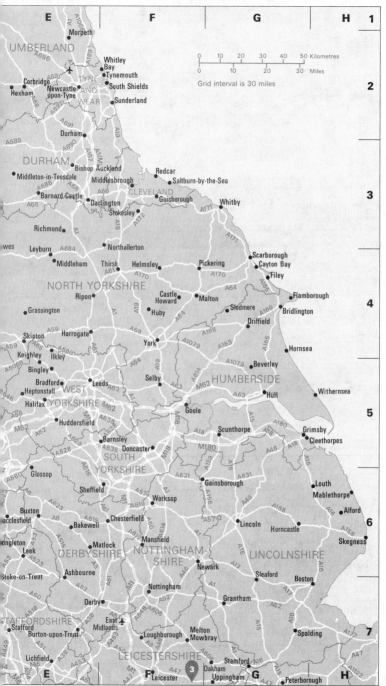

Map 6

Grid interval is 30 miles

0 10 20 30 40 50 Kilometres
0   10   20   30 Miles